The Six-Minute Solution:
A Reading Fluency Program
(Intermediate Level)

Gail N. Adams, M.Ed.
Sheron M. Brown, M.A., M.S.

Grades 3–6

Published and Distributed by

Sopris West™
EDUCATIONAL SERVICES

A Cambium Learning™ Company

4093 Specialty Place • Longmont, Colorado 80504 • (303) 651-2829
www.sopriswest.com

132484/6-10

Acknowledgments

We would like to express our appreciation to:

Dr. Anita Archer, the most gifted teacher we have ever known. Her inspiration, friendship, and encouragement were instrumental in the development of this book.

Susan Van Zant and Teri Middleton, our dear friends and colleagues, for their willingness to assist us in writing and editing some of the material in this book.

Judy Wollberg of Sopris West, whose support and guidance were invaluable to us during this project.

Our immediate family members—Larry Adams, Jack Brown, and Jennifer Adams—for their patience, understanding, and love.

Our mothers—Ruth Novelli and Joan Miscall—who first instilled in us a love of reading.

Gail N. Adams
Sheron M. Brown

About the Authors

Gail N. Adams is a veteran teacher with 30 years of experience in elementary and middle schools. In addition to working as a resource specialist for the Poway (California) Unified School District, Adams served as an educational consultant for the San Diego Office of Education and the North County Professional Development Federation. As such, she was a contributing author and trainer for the materials developed under two California reading grants. Adams is also a nationally certified trainer for the *REWARDS*, *Effective Reading Intervention Academy*, *Summer Reading Camp*, and *Read Naturally* programs. She holds a master's degree in education with an emphasis in reading and is certified in general education, special education learning disabilities, and as a reading specialist.

Sheron M. Brown, a retired elementary reading specialist, was an educator for 38 years. She holds master's degrees in curriculum and instruction, reading, and educational administration. Brown began her teaching career in her home state of New Jersey and taught in Florida, Texas, Alaska, and California. She was a classroom teacher for grades 1–10 and an elementary administrator. Brown has also been an educational consultant for the San Diego County Office of Education and the North County Professional Development Federation. She conducts workshops and teacher trainings for school districts and conferences throughout the United States and is the author of four books of word-sorting and word-study activities: *All Sorts of Sorts*, *All Sorts of Sorts 2*, *All Sorts of Sorts 3*, and *Words They Need to Know* (with Sally Oppy). All are published by the Teaching Resource Center in San Diego, California.

Contents

Introduction

Nothing is more painful and frustrating to a teacher than to hear a student arduously read a sentence word by word, seeming to have to physically drag himself or herself to the end of the sentence. As educators, we have all heard students read in this manner time and again and have wanted to do something—anything—to help these disfluent students become good readers.

Six-Minute Solution Intermediate will help students do just that. This research-based, highly effective instructional procedure for students in grades 3–6 builds reading fluency in only six minutes of the instructional day. For an overview of the instructional format, see the table below.

SIX-MINUTE SOLUTION INTERMEDIATE INSTRUCTIONAL FORMAT		
Time	**Materials**	**Procedures**
1 minute	■ Timer ■ One portfolio for each set of student partners that contains: a. Two copies of the same *Grade-Level Practice Passage* (laminated or placed inside plastic sleeves). b. Two copies of the *Fluency Record* or *Fluency Graph* (one for each student). c. One dry-erase marker and erasing cloth inside a zipper-lock plastic bag.	**Get Ready** ■ Teacher announces that fluency timings will begin. ■ Student partners remove fluency materials from the partnership's portfolio. ■ Partners record today's date on their respective *Fluency Record* or *Fluency Graph*. ■ Teacher monitors to ensure students are ready to begin their timings.
1 minute		**Partner 1 Reads** ■ Teacher sets the timer for 1 minute and says, "Begin." ■ Partner 1 reads until the timer sounds. ■ Partner 2 marks Partner 1 reading errors and stopping point on his/her copy of the *Practice Passage*.
1 minute		**Partner 2 Gives Feedback** ■ Partner 2 tells Partner 1 how many words he/she read, the number of errors he/she made, and does the error-correction procedure (see *Chapter 4*). ■ Partner 1 records the numbers on his/her *Fluency Record* or *Fluency Graph*. ■ Partner 2 wipes off the markings on his/her *Practice Passage* and gives the marker to Partner 1.
1 minute		**Partner 2 Reads** ■ Teacher again sets the timer for 1 minute and says, "Begin." ■ Partner 2 reads the same *Practice Passage* to Partner 1 until the timer sounds. ■ Partner 1 marks Partner 2 reading errors and stopping point on his/her copy of the *Practice Passage*.

1 minute		**Partner 1 Gives Feedback** ■ Partner 1 tells Partner 2 how many words he/she read, the number of errors he/she made, and does the error-correction procedure (see *Chapter 4*). ■ Partner 2 records the numbers on his/her *Fluency Record* or *Fluency Graph*. ■ Partner 1 wipes off the markings on his/her *Practice Passage*.
1 minute		**Students Put Away Materials** ■ One partner returns the copies of the *Practice Passage*, *Fluency Record* or *Fluency Graph*, dry-erase marker, and erasing cloth in the zipper-lock plastic bag to the partner portfolio.

Struggling readers as well as good readers benefit from *Six-Minute Solution Intermediate*'s daily fluency practice. Struggling readers gain fluency first at the word level and then at the passage level, while competent readers are challenged to read more expressive texts that are increasingly more difficult and sophisticated. All students benefit from fluency practice because as they encounter more challenging texts, they need to continue to grow as fluent readers.

Rereading to Build Fluency

As the saying goes, "Practice makes perfect"—whether it's shooting basketballs, playing the piano, or processing text in a smooth, efficient, and accurate manner. The benefits of repeated readings of the same passage to build reading fluency have been well documented in many research studies (Levy, Nicholls, & Kroshen, 1993; Meyer & Felton, 1999; Samuels, 1979). *Six-Minute Solution Intermediate* helps students succeed at reading fluency using an instructional model that is based on repeated-reading research and partnering students with closely matched instructional and fluency levels. Research supports the fact that students' reading skills improve when they work with peers in structured reading activities (Greenwood, Delquadri, & Hall, 1989; Rosenshine & Meister, 1994; and Stevens, Madden, Slavin, & Famish, 1987).

Partnering Students to Build Fluency

In *Six-Minute Solution Intermediate*, students' current instructional reading levels are determined and then students are placed in fluency partnerships. In these partnerships, one student reads the passage to his/her partner for one minute while the partner tracks the words read correctly as well as the reading errors. Partners then switch roles, with each partner charting his/her own progress. The entire procedure takes only six minutes.

Decoding & Fluency

Experts may disagree as to what exactly is the best approach to teach students how to read, but they are in agreement as to what good reading "sounds" like. According to Carnine, Silbert, and Kame'enui (1997), fluency is "reading smoothly, easily, and quickly." In order to read fluently, the reader must be able to decode the vast majority of words automatically, with approximately 95 percent accuracy. However, although there is a clear link between fluency and decoding skills, fluency practice alone will not improve a student's decoding skills. Any underlying decoding problems must also be addressed either prior to or in conjunction with fluency practice.

Comprehension & Fluency

Research also shows a high correlation between reading *comprehension* and reading *fluency* (Farstrup & Samuels, 2002; Foorman & Mehta, 2002; LaBerge & Samuels, 1974). Reading comprehension suffers when students lack fluency. If a student is focusing his/her cognitive energies on word decoding and recognition, those energies are not available for comprehension. In the words of Farstrup and Samuels (2002), fluency consists of "optical, perceptual, syntactic, and semantic cycles, each melting into the next as readers try to get meaning as efficiently as possible using minimal time and energy."

Independent Reading & Fluency

Fluent readers generally find reading to be a pleasurable activity; as a result, they read more. When the amount of time spent on independent reading increases, there are accompanying gains in reading-related skills. As students read more, they increase not only their comprehension but also their vocabulary, background knowledge, decoding, and fluency skills. The "Matthew effect"—a term coined by reading researcher Dr. Keith Stanovich—refers to the effect that in reading, as in other areas of life, "the rich get richer while the poor get poorer" (Stanovich, 1986).

Work Completion & Fluency

Fluent readers will be better able to complete both class assignments and homework. This is significant when you consider the amount of reading assigned to upper elementary, middle school, and high school students. As an example: Student A, a fluent reader, is able to read an average of 180 correct words per minute (cwpm); Student B, a struggling reader, has an average fluency rate of 60 cwpm. Both students are assigned the same amount of reading. Student A, with an appropriate fluency rate, is able to complete the assignment in two hours. Student B, who reads at only one-third the rate of Student A, needs six hours to complete the same assignment.

Reading Achievement & Fluency Practice

Although the National Assessment of Educational Progress (Pinnell, Piluski, Wixson, Campbell, Gough, & Beatty, 1995) found that 44 percent of fourth graders were not fluent readers, research shows that educators have the knowledge and tools to affect this problem. After analyzing many fluency studies, the National Reading Panel (NICHD, 2000) reported that fluency can be taught and that guided, repeated, oral reading procedures are "appropriate and valuable avenues for increasing reading fluency and overall reading achievement." Skilled readers read words quickly, correctly, and without hesitation. Students who have not become fluent readers continue to plod slowly through each sentence without experiencing the joy of quick, automatic, fluent reading. By its very nature, fluency practice supports comprehension. It provides a skill-building activity that enables students to move quickly through text. As students build fluency through rereading, they amass a larger reading vocabulary. As they begin to read with automaticity, their cognitive attention can be focused on the text's meaning instead of on word identification. The National Reading Panel (NICHD, 2000) found that repeated oral reading, accompanied by feedback and guidance, resulted in significant reading achievement.

Six-Minute Solution Intermediate uses both of these research-validated components—repeated readings of the same passage and oral feedback from peers—to build fluency.

Six Simple Steps for Getting Started

The *Six-Minute Solution Intermediate* partner fluency model can be easily implemented in a variety of settings. The following is a list of the steps needed to get started and an estimate of how long each step will take.

Step 1. Assessment (Chapter 1)
Estimated Time 1-2 hours
- Give each student a one minute timing on a grade level passage to determine oral fluency rate.
- Give each student a test to determine instructional reading level—San Diego Quick, silent reading test or a passage placement accuracy test.

Step 2. Select Fluency Partners and Instructional Groups (Chapter 2)
Estimated Time 1 hour
- Using a class roster, list students by fluency score and then by instructional reading level.
- Assign partners by ranking. For example, students ranked #1 and #2 would be partners and students ranked #3 and #4 would be partners. Partners must be closely matched (fluency rates should be within 10-15 words of each other).
- Designate the stronger of the two as partnership #1 and the other #2.

Step 3. Introduce the Fluency Concept (Chapter 3)
Estimated Time 20-30 minutes
- Teacher demonstrates whisper reading the sample passage, tracking while reading, underlining unknown words and marking the last word read when the timer sounds.
- Teacher demonstrates totaling correct number of words read and graphing.
- Students whisper read passage for one minute, figure out the number of correct words read and graph. Procedure is repeated for a second minute.
- Students compare number of cwpm on each of their timings. Teacher leads class discussion on the benefits of repeated reading.

Step 4. Establish Partner Behavior (Chapter 4)
Estimated Time 10-20 minutes
- Teacher models and discusses cooperative and respectful partnerships.
- Teacher selects a student partner to demonstrate correct partner behavior during reading—"lean in and whisper read."
- Teacher demonstrates giving polite feedback to the partner.

- Teacher demonstrates gently correcting errors using tell and repeat method.
- Teacher states "No Arguing" rule and demonstrates how arguing wastes time.

Step 5. Train Students in the Partnership Model (Chapter 5)
Estimated Time 20-30 minutes
- Teacher demonstrates partner procedure with a student.
- Teacher sets timer for one minute and instructs all partner 1s to read and all partner 2s to follow along and underline errors.
- After the timer sounds, teacher instructs all partner 2s to give feedback to all partner 1s—total words read, number of errors, and correct words per minute.
- Teacher instructs all partner 1s to graph or record their score.
- Teacher instructs students to change roles and get ready for the second timing. Students repeat procedure for a second minute.
- Procedure is repeated. **Note:** Teacher should walk around the room and monitor carefully at all times.

Step 6. Train Students to Manage Materials (Chapter 6)
Estimated Time 10-15 minutes
- Teacher shows students where portfolios and passages are kept.
- Teacher demonstrates choosing new passages and filing old passages.
- Teacher demonstrates storing the pen, cloth or sponge.

Sample Schedule

The following is a sample of a weekly (5 day) schedule for the *Six-Minute Solution Intermediate* partner fluency model. Notice that the first day of the week includes an accuracy check and the last day of the week may include optional comprehension and writing activities.

Six-Minute Solution Intermediate Sample Schedule	
Monday	▪ All partnerships have new *Practice Passages*. Partners preview the entire passage for accuracy by whisper-reading or silently reading, underlining unknown words. Teacher monitors and identifies any words unknown to either partner. – **Option 1:** No timings on Mondays. Have partners use the allotted six minutes for previewing *Practice Passages*. – **Option 2:** Allow extra time (10–15 minutes) on Mondays. Have partners first preview their *Practice Passage* for accuracy. Then, conduct partner fluency practice during the allotted six minutes.
Tuesday through Thursday	▪ *Six-Minute Solution Intermediate* procedure: Fluency practice.
Friday	▪ Partners turn in the week's *Practice Passage* and select a new one for the following week. – **Option:** Extend the amount of time to incorporate student practice with comprehension or summary writing strategies. Partners can use the current *Practice Passage* for these optional activities before turning it in and selecting a new passage for the following week. See *Chapter 8* for suggestions.

Program Overview

Six-Minute Solution Intermediate can be easily implemented in a variety of educational settings by following six easy steps, each of which is discussed in the first several chapters.

Chapter 1: Assessments

Assessment is critical in determining student fluency partnerships and in selecting the appropriate reading level of *Practice Passages*. This chapter provides step-by-step procedures for assessing students' oral reading fluency rates and instructional reading levels. It also includes recommended grade-level oral reading fluency rates.

Chapter 2: Selecting Fluency Partners and Instructional Groups

Careful selection of student fluency partnerships is critical to the success of *Six-Minute Solution Intermediate*. This chapter describes the procedures for selecting partners based on assessment data that has been collected via spreadsheet software or manual sorting. We also offer suggestions for program implementation in different configurations: entire classrooms, small groups, special-needs classes, intervention programs, and cross-age tutoring programs.

Chapter 3: Introducing the Fluency Concept

This chapter provides the necessary steps for introducing the concept of repeated reading to students.

Chapter 4: Establishing Partner Behavior

Training students to work in a cooperative manner and to provide polite feedback to each other are the focuses of this chapter.

Chapter 5: Training Students in the Partnership Model

Taking the time to properly train students in *Six-Minute Solution Intermediate* procedures will ensure that the program runs smoothly. This chapter discusses how to teach students to correctly carry out fluency procedures.

Chapter 6: Managing Materials

Well-organized program materials that are easily accessible to students will assist in the establishment of effective fluency routines. In this chapter, we include ideas for initial implementation and ongoing management of materials.

Chapter 7: Student Progress and Record Keeping

It is essential to monitor individual student progress and to make instructional decisions based on that progress. This chapter provides examples of how to interpret fluency data, adjust reading goals accordingly, and support students who are not making adequate progress.

Chapter 8: Comprehension and Writing Strategies

Although *Six-Minute Solution Intermediate* is primarily a fluency-building program, its *Practice Passages* may be used to instruct students in a variety of comprehension strategies as well. This chapter offers suggestions for teaching students how to summarize, paraphrase, retell, describe, sequence, compare, solve problems, and determine cause and effect. *Practice Passages* may also be used as models for teaching students the writing form of short summary. Examples of paragraph frames are included.

Conclusion: More Than Six Minutes a Day

With the *Six-Minute Solution Intermediate* fluency partnership model, students can increase their oral reading fluency by practicing for only six minutes a day on a regular basis. There will be times, however, when teachers will need to devote more than six minutes a day to fluency practice. The *Conclusion* outlines some situations that may require implementing extended fluency practice.

Assessment

The *Assessment* section includes the following components:

Assessment Passages

The *Assessment Passage* set consists of one passage per grade-level readability (grades 1–6), for a total of six passages. *Assessment Passages* can be used for two purposes:

1. To obtain a student's fluency score on a grade-level passage.
2. To determine a student's instructional level.

Using the *Six-Minute Solution Intermediate* Assessment Passages. Consult these directions for assessing cwpm, determining reading instructional level, collecting pretest/posttest data, and determining student progress.

San Diego Quick Assessment of Reading Ability

- *San Diego Quick Assessment of Reading Ability* (includes Teacher Record and Student Form). This assessment may be used to determine students' instructional reading levels.

Fluency Building Sheets

Practice Passages

Practice Passages are organized by Flesch-Kincaid readability level in sets of five for grades 1–6 (total of 150). The nonfiction, informational *Practice Passages* focus on science, social studies, history, and biographical topics. We use nonfiction passages for two important reasons:

1. Struggling readers often lack general background knowledge in topics that *Practice Passages* cover. Students benefit from fluency practice with reading material that offers general-knowledge information.

2. It is easier to "hide" readability level in nonfiction material. To improve reading fluency, a student needs to practice rereading passages at his/her *instructional* reading level, which, in many cases, is below chronological grade-level placement.

The *Practice Passages* within each grade level are not thematic or dependent on one another. **Note:** While *Practice Passages* are available for grades 1 and 2 readability, their content is appropriate for older, rather than primary, students.

Automatic Word Lists

These lists include words that are most often encountered in written English. The words are grouped in sets of 25 and are repeated three times within each list.

Fluency Building Sheets: Vowels and Vowel Combinations, Prefixes, and Suffixes

In order to fluently read multisyllabic words, students must be able to quickly break words into decodable chunks. Knowing vowel combinations and word parts automatically is a necessity for advanced decoding. Students who need to develop this preskill will benefit from practicing with these fluency building sheets.

Appendix

The *Appendix* includes the following components:
- Frequently Asked Questions
- *Fluency Assessment Report*
- *Initial Assessment Record* (to rank and partner students)
- *Fluency Record* (data-collection form students use to record their cwpm scores)
- *Fluency Graphs 1, 2,* and *3* (data-collection forms students use to graph their cwpm progress). Choose the graph that best represents the current cwpm and goal cwpm for a student.
- Three *Six-Minute Solution* field tests (for readers who would like more information about the implementation and validation of *Six-Minute Solution* procedures).
- Blackline masters for introducing fluency concepts to students:
  - Summary Paragraph Frame 1
  - Summary Paragraph Frame 2
  - What Is Reading Fluency?
  - Why Is Reading Fluency Important?

CHAPTER 1

Assessments

Assessment is an important step to implementing *Six-Minute Solution Intermediate*. Determining students' reading levels helps you to select practice passages, assign student partners, and establish a baseline to measure student progress.

Materials:
- Two copies of a grade-level passage—one for the student to read from and another for the teacher to use to record total words read and errors. **Note:** Every student must read the same passage for the purpose of assessment. The teacher could have a laminated copy on which to record errors and stopping point with a water based or dry erase marking pen. The teacher would then erase between students. Or the teacher could run multiple copies of the same passage and use a separate one to record errors and stopping point for each student.
- Data sheet for the teacher to record correct words per minute and timer.
- Materials to determine instructional reading level (San Diego Quick Test of Sight Word Recognition, silent reading test or a placement accuracy test.)

Estimated Time:
1–2 hours

Assess Students

The first step in implementing *Six-Minute Solution Intermediate* is to determine students' oral reading fluency rates and instructional reading levels. This initial assessment will guide *Practice Passage* selection, provide data for selecting partners, and provide baseline information so that student growth can be evaluated. More specifically, the two-part assessment that follows (Assessment 1 and Assessment 2) will determine:

1. A student's **oral reading fluency rate** (i.e., correct words per minute [cwpm] reading of a *Assessment Passage* at the student's grade-level placement).

2. A student's **instructional reading level** as determined by using one of the following measures: word recognition test (*San Diego Quick Assessment of Reading Ability*, see *Assessment*), a silent reading test or a passage placement accuracy test to indicate the level at which a student can read with 91 percent–96 percent accuracy. **Note:** If you already use an informal reading inventory, you may use this data to determine a student's instructional reading level.

We recommend that students be assessed for fluency three times a year (e.g., in September, January, and May) to ensure appropriate student progress and to validate that student partners are working well together and recording scores accurately. In addition, it is always a good idea to keep parents informed of their children's fluency levels. The *Fluency Assessment Report* (see *Appendix*) can be used for this purpose.

Students who have significant reading problems may need a more extensive assessment than is described in this program in order to determine the nature and severity of their reading problems. The more extensive assessment information can either replace *Six-Minute Solution Intermediate* assessments or be used in conjunction with them. Use the assessment information you gather to guide you in addressing underlying deficits in skills, such as phonemic awareness and decoding. Instruction in these important skills may be conducted prior to or along with the implementation of *Six-Minute Solution Intermediate*.

Assessment 1

Oral Reading Fluency

Materials:
- One copy of an *Assessment Passage* (see *Assessment*) for the student to read at the student's grade-level placement, laminated or enclosed in a plastic sleeve. Each student in the class will read the same *Assessment Passage* individually (e.g., all sixth-grade students will read the same Level 6 *Assessment Passage*). **Note:** When listening to an individual student read, sit apart from the other students so that they are not within hearing distance. This would give them prior knowledge of the passage.
- One copy of the same laminated *Assessment Passage* on which to record each student's reading errors and stopping point. **Note:** You may wish to have a laminated copy of the same *Assessment Passage* for each student on which to permanently record reading errors and stopping point. In that case, you will need as many copies as there are students in the class.
- A digital timer or stopwatch, a marking pen, and a clipboard.

Special circumstances: When working with groups of students who read significantly below grade level, it would not be appropriate to ask them to read a grade-level *Assessment Passage*. Instead, assess remedial students with a *Assessment Passage* at their estimated reading level. Continue assessing to determine the level at which a student reads with 95 percent accuracy (i.e., 5 errors in a 100-word passage). This would be the appropriate level for a student to begin building fluency.

Estimated time:
2.5 minutes per student

Procedure:
1. Give each student the laminated copy of the grade-level *Assessment Passage* and say, "The title of this passage is _____ . When I say, 'Please begin,' I would like you to start reading here (point to the first word) and read out loud quickly and carefully until the timer sounds. If you do not know a word, I will tell it to you. Are you ready?"
2. Set the timer for one minute and say, "I will start the timer when you begin reading."
3. Using a clipboard to hold the teacher copy of the *Assessment Passage*, follow along as the student reads, underlining errors. Mark a diagonal line when the timer sounds, indicating the point at which the student stopped reading. The use of the clipboard will keep the student from being distracted by any marks you may make.

4. Tell the student, "Thank you. Please return to your seat and ask _____ (the next student) to come over to read."
5. During the interval between students, determine the total number of words the student read, subtract any errors, and note the correct words per minute (cwpm) read.
6. After all students have read the *Assessment Passage*, record their cwpm scores on the *Initial Assessment Record* (see *Appendix*).

Oral reading errors:
- Mispronunciations, unless attributed to accent or dialect.
- Words supplied by the teacher.
- Word omissions.
- Dropped word endings, unless attributed to accent or dialect.
- Substitutions, even if the word meaning is unchanged (e.g., "home" for "house").
- Reversed order of words (e.g., "he was" for "was he") counts as two errors.
- Mispronunciation of proper nouns counts as one error every occurrence.

Notes:
- Repetitions (e.g., "the boy, the boy") are *not* counted as errors.
- Insertions are *not* counted as errors or as words read.

Assessment 2

Instructional Reading Level

Any of three types of assessments may be used to obtain a close approximation of a student's instructional reading level:
- Word recognition test *or*
- Group silent-reading test *or*
- Passage placement accuracy test

Although these three types of assessments may seem unrelated, they are good informal indicators of a student's reading ability. It is not necessary to administer all three tests to determine a student's instructional reading level. The advantage to using a group silent-reading test is that it can be administered to all students at the same time. While the class is taking the test, you can read with individual students to obtain their oral reading fluency rate. Alternatively, word recognition tests are given to each student individually, with students reading the words orally to you. Passage placement reading tests must also be administered individually. Word recognition tests and/or oral passage placement tests may be administered individually to students at the same time as the oral reading fluency test (Assessment 1).

Word Recognition Test

Materials:
- *San Diego Quick Assessment of Reading Ability* (see *Assessment*).

Estimated time:
2.5 minutes per student

Procedure:
1. Make copies of the *Student Form, Teacher Record,* and *Errors & Reading Levels* scoring sheet.
2. Administer the test per the directions in the introductory paragraph.
3. Transfer student scores to the scoring sheet.

Group Silent Reading Test

Materials:
- Copies of a silent reading test for all students in the class.

Estimated time:
- Will vary, depending on the test.

Procedure:
1. Choose a silent reading test that can be administered to the entire class during one class period. The selected silent reading test may be teacher-prepared or commercial. The most important function of a silent reading test is to yield a measurable score that can be used to rank students according to their instructional reading levels. Examples of commercially prepared tests that lend themselves well to this procedure include:
   a. Scholastic Reading Inventory (SRI) (Scholastic, 2003). Scores are reported in Lexile levels.
   b. Gates-MacGinitie (MacGinitie, MacGinitie, Maria, & Dreyer, 2003). Scores are reported in percentiles.
   c. McLeod Test of Reading Comprehension (Consortium on Reading Excellence; CORE, 1999). Scores are reported in grade-level scores.
   d. Measure of Academic Progress (MAPs). This is a standardized computer test with scores reported in RIT (Rasch Unit) scores.
2. Explain the test directions to the class and complete the practice items with the entire group.
3. Instruct students to begin working on the silent reading test. Make sure that students have something they can do independently when they finish the test.
4. After all students have completed the test, record their scores.

Passage Placement Accuracy Test

Procedure:
1. Select a few grade-level *Assessment Passages* (see *Assessment*) based on your estimation of the student's reading level.
2. Tell the student, "We need to find a reading level that is just right for you to practice reading. That means that the passage must be comfortable for you—not too easy and not too hard. In order to find that level, I am going to ask you to read a few passages to me."
3. Give the student a copy of the *Assessment Passage* and say, "The title of this passage is _____ . Please begin here (point to the first word) and read out loud to me. If you do not know a word, I will tell it to you. Are you ready? Please begin." **Note:** The oral passage reading test is untimed.

4. When the student finishes reading the passage, ask, "How did you feel when you were reading the passage? Was it too easy? Was it too hard? Was it just right?"

Use the *Determining Reading Levels Chart* (following) to determine whether or not the student is reading the *Assessment Passage* at his/her independent, instructional, or frustration level. The frustration level is one at which the passage is simply too difficult for the student to read, and little or no learning will occur. The instructional level is one at which the material can be read by the student, but some teacher guidance and instruction are necessary for content comprehension. The instructional level is the most important level to determine since it is at this level that learning truly occurs. The independent level is one at which the student can read the passage easily and without teacher assistance or instruction.

Determining Reading Levels Chart (Using a 100-word passage)		
Passage Errors Allowed	**Passage Reading Level**	**Comprehension Level**
3 or fewer errors	Independent (97%–100%)	Good to Excellent
4–9 errors	Instructional (91%–96%)	Good to Satisfactory
10 or more errors	Frustration (90% & below)	Satisfactory/Fair/Poor

Examples:
- A student who reads a 100-word passage with 2 errors has an accuracy rate of 98 percent, which indicates that the passage is at the student's *independent* reading level.
- A student who reads a 100-word passage with 5 errors has an accuracy rate of 95 percent, which indicates that the passage is at the student's *instructional* reading level.
- A student who reads a 100-word passage with 12 errors has an accuracy rate of 88 percent, which indicates that the passage is at the student's *frustration* level.

Students may be placed at their instructional or independent level for the purpose of building fluency. They should never practice fluency with a passage in which their reading is less than 90 percent accurate. Accuracy *must* precede fluency, so it is essential that students be monitored for accurate reading before repeated reading practice takes place. **Note:** Refer to "Using the *Six-Minute Solution Intermediate* Assessment Passages" (see *Assessments*) for information about determining reading instructional level, assessing cwpm, and collecting pretest/posttest data.

Many teachers assign students fluency passages at their instructional level with the intent of having them progress more quickly. Other teachers—especially those of reluctant readers—assign students fluency passages at their independent level with the intent of having them experience immediate success, resulting in increased motivation and self-esteem.

Special Circumstances: Students who are enrolled in Title 1, remedial reading, special education, or English Language Learner (ELL) classes or who have significant reading problems may be more appropriately assessed with an individually administered reading test such as the Woodcock Reading Mastery Test (Woodcock, 2000). This test will help you determine instructional reading levels and gather information about underlying reading problems.

Appropriate Fluency Rate

A student's target fluency rate is based on his/her *instructional reading level*, not the current grade-level placement. For example, the initial goal for a sixth-grade student reading at a third-grade instructional level is 70–110 cwpm, which is the recommended oral reading rate for third-grade readers. Once the student has met the initial goal, increase the cwpm goal to the upper range or move the student to *Practice Passages* at the next grade level.

Keep in mind that student partners always read the same *Practice Passage* at the same time. A fifth-grade ELL student reading at a third-grade level may be partnered with a fifth-grade special education student also reading at the third-grade level. Occasionally, there may be an "outlying student"—one whose instructional reading level does not match that of any other student. In that case, the outlying student may need to be partnered with a teacher, an aide, or a classroom volunteer.

Refer to *Table 1.1* (Hasbrouck & Tindal, 2005) for cwpm standards by grade level and school season. As a general rule, students scoring below the 50th percentile benefit from participating in a fluency building program.

Table 1.1
2005 Hasbrouck & Tindal Oral Reading Fluency Data

Jan Hasbrouck and Gerald Tindal completed an extensive study of oral reading fluency in 2004. The results of their study are published in a technical report entitled, "Oral Reading Fluency: 90 Years of Measurement," which is available on the University of Oregon's website, **brt.uoregon.edu/tech_reports.htm.**

The table below shows the mean oral reading fluency of students in grades 1 through 8 as determined by Hasbrouck and Tindal's data.

You can use the information in this table to draw conclusions and make decisions about the oral reading fluency of your students. **Students scoring below the 50th percentile using the average score of two unpracticed readings from grade-level materials need a fluency-building program.** In addition, teachers can use the table to set the long-term fluency goals for their struggling readers.

Note that there is a difference between monitoring and placement. **Monitoring** with an assessment tool such as *Reading Fluency Monitor* can help you identify students who need to improve their fluency and monitor their progress over time.

Placement is the process of selecting an appropriate level of reading material and setting a reading rate goal within the context of a fluency-building program, such as READ NATURALLY. To place students in READ NATURALLY, use the READ NATURALLY placement table.

Grade	Percentile	Fall CWPM*	Winter CWPM*	Spring CWPM*
3	90	128	146	162
	75	99	120	137
	50	71	92	107
	25	44	62	78
	10	21	36	48
4	90	145	166	180
	75	119	139	152
	50	94	112	123
	25	68	87	98
	10	45	61	72
5	90	166	182	194
	75	139	156	168
	50	110	127	139
	25	85	99	109
	10	61	74	83
6	90	177	195	204
	75	153	167	177
	50	127	140	150
	25	98	111	122
	10	68	82	93
7	90	180	192	202
	75	156	165	177
	50	128	136	150
	25	102	109	123
	10	79	88	98
8	90	185	199	199
	75	161	173	177
	50	133	146	151
	25	106	115	124
	10	77	84	97

Grade	Percentile	Fall CWPM*	Winter CWPM*	Spring CWPM*
1	90		81	111
	75		47	82
	50		23	53
	25		12	28
	10		6	15
2	90	106	125	142
	75	79	100	117
	50	51	72	89
	25	25	42	61
	10	11	18	31

*CWPM = Correct Words Per Minute

CHAPTER 2

Selecting Fluency Partners and Instructional Groups

The appropriate selection of student fluency partnerships is essential to the success of the program. This chapter describes the procedure for ranking students based on assessment results and forming partnerships based on the data.

Materials:
- Fluency data for each student (i.e., a fluency score and an independent/instructional reading level score).
- A student ranking sheet or a computer spreadsheet program that generates ranking order.

Estimated time:
1 hour

Selecting Partners

When selecting fluency partners, match students as closely as possible by both *oral reading fluency rates and instructional reading levels*. Assign partners based on ranking. For example, if using a spreadsheet program, sort first for fluency score and then for reading level. Students ranked as #1 and #2 would be partners, students ranked as #3 and #4 would be partners, and so on. *Partners must be closely matched. As a general rule, their fluency rates should be within 10–15 words of each other.* An appropriate match is critical to success.

An example of an appropriate partnership match would be two sixth-grade students at grade 3 instructional reading level with oral fluency rates within 10–15 words of each other. If one of these students had an oral reading fluency rate of 85 cwpm and the other student had an oral reading fluency rate of 45 cwpm, they would not be matched as fluency partners. The reason for this is that the student with the lower cwpm oral fluency rate would not be able to follow along with the partner's more rapid rate of reading.

Keeping in mind that student partners must always read the same *Practice Passage*, you could partner a fifth-grade ELL student reading at the third-grade level with a fifth-grade special education student who is also reading at the third-grade level. Occasionally, there may be an "outlying student"—one whose instructional reading level does not match that of any other student. This student may be partnered with a teacher, an aide, or a classroom volunteer.

Once partnerships are selected, label the partners as Partner 1 and Partner 2. Partner 1 should be the stronger of the two partners. For example, two sixth-grade students—each with an instructional level of fourth grade—are partners. Partner 1 has a fluency rate of 72 cwpm and Partner 2 has a fluency rate of 68 cwpm. **Note:** Students must be assigned *Grade-Level Practice Passage* timings at their independent or instructional grade level.

Fluency partners may be selected by using spreadsheet software or by manually sorting students' oral reading fluency and instructional reading-level scores.

Using Spreadsheets to Select Fluency Partners

For large groups of students, the easiest way to select fluency partners is to use spreadsheet software. The following steps will help you create the spreadsheet:

1. Begin by opening a new document (blank spreadsheet) and naming it (e.g., Language Arts Period 3, Mr. Smith's Sixth-Grade Class).
2. Label six columns with the following headings: Last Name, First Name, Date, Grade, Oral Reading Fluency Score (cwpm), and Instructional Reading Level.
3. Enter data in the six columns for each student.
4. Sort the data first by fluency (cwpm) and then by instructional reading level, in either ascending or descending order.
5. Assign fluency partners based on the sort (e.g., the first two students on the list would be partners, the second two students would be partners, and so on).

Manually Sorting Scores to Select Fluency Partners

Another method you can use to select fluency partners is manual sorting. The following steps will help you rank student scores more easily:

1. Sort your students' oral fluency scores from Assessment 1 (see *Chapter 1*) in ascending order—from lowest to highest.
2. In the first column on the Initial Assessment Record (see *Appendix*), list students in the order of their oral-reading fluency scores.
3. In the second column, list the oral-reading fluency score for each student.
4. In the third column, list the students' instructional reading-level scores—from the *San Diego Quick Assessment* (see *Assessment*).
5. Match students as closely as possible based on the data, making sure that each partner's fluency score is within 10–15 words of one another and that both students are reading at the same instructional level.

Selecting Instructional Groupings

Although *Six-Minute Solution Intermediate* is fundamentally designed for the entire classroom, the following group configurations may be used successfully as well:

- Small groups within a class
- Individual fluency programs
- Parent-student partnerships
- Cross-age partnerships

Entire Classroom

In this instructional grouping, the entire classroom is assessed and fluency partnerships are assigned. All Partner 1s read the assigned *Practice Passage* to their partners for one minute. While they are reading, Partner 2s mark Partner 1 errors and stopping point on their own laminated copy of the passage. Partner 1s then record their own cwpm score on their *Fluency Record* or *Fluency Graph* (see *Appendix*). All Partner 2s then read the same *Practice Passage* for one minute. Results are tracked by Partner 1s on their laminated copy of the passage. Partner 2s then record their own cwpm score on their *Fluency Record* or *Fluency Graph*. When fluency practice is completed for the day, partners store their portfolio, which contains the laminated *Practice Passage*, *Fluency Records* or *Fluency Graphs*, and a zipper-lock plastic bag with a dry-erase pen and erasing cloth.

Small Groups Within a Class

Repeated reading practice can also be implemented in a small-group setting—such as within a guided reading group—using the same *Practice Passage* for students who read at the same instructional level. Sample Schedule is as follows:

Monday
- The teacher and students preview the passage for accuracy.
- The teacher sets a timer for one minute. Students whisper-read the passage to themselves, underlining difficult words.
- When the timer sounds, students calculate their cwpm score and note the number on their own *Fluency Record* or *Fluency Graph*. This is their initial reading score.

Tuesday, Wednesday, Thursday
- The teacher and students choral-read the passage together for one minute.
- The teacher then sets a timer for one minute. Students whisper-read the passage to themselves.
- When the timer sounds, students calculate their cwpm score and note the number on their *Fluency Record* or *Fluency Graph*.

Friday
- Final timing, using one of two options:
  Option 1—Students pair up. The teacher sets a timer for one minute. One student reads while the partner follows along, underlining any reading errors and circling the last word read. Partner tells the reader how many cwpm were read, and reader records the number on his/her *Fluency Record* or *Fluency Graph*. This is the final timing. The teacher then resets the timer for one minute. Students repeat the process, with roles reversed.
  Option 2—The teacher listens to each student read for one minute while the other students follow along silently. The teacher tells each student his/her cwpm read on the final timing. Students graph their own results.

Individual Fluency Programs

Although all struggling readers should have reading fluency practice as an instructional goal, the partnership model is not appropriate in all educational settings. In a special education, remedial, or resource room—where students' instructional reading levels may be very diverse—it is often not possible to select evenly matched fluency partners. In these cases, individual fluency programs should be developed.

To establish an individual fluency program, the teacher will need to assess each student to determine the appropriate level for fluency practice. Students should be introduced to the concept of repeated reading and given a rationale as to why they will be engaging in the practice. Finally, each student will need his/her own fluency folder containing two *Practice Passages*—one for the student to read from and the other for the teacher to follow along with—a *Fluency Graph*, and a marking pen for filling in the graph each day.

There are two options for conducting individual fluency programs. With Option 1, each student reads a *Practice Passage* at his/her individual instructional level, and all students follow the same steps every day. With Option 2, each student reads a *Practice Passage* at his/her individual instructional level, and then proceeds through the steps at his/her own rate.

Option 1

- **Monday**—Each student selects a new *Practice Passage* at his/her own instructional level. Students read the passage on their own, underlining difficult or unknown words. The teacher meets with each student individually. The teacher reads the entire passage with the student for accuracy, modeling fluent reading. Then, the student reads the passage while being timed for one minute to obtain an initial cwpm score. The student graphs the cwpm score on his/her *Fluency Graph*.
- **Tuesday, Wednesday, Thursday**—All students take turns reading their *Practice Passage* to the teacher while being timed for one minute. Each student then graphs his/her cwpm score on his/her *Fluency Graph*. When not meeting with the teacher, students practice whisper-reading their passage.
- **Friday**—All students take turns reading their *Practice Passage* to the teacher while being timed for one minute in order to obtain a final score. Each student then graphs the final cwpm score on that particular passage on his/her *Fluency Graph*.

Option 2

- **Step 1**—Each student selects a new *Practice Passage* at his/her own instructional level.
- **Step 2**—The teacher meets with each student individually and together they choral-read the passage for accuracy (untimed).
- **Step 3**—Each student reads the passage to the teacher for one minute. The teacher tells the student how many cwpm he/she read. This is the student's initial score.
- **Step 4**—The teacher and the student select a target goal together. The goal should be 20–40 words above the initial timing. For example, if a student reads 50 cwpm on an initial timing, the target goal could be 80. **Note:** Select a target goal that is reasonably attainable for the student, taking into consideration his/her reading level and motivation.
- **Step 5**—Every day during fluency practice, the student reads his/her *Practice Passage* to the teacher for one minute and graphs the cwpm on his/her *Fluency Graph*. When students reach their oral reading goal with fewer than five reading errors, they have "passed" the passage. **Note:** Some students may be able to fluently read a passage in one week or less, while others may need to practice reading the same passage for two or more consecutive weeks before they reach their predetermined goal.

Parent-Student Partnerships

Parents can be easily trained to conduct one-minute fluency timings and data-recording procedures either at the school or at home. Working with their children on *Automatic Word Lists*, *Fluency Building Sheets*, and *Practice Passages* is a highly effective way for parents to support a school's readers. Home data-recording sheets can be brought to school and checked by the teacher. Additional *Practice Passages* can be sent home based on the data. As parents conduct fluency timings at home, they will acquire first-hand knowledge of their children's reading improvement on a daily basis.

Cross-Age Partnerships

Older students may be assigned as fluency partners to younger students. The older students conduct one-minute fluency timings and record the data of their younger partners.

CHAPTER 3

Introducing the Fluency Concept

This chapter provides a model for introducing the concept of fluency to students. We believe that students deserve an explanation prior to engaging in any new procedure. They are more likely to be enthusiastic participants when they understand the "what" and the "why." In the words of noted educator Dr. Anita Archer, "Rationale reduces resistance."

Materials:

- A copy of a sample *Practice Passage* (see *Fluency Building Sheets*) for each student. **Note:** The readability level of the passage should match that of the lowest reader in the class.
- A copy of a *Fluency Graph* (select from *1, 2,* or *3* in the *Appendix*) for each student.
- Overhead transparencies of the sample *Practice Passage* and the selected *Fluency Graph*.
- **Optional:** Overhead transparencies of blackline masters "What Is Fluency?" and "Why Is Fluency Important?" (see *Appendix*).
- Marking pens for students and an erasable marking pen for the teacher.
- Color markers for teacher and students.
- A timer.

Estimated time:
20–30 minutes

Use Activity Procedure or Scripted procedure

Activity Procedure

- **Step 1: Select the *Practice Passage*.** Select one passage for classroom demonstration and training. The readability of the selected passage should match the lowest level of reading in the class. For example, in a sixth-grade class, if the student who reads at the lowest level reads at the third-grade level, the passage selected for training should be at a third-grade readability level. It is important that students do not struggle while reading the *Practice Passage*.
- **Step 2: Introduce the concept of fluency.** Conduct the *Activity Procedure* or the *Scripted Procedure*, following.
  - Using grade-appropriate language, introduce students to the value of building fluency. You may paraphrase the information in the *Introduction* section and discuss the benefits of rereading, the concept of "practice makes perfect," and the correlation among fluency, comprehension, and work completion.

Optional Scripted Procedure

- Present the overhead transparency of "What Is Reading Fluency?" and say:
  - "Our class will be starting a daily reading fluency program. Before I explain the program to you, I want to talk about what fluency is and why it is important. Reading fluency is the ability to read text accurately. That means that you know the words. Reading fluency is also

the ability to read text quickly. However, fluency is not speed-reading. Good readers read quickly, but not *too* quickly. Finally, reading fluency is the ability to read with expression. As readers, we want to be sure to stop at the punctuation marks and read so that other people can understand what we are saying. That means that we need to clearly say each word, not read so fast that the words run together. We need to remember the three parts to fluent reading: reading accurately, reading quickly, and reading with expression."

– "Listen. When we read fluently, we are reading accurately, quickly, and with expression."

– "Everyone, when you read fluently, you are reading how? (Students should respond, "accurately.") You are also reading how? (Students should respond, "quickly.") But you are also reading with what, everyone?" (Students should respond, "with expression.")

– "So, reading fluently is reading accurately, quickly, and with expression. Say it with me, everyone." (Students should respond, "Reading fluently is reading accurately, quickly, and with expression.")

– Present the overhead transparency of "Why Is Reading Fluency Important?" and say:

– "It is important to work on improving reading fluency for three main reasons. How many reasons?" (Students should respond, " three.")

– "The most important reason is because reading fluency is related to reading comprehension. Fluent readers understand what they are reading. Fluent readers have good what, everyone?" (Students should respond, "comprehension.")

– "If we can read words easily or fluently, we can pay better attention to what we are reading. So the main reason we are going to work on reading fluency is that we will improve our what, everyone? Our … " (Students should respond, "comprehension.")

– "Fluent readers like to read because reading is easy for them. If reading is easy for us, we will read more and if we read more, we will learn more. So, another reason for improving reading fluency is to be able to read more independently. We are going to practice reading fluency so that we will become what kind of readers, everyone?" (Students should respond, "independent.")

– "Finally, fluent readers need less time to complete their class assignments and their homework. Fluent readers read faster, so they finish work faster and have more time for outside activities. Raise your hand if you would like to be able to finish your homework in less time. (*Pause for students' response.*) So, we will practice reading fluency so that we will improve our what, everyone?" (Students should respond, "work completion.")

Activity Procedure

- **Step 3: Explain the *Practice Passage*.** Pass out copies of the selected *Practice Passage* to students. Point out the numbers at the beginning of each line in the passage. Explain to students that these numbers will help them keep track of how many words they read in one minute.

- **Step 4: Model the reading fluency procedure.**
  - Explain to students that when they read a passage, they will start with the first word and read until the timer sounds. As they read, they should track with a pen (without making marks) and underline any unknown or difficult words. When the timer sounds, they will draw a diagonal line after the last word read.
  - Demonstrate the above procedure with the overhead transparency of the selected *Practice Passage*.
  - Continue using the transparency to demonstrate **how to count the total number of words read**. Starting at the number at the beginning of the last line read, simply count from that number to the last word read. This is the total number of words read. Write that number in the calculation notation at the bottom of the passage page. Count the number of underlined (i.e., unknown or incorrect) words. Write that number in the calculation notation at the bottom of the passage page. Subtract the number of underlined words from the total number of words to determine the **correct words per minute (cwpm)**. Write that number in the calculation notation at the bottom of the passage page.

Optional Scripted Procedure

- "Listen. When we read a passage, we will start with the first word of the passage (point) and read until the timer sounds. Where will we start, everyone?" (Students should respond, "with the first word of the passage.")
- "As we read, we should track with our finger or pen and be ready to underline any unknown or difficult words. A difficult word is a word that we cannot figure out within a couple of seconds. What will we do with difficult words, everyone?" (Students should respond, "underline them.")
- "When the timer sounds, we will draw a diagonal line after the last word we read. Watch me." (Demonstrate drawing a diagonal line.)
- "Next, we need to figure out the total number of correct words we read. To do this, we look at where we put the diagonal line after the last word we read. What do we do first, everyone?" (Students should respond, "find the last word we read.")
- "Then we go back to the beginning of that line. Where do we go, everyone?" (Students should respond, "to the beginning of the last line we read.")
- "We find the number count on that line. What do we find, everyone?" (Students should respond, "the number count.")
- "Then we count from that number to the last word read. That is the total number of words we read. What is it, everyone?" (Students should respond, "the total number of words read.")
- "We write that number on this line at the bottom of the page." (Write the number on the "Total Words Read" line.)
- "Next, we count the number of underlined words. What do we count, everyone?" (Students should respond, "the number of underlined words.")

- "We write that number on this line." (Write the number on the "Errors" line.)
- "Then, we subtract the number of underlined words from the total number of words read. The answer gives us the number of correct words read per minute, or the cwpm. (Write the number on the "CWPM" line.) What does it tell us, everyone?" (Students should respond, "the number of correct words read per minute.")

Activity Procedure

- **Step 5: Students whisper-read the Practice Passage.** Conduct the *Activity Procedure* or the *Scripted Procedure*, following.
  - Set the timer for one minute and ask students to whisper-read the passage, following the procedures of tracking, underlining unknown/ difficult words, and drawing a diagonal line after the last word read when the timer sounds. **Note:** Students must whisper-read in order to simulate oral reading.
  - When the timer sounds, ask students to count the total number of words read, count the number of underlined words, and subtract the number of underlined words to determine their cwpm scores. Monitor students carefully.
  - Set the timer for another minute, and ask students to reread the passage, beginning with the first word.
  - When the timer sounds, ask students to determine their cwpm scores.
  - Lead a group discussion about fluency practice. Ask students to raise their hands if their cwpm scores were higher with the second reading. Solicit student reflection on why they might have read more words the second time.

Optional Scripted Procedure

- "Now it is your turn. I am going to set the timer for one minute. When I tell you to begin, I want you to whisper-read the passage, beginning with the first word. It is important that you whisper-read because we are practicing oral—not silent—reading. As you read, underline any unknown or difficult words. When the timer sounds, draw a diagonal mark after the last word you read. Let's check: Will you read silently? (Students should respond, "no.") How will you read? (Students should respond, "whisper-read.") What will you do when the timer sounds? (Students should respond, "draw a slash mark after the last word I read.")
- When the timer sounds, say, "Draw a diagonal mark after the last word you read. Go back to the beginning of that line. Say the number and continue counting until you reach the last word read. That is your total number of words. Write that number down at the bottom of the passage page." Monitor students carefully.
- "Now, go back to the beginning of the passage and count the number of underlined words. Write that number down at the bottom of the page." Monitor students carefully.
- "Subtract that number from your total number of words, and write it on the last line." Monitor students carefully.

- "Now you have your number of correct words per minute, or cwpm."
- "Now you are going to whisper-read the passage again. Start with the first word of the passage, whisper-read, and underline unknown or difficult words. When the timer sounds this time, circle the last word you read instead of drawing a diagonal line. Ready, please begin."
- When the timer sounds, say, "Circle the last word you read. Go back to the beginning of that line. Say the number and continue counting until you reach the last word read. That is your total number of words. Write that number down." Monitor students carefully.
- "Now go back to the beginning of the passage, and count the number of underlined words. Write that number down. Subtract that number from your total number of words." Monitor students carefully.
- "Now you have your cwpm score for your second reading."
- "Compare your first timing score with your second timing score. (*Pause as students compare.*) Raise your hand if you read more words the second time than you read the first time." The vast majority of students will have read more words the second time.
- "Turn to your neighbor (partner) and tell why you think you read more words the second time." Monitor students carefully.
- "As I monitored, I heard many of you say that when you read the second time, you already knew the words. You were familiar with the passage, so you could read faster the second time. There were no surprises on the second reading. You are exactly right. The more you practice a skill, the better you get. So in order to become more fluent readers, we are going to practice every day."

Activity Procedure

- **Step 6: Students graph their cwpm scores.** Conduct the *Activity Procedure* or the *Scripted Procedure*, following.
  - Using the overhead transparency of the *Fluency Graph*, demonstrate how to use it to record cwpm scores.
  - Using their copy of the *Fluency Graph*, have students practice graphing their cwpm scores on their first and second readings of the demonstration passage.

Optional Scripted Procedure

- "Now we are going to look at how to graph cwpm scores. Each one of you has a graph that looks like this (show the example *Fluency Graph*). At the top, you will write your name, your partner's name, the class you are in, and the date you first started using this graph. For today's practice, just fill in your name."
- "Notice that there is a place for the date and the passage number at the bottom of the graph. Fill in today's date and the practice passage number. Since all of us are reading the same passage on the same day, we will all have the same date and passage number."
- "Now look at the numbers on the left side of the graph. Those numbers represent the number of correct words you read in one minute. What do the numbers stand for?" (Students should respond, "number of correct words read in one minute.")

- "Do you see a place for errors on this graph? (Students should respond, "no.") You will not be recording errors on this graph. You will record only correct words per minute, or cwpm, from the practice passage onto the graph."
- "Look at the bottom of the graph. Do the numbers start with 1? (Students should respond, "no.") What do they start with? (Students should respond, "5.") That's right; the numbers are in increments of 5."
- "Let's pretend that I read 45 cwpm on my initial timing. Put your finger on the number 45. I will color in the squares from 5 to 45 to graph my initial timing."
- "Let's pretend that on my second timing, I read 52 cwpm. Is the number 52 on the graph? (Students should respond, "no.") So I will have to estimate. To do that, I will go to the number closest to 52. What number will that be? (Students should respond, "50.") Then I will fill in the column just a little higher than 50 to show that I read more than 50 cwpm. This time I will color in the squares from 5 to just past 50 to graph my second timing."
- "Now it's your turn. Graph your first and second timing scores. Raise your hand if you need help." Walk around the classroom and monitor as students graph their cwpm scores.

CHAPTER 4

Establishing Partner Behavior

In order for the partnership model to be successful, students need to work together in a polite and respectful manner. This chapter offers suggestions for introducing the concept of a working relationship within a cooperative partnership.

Students need to be instructed in appropriate fluency partnership behavior (e.g., leaning in and whispering), remembering that the only people who need to hear them are their partners, and providing appropriate corrective feedback on missed words. Addressing classroom noise level during training is key to preventing many potential problems. Teachers are often amazed at the low level of classroom noise when fluency timings are in progress.

Materials:
None

Estimated time:
10 minutes

Use Activity Procedure or Scripted Procedure

Activity Procedure

- Tell students that they will be working with a fluency partner for six minutes each day, emphasizing that the partnership is a *working relationship* and not necessarily a friendship. You may want to give an example of cooperation within a workplace, relating that although people do not necessarily like everyone they work with and they may not want to be close friends, they still need to treat each other with respect. You may also want to explain that the partnerships were assigned based on assessment information and the fact that "the computer assigned the partners." **Note:** If the concept of fluency is discussed completely with the class, there are generally fewer problems within partnerships. However, very occasionally, there may be partners who simply do not work well together. In that case, partners may need to be reassigned.
- Set rules about the appropriate noise level during fluency practice. Remind students that half the class will be reading aloud at the same time, and that the only people who need to hear them are their fluency partners. Tell students that they will "lean in and whisper" when reading to their partners. Model the procedure, giving positive and negative examples.
- Teach students to give polite feedback during the error-correction procedure (see *Figure 4.1*).

Figure 4.1
An Example of the Error-Correction Procedure

While the reader is reading aloud for one minute, the fluency partner follows along and underlines any errors. When the timer sounds, the partner notes the last word read, then provides polite feedback in the following manner.

Partner: "You read _____ (total number of) words. I heard _____ (number of) errors." The partner then points to each underlined (incorrect) word and pronounces it correctly for the reader. The partner asks the reader to repeat the word correctly.

Reader: Records the cwpm on the *Fluency Graph*.

Note: Establish a "No Arguing" rule between partners at this point in the training.

Optional Scripted Procedure

- "We are going to be working in partnerships to practice reading fluency for six minutes every day. Let me tell you about partnerships. Partnerships are a working relationship. What are they, everyone? (Students should respond, "a working relationship.") A working relationship means that you work together. You do not have to be friends with your partners. You do not have to eat lunch together or walk down the hall together. You do not have to talk to each other outside of this class. But here is what you do need to do. For the six minutes that you are working in the partnership, you have to be polite and respectful. What do you have to be, everyone?" (Students should respond, "polite and respectful.")

- "In your partnerships, one of you will be Partner 1 and one of you will be Partner 2. All Partners 1s will read at the same time while all Partner 2s will listen, follow along, and underline any reading errors. That means that half the class will be reading at one time. If all Partner 1s read in a regular speaking voice, is it possible that the noise level in the room will be too high? Yes or no? (Students should respond, "yes.") In order to keep the noise level down so that partners can hear each other read, you will lean in and whisper. What will you do, everyone?" (Students should respond, "lean in and whisper.").

- Choose a student partner to demonstrate the procedure: "I am (Juan's) partner. Watch me read to Juan." Demonstrate reading in a normal speaking tone while looking straight ahead. "Did I lean in and whisper? Yes or no? (Students should respond, "no."). Watch me again." Demonstrate the "lean in and whisper" procedure. "Did I lean in and whisper?" (Students should respond, "yes.")

- "While your partner is reading, you will follow along and underline any errors you hear. What will you do, everyone? (Students should respond, "follow along and underline errors.") When the timer sounds, you will draw a diagonal line after the last word your partner read. What will you do when the timer sounds, everyone? (Students should respond, "draw a diagonal line after the last word my partner read.") Then you will figure out your partner's correct words per minute, or cwpm, score. What will you do, everyone?" (Students should respond, "figure out my partner's correct words per minute score.")

- "The next step is reporting to your partner. What is the next step, everyone? (Students should respond, "reporting to my partner.") First, you will tell your partner the total number of words that he/she read. Say, 'You read _____ words.' What do you say, everyone?" (Students should respond, "you read _____ words.")

- "Then you say, 'I heard _____ errors.' What do you say, everyone? (Students should respond, "I heard _____ errors.") Why do you suppose I want you to say 'I heard _____ errors' rather than 'You made _____ errors'? (Students should suggest it sounds better.) Yes, it sounds kinder. Then you tell your partner their correct words per minute. That is the number they will graph at the end of the session."

- "Finally, you will point to any reading errors your partner made, one word at a time, and pronounce the word correctly for your partner. Your partner will then read the word again correctly."

- "There is one very important rule you need to follow when working with your partner. The rule is 'No Arguing.' What is the rule, everyone? (Students should respond, "no arguing.") The reason we have a 'No Arguing' rule is that arguing wastes time. What does it do, everyone? (Students should respond, "it wastes time.") If your partner underlines a word that you think you read correctly, you could stop reading and tell your partner that he/she made a mistake. But if you do that, you will miss the rest of the timing for the day and won't be able to record a score. So, if your partner hears you read a word incorrectly, it is counted as an error because there is no what? (Students should respond, "no arguing.") The best thing for partners to do is to treat each other fairly."

CHAPTER 5

Training Students in the Partnership Model

Taking the time to properly train students in *Six-Minute Solution Intermediate* procedures will ensure that the program runs smoothly. This chapter discusses how to teach students correct fluency procedures. Once students are properly trained, the entire fluency practice should take only six minutes of the reading period each day.

Devote a *minimum* of two to three class periods to training (Steps 3–6 in *Chapters 3–6*). We recommend that an explicit instructional model be employed when teaching the procedures. Each procedure should be introduced through modeling, then considerable guided practice time should be allowed with the teacher walking around the classroom to monitor, give feedback, and remodel procedures as necessary before students practice the procedure independently.

Teachers may want to randomly assign or specifically select partners for this step so that students can practice the procedure before teaming up with their ultimately assigned partners. Once all students feel comfortable with the procedure, they can then be placed with their assigned fluency partners.

Materials:
- For each fluency partnership, one pocket portfolio that includes two copies of a preselected *Practice Passage* (either laminated or placed in a plastic sleeve) and two copies of a *Fluency Graph* (one for each partner).
- For each fluency partnership, a zipper-lock plastic bag containing a dry-erase marker and erasing cloth.
- A *Fluency Graph* for each student.
- Overhead transparencies of the selected *Grade-Level Practice Passage* and *Fluency Graph*.
- A timer.

Estimated time:
20–30 minutes

Use Activity Procedure or Scripted Procedure

Activity Procedure
- Select a *Practice Passage* at the readability level that matches the lowest reading level in the class.
- Seat students with fluency partners (randomly assigned or specifically selected) and assign them the numbers 1 and 2.
- Using the overhead transparency of the selected *Practice Passage*, model the fluency partnership with a student partner, emphasizing how the listener should track the words being read by the partner. Tracking helps students keep their place as their partners read and makes marking errors easier.
- Model the procedure for marking errors and noting the stopping point.
- Model the error-correction procedure (see *Figure 4.1* in *Chapter 4*).
- Model how to calculate cwpm by counting the total number of words read and subtracting errors. For example:

Total Words Read   _____ *120* _____

− Errors   _____ *5* _____

= CWPM   _____ *115* _____

- Using the overhead transparency of the *Fluency Graph*, review how to graph cwpm scores.
- After reviewing and modeling all aspects of fluency partnership activities, have students practice the fluency procedure. Set the timer for one minute, and ask all Partner 1s to read. Remind them to lean in and whisper-read to their partners. Remind Partner 2s to track their partner's reading.
- Instruct Partner 2s to give polite feedback to Partner 1s.
- Set the timer again for one minute and ask Partner 2s to read. Remind them to lean in and whisper-read to their partners. Remind Partner 1s to track their partner's reading.
- Instruct Partner 1s to give polite feedback to Partner 2s.

Optional Scripted Procedure

- Select a student with whom to demonstrate the partner procedure. Ask the student to read, and instruct him/her to make a few reading errors. Say, "Watch as my partner Sarita and I conduct our fluency timings. Sarita is Partner 1, so she will read first. Watch and see what I do while she is reading."
- Set the timer for one minute and ask the student to begin reading. Model tracking with a pen and underlining reading errors as the student reads.
- After the timer sounds, ask, "What did you observe me doing with my pen as my partner was reading? (Students should respond, "tracking.") Yes, it is important to follow along by tracking under each word as my partner reads. What did I do when I heard an error? (Students should respond, "you underlined it.") Yes, I underlined the word and kept tracking. Did I make any extra marks on the passage? (Students should respond, "no.") That's correct. I made a mark only if I heard an error. If I had drawn a line under each word my partner read, would I have been able to tell when she made an error? Yes or no? (Students should respond, "no."). Also, marking under all of the words would be messy and hard to clean off in only one minute."
- "Now listen to me give polite feedback to Sarita: 'You read 86 words. I heard 2 errors. 86 − 2 = 84. 84 is your cwpm score. Mark that number on your graph. You will color in the squares later.' "
- "Now I need to tell Sarita the words she missed and ask her to repeat them." Point to the first error and say, "This word is _____ . What word?" Continue with the other missed words.
- "Now it is everyone's turn. Raise your hand if you are Partner 1s. Raise your hand if you are Partner 2s. When I say, 'Please begin,' all Partner 1s will lean in and whisper-read to their partners. All Partner 2s should have their pens and be ready to track their partner's reading, mark reading errors, and draw a diagonal line at the stopping point. Please begin."

- When the timer sounds, say, "All Partner 2s, give polite feedback to Partner 1s." Partner 1s mark their cwpm scores on their graph. Monitor students carefully.
- "Now it is Partner 2's turn. When I say 'Please begin,' all Partner 2s will lean in and whisper-read to their partners. All Partner 1s should have their pens and be ready to track their partner's reading, mark reading errors, and draw a diagonal line at the stopping point. Please begin."
- When the timer sounds, say, " Now, Partner 1s should give polite feedback to Partner 2s." Partner 2s mark their cwpm scores on their graph. Monitor students carefully.
- At the end of the timings, have one partner from each partnership put the materials away.

CHAPTER 6

Managing Materials

Well-organized materials that are easily accessible to students will assist in the establishment of effective fluency routines. This chapter includes ideas for initial implementation and ongoing management of *Six-Minute Solution Intermediate* materials.

Materials:
- One pocket portfolio for each partnership. Label each portfolio with the names of Partner 1 and Partner 2.
- Each portfolio should hold two copies of the same *Practice Passage* (laminated or enclosed in a plastic sleeve), a *Fluency Graph* for each student, and a zipper-lock plastic bag containing a dry-erase marker and erasing cloth.
- Stored Practice Passages in a central file that is accessible to students in order of readability.

Estimated Time:
10–15 minutes

Activity Procedure
- *Practice Passages* for each partnership. (*Practice Passages* are number-coded by grade level [e.g., all fifth-grade-level passages are numbered in the 500s, all sixth-grade-level passages are numbered in the 600s]. This coding system enables teachers to note reading levels without the levels being obvious to students.)
- Tell the class where the *Practice Passages* and partnership portfolios will be located.
- Demonstrate the process for choosing a new passage on Friday for fluency practice the next week:
  —Take the currently used *Practice Passages* out of the plastic sleeves.
  —Return the passages to the designated file and select two copies of a different *Practice Passage* within the same readability level or per the teacher's instruction.
- Teach students to return their partnership portfolios—with all materials—to the designated location.

Additional Fluency Tips
- Once students are trained in the *Six-Minute Solution Intermediate* instructional format (see *Table I.1* in the *Introduction*), use the *Six-Minute Solution Intermediate Sample Schedule* (see *Program Overview*). It is most effective and efficient for students to begin reading a new *Practice Passage* on the first day of the school week.
- Make certain that each partnership knows who is Partner 1 and who is Partner 2. Partner 1 is the stronger reader and always reads first. However, do not share that information with students; simply state that Partner 1 reads first for management purposes.

- Tell students where they will sit during fluency practice. For example, some teachers make a seating arrangement for the language arts period that places partners next to each other. Other teachers have Partner 1s move beside Partner 2s' desks.
- Begin the first fluency practice session of the week with an accuracy check. Have students read the *Practice Passage*—untimed—to determine any unknown or difficult words. If neither of the partners knows a word, supply it for them. This accuracy check should occur only on the first day of a new *Practice Passage* each week.
- Remember that students need a minimum of three to five repeated readings of the same *Practice Passage*. Since both partners will be reading the same *Practice Passage*, they will hear it twice a day. Practice Passages should be changed once a week so that students are not able to memorize them. **Note:** The reading level of a Practice Passage is changed only after teacher review and assessment.
- Remind students that they are responsible for keeping to the six-minute time frame:
  - 1 minute for the partners to get ready.
  - 1 minute for Partner 1 to read.
  - 1 minute for Partner 2 to tell Partner 1 the total number of words read, the errors, corrections, and cwpm. Partner 1 quickly records his/her cwpm.
  - 1 minute for Partner 2 to read.
  - 1 minute for Partner 1 to tell Partner 2 the total number of words read, the errors, corrections, and cwpm. Partner 2 quickly records his/her cwpm.
  - 1 minute for both partners to color in their own graphs and put materials away.
- Generally speaking, fluency partners provide accountability for each other. Occasionally, a partnership may appear to be awarding inflated scores. A word or two in private to the "suspects" should solve the problem, along with maintaining close proximity while the partnership is conducting its timings.
- *Continually* monitor students closely during the six-minute fluency practices.

CHAPTER 7

Student Progress and Record Keeping

Record keeping is an essential component of *Six-Minute Solution Intermediate*. It is critical to monitor improvement and make instructional decisions based on individual student progress. This may be accomplished by using either the *Fluency Record* or the *Fluency Graphs* (see *Appendix*). Teach students how to graph their own progress. Students tend to enjoy using *Fluency Records* and *Fluency Graphs*, as these tools make it easy for them to see their progress. Graphs can be especially motivating to students who have not had much reading success in the past. It gives them a concrete way to see their reading skills improve.

As a general rule, students who repeatedly read *Practice Passages* at the correct instructional level make weekly progress—even if only by an increase of a few correct words per minute. Give special attention to any student whose reading rates are not increasing from week to week.

Determine whether students are reading at the expected rate for their instructional reading levels (see *Table 1.1* in *Chapter 1*). Remember, each student should read at the rate commensurate with the *instructional reading level*, not the grade-level placement. Reading rates increase as students are able to read more difficult material.

Check your students' *Fluency Records* or *Fluency Graphs* on a regular basis in order to determine that:

- Adequate progress is being made.
- Students have been assigned appropriate *Practice Passages*—neither too easy nor too difficult.
- Students have been assigned appropriate fluency partners.
- It is the appropriate time to increase the difficulty level of the *Practice Passage* being used by partners.

Making Instructional Decisions Based on Fluency Graphs

The following examples demonstrate how the information on a student's *Fluency Record* or *Fluency Graph* can help you make important instructional decisions.

Example 1: Kevin

Kevin is a fifth-grade student with a second-grade instructional reading level. Based on *Table 1.1* (Hasbrouck & Tindal, 2005) in *Chapter 1*, he is within the expected reading rate for his instructional level. Kevin is also making adequate progress. The first five days on his *Fluency Graph* (see *Figure 7.1*) reflect rereading the same *Practice Passage*. His first reading on Monday was 60 cwpm. After practicing the passage four more times, his ending fluency rate was 70 cwpm.

Notice what happens the following week (see March 9 column). Kevin is now reading a new *Practice Passage*. However, his beginning fluency rate has increased by five words (from 60 to 65 cwpm) when compared to the previous Monday—even though this is a new *Practice Passage*. As Kevin continued to reread this passage during the second week, his reading rate steadily improved. As Kevin's reading rate continues to improve and he begins to approach 80 cwpm, he will most likely be ready to start practicing *Practice Passages* at the third-grade level. Kevin's expected fluency rate goal would then range from 70 to 110 cwpm.

Figure 7.1
Kevin's Fluency Graph

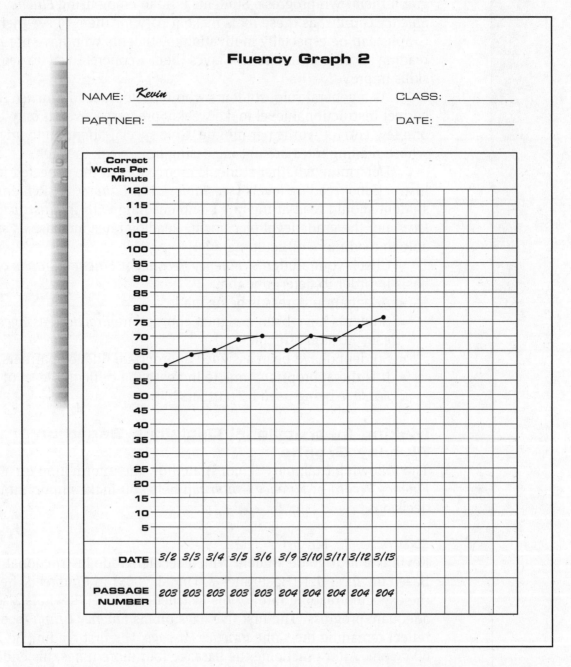

Example 2: Sarita

Sarita is reading at a third-grade instructional level and was assigned a third-grade *Practice Passage*. Based on *Table 1.1* (Hasbrouck & Tindal, 2005) in *Chapter 1*, the appropriate goal for Sarita is to read 70–110 cwpm.

A glance at Sarita's *Fluency Graph* (see *Figure 7.2*) reveals that she is reading below her expected range. In this case, the teacher decides that he needs to reevaluate whether Sarita has been placed correctly at her instructional level. Based on the reevaluation, the teacher will decide whether or not to: (1) lower the *Practice Passage* reading level; (2) add practice with the *Automatic Word Lists*; or (3) incorporate additional instructional strategies such as the ones in the following section, "Helping the Student Who Is Not Making Adequate Progress." (Refer to the *Practice Passages* and the *Automatic Word Lists*—both in the *Fluency Building Sheets* section—for choosing *Automatic Word Lists* to use with your students.)

Figure 7.2
Sarita's Fluency Graph

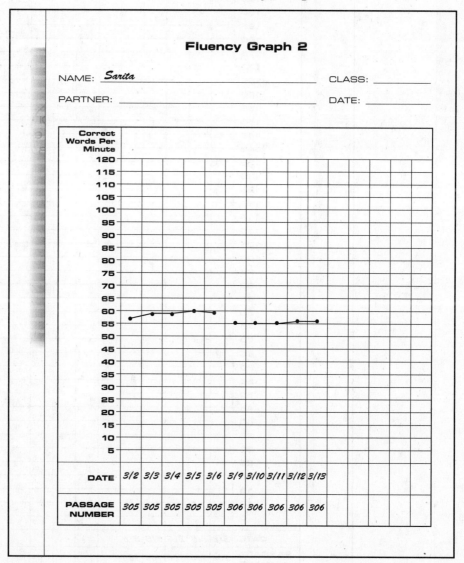

Example 3: José

José is a fourth-grade student with a fourth-grade instructional reading level. His fluency goal, as shown in *Table 1.1* (Hasbrouck & Tindal, 2005) in *Chapter 1*, is 125 cwpm. When José's teacher reviewed his *Fluency Graph* (see *Figure 7.3*), she noticed that his reading rate is above his goal rate. She decided to assign fifth-grade *Practice Passages* to José, which may be more challenging for him.

Figure 7.3
José's Fluency Graph

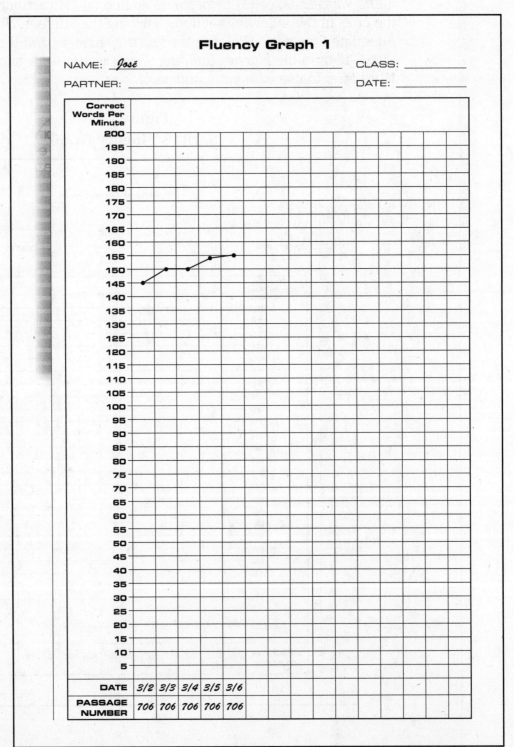

Helping the Student Who Is Not Making Adequate Progress

If a student is not making progress in the passage fluency and word-building activities in *Six-Minute Solution Intermediate*, the reason may be is that the assigned *Practice Passages* do not match the student's instructional reading level. A student must be placed at the correct instructional reading level in order to make the expected progress. When students practice fluency at their correct instructional levels, the vast majority of them make excellent progress. However, if after examining a student's *Fluency Graph* or *Fluency Record* you determine that little progress has been made in two or more weeks, consider the following:

- If a student reads fewer than 40 cwpm, an intensive comprehensive reading program should be used instead of, or in addition to, *Six-Minute Solution Intermediate*. A student who does not read more than 40 cwpm needs explicit instruction in underlying reading skills before reading fluency can be developed.

- Read the *Practice Passage* with the student to ascertain if he/she has been placed at the correct instructional reading level. The student should be able to correctly read approximately 95 percent of the words when reading at the appropriate instructional reading level. Note the errors the student is making. Perhaps many of the words the student is having difficulty with are high-frequency sight words. In this case, the student is likely to benefit from additional practice using the *Automatic Word Lists*. These lists contain sets of the most commonly encountered (i.e., high-frequency) words in the written English language.

- If you observe that a student is having great difficulty reading an assigned *Practice Passage*, select another one that is one grade level below. If the student reads less than 95 percent of the words correctly in the new passage, have him/her read a *Practice Passage* at an even lower reading level.

- A student's reading fluency problems may be associated with poor decoding skills. Assess whether the student would benefit from extra instruction in decoding.

- When students are first presented with new *Practice Passages*, make a point of meeting with the partnerships of struggling readers to ensure that they are demonstrating adequate accuracy. Consistently and carefully monitor partnerships of struggling readers throughout the week.

- A stronger reader may be paired with a struggling reader as a practice partner. The stronger reader reads the *Practice Passage* while the struggling reader follows closely behind, echoing the words of the stronger reader. The struggling reader will gain additional reading strength by having the passage read almost simultaneously. Practice partnership sessions should take place in addition to the regular *Six-Minute Solution Intermediate* sessions.

- Give fluency partners extra untimed reading-practice opportunities. Partners can whisper-read to each other, thus gaining additional rereadings of the same *Practice Passage* before taking their formal one-minute timings. Whisper-reading will help to build the confidence of struggling readers before their actual word counts are recorded.

- Fluency partners may also "ping-pong read" sentences back and forth to each other as another form of practice. This practice will also help students gain confidence and familiarity with the *Practice Passage* prior to the formal fluency timing.

CHAPTER 8

Comprehension and Summary Writing Strategies

Comprehension strategies (e.g., summarizing and paraphrasing) and the use of graphic organizers can be taught and practiced using the *Practice Passages* in *Six-Minute Solution Intermediate*. We recommend that students be taught comprehension strategies and how to use graphic organizers directly through modeling and guided practice, bolstered by independent practice. Oral activities can easily be extended into a mini-lesson on how to take notes on expository material using the indentation note-taking strategy as described in the *Skills for School Success Series* (Archer & Gleason, 2002). Examples of effective comprehension strategies for nonfiction include:

- Summarizing
- Paraphrasing
- Retelling
- Describing
- Learning expository text structure

Summarizing

One method of improving students' comprehension skills is to teach summarizing. First, model summarizing by pausing after reading aloud each paragraph of a *Practice Passage* from an overhead transparency. Then, "think aloud" while you determine the main idea of each paragraph, limiting the number of words you use to summarize. Counting the words as they are spoken is a powerful way to illustrate this point. Another effective way to teach summarizing is to use "paragraph-shrinking" techniques (Fuchs, Fuchs, Kazlan, & Allen, 1999).

Once you have modeled oral summarizing, you can assign student partners alternate paragraphs from their *Practice Passage* to orally summarize. Then, have the partners practice orally summarizing the whole passage. With additional instruction, this oral summarization practice can be extended to summary writing. After students complete their oral summarizations, ask them to turn over the *Practice Passage* and write a short summary of it.

Paraphrasing

To model paraphrasing, read aloud a *Practice Passage*—paragraph by paragraph—from an overhead transparency. After reading each paragraph, stop and announce, "I can put the information in this paragraph into my own words by saying …. " Point out to students that it is easier to learn new information when you put it into your own words instead of trying to remember the text's language.

After modeling, have student partners paraphrase alternate paragraphs of their *Practice Passage*. Another effective method for teaching paraphrasing is the "read-cover-recite-check" strategy from the *Skills for School Success Series* (Archer & Gleason, 2002).

Retelling

Read aloud a *Practice Passage* from an overhead transparency. Then, model a brief retelling of the passage, using the main ideas of the paragraphs to formulate the retelling. By using phrases such as "The passage began with … ,"

"Next, I read … ," and "Then I learned … ," you can effectively model retelling of information.

Describing

You can model describing by listing the characteristics, features, and examples of a topic. As you model, include key vocabulary words and phrases generally found in descriptive texts such as "for example," "characteristics," "for instance," "such as," and "to illustrate." You may use a spider-web graphic organizer (as in *Figure 8.1*) in which the topic of the passage is listed in a circle in the center and the features are written on lines extending out from the circle, forming a web.

Students can take turns orally describing their *Practice Passage* paragraphs to their partners while the partners take notes on the passage.

Figure 8.1
Spider-Web Graphic Organizer

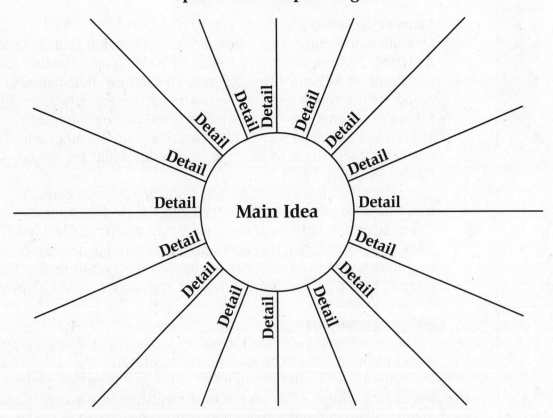

Learning Expository Text Structure

Students can be taught about how text is structured using the following methods:

- Sequencing
- Comparing
- Analyzing cause and effect
- Problem solving

Sequencing

Some of the *Practice Passages* list items or events in numerical or chronological order, or in sequences. When teaching students a comprehension strategy for this type of passage, call attention to key vocabulary words such as "first," "second," "third," "next," "then," "finally," "yesterday," "today," "now," "later," "before," and "after." Extend this sequencing comprehension activity to include writing by using a graphic organizer to list information sequentially (see *Figure 8.2*).

Figure 8.2
Sequencing Graphic Organizer

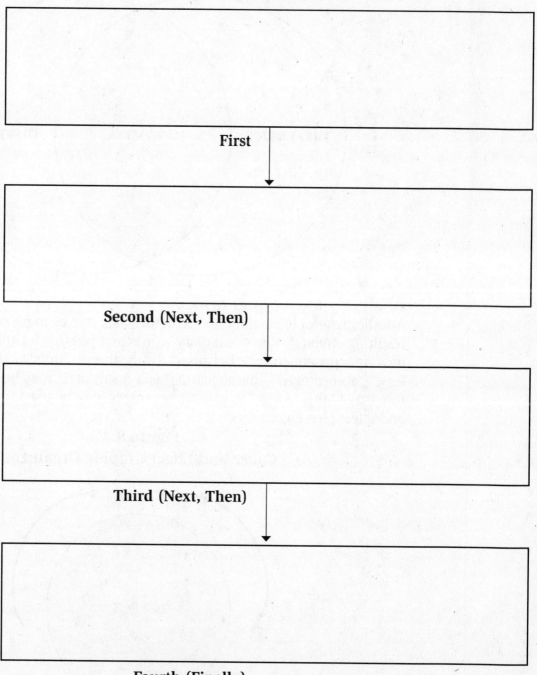

Comparing

Some of the *Practice Passages* explain how two or more things are alike or different. Call attention to key vocabulary words and phrases in these passages such as "alike," "same as," "different from," "in contrast," "on the other hand," "but," "yet," "however," "although," "opposite of," "as well as," "while," and "unless." Venn diagrams are excellent graphic organizers to use for showing the similarities and differences in comparison text. A Venn diagram consists of two or more overlapping circles (see *Figure 8.3*).

Figure 8.3
Venn Diagram

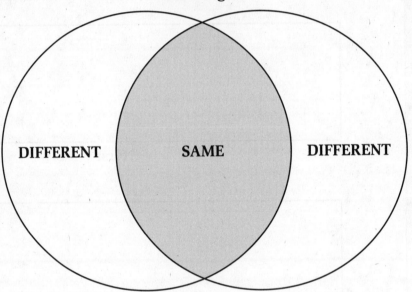

Analyzing Cause and Effect

Another type of expository text structure lists one or more causes and the resulting effect(s). Key vocabulary words and phrases for this type of text include "consequently," "because," "if ... then," "thus," "since," "neverthe- less," "accordingly," "because of," "as a result of," "may be due to," "there- fore," and "this led to." A graphic organizer may be used to illustrate cause and effect (see *Figure 8.4*).

Figure 8.4
Cause and Effect Graphic Organizer

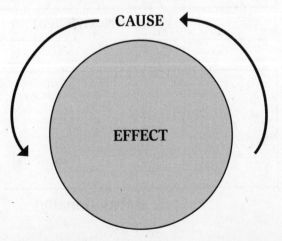

Problem-Solving

This type of expository text structure states a problem and lists one or more solutions. Key vocabulary words and phrases include "the problem is," "the question is," "furthermore," "one reason for," "a solution," and "another possibility." An example of a graphic organizer for problem-solving text is shown in *Figure 8.5*.

Figure 8.5
Problem-Solving Graphic Organizer

Problem:

Solutions:

Summary Writing Strategies

Teachers may elect to incorporate summary writing strategies into the *Six-Minute Solution Intermediate* fluency model. In that case, on the last day of fluency practice, partners write a short summary of the assigned *Practice Passage*. It is recommended that teachers demonstrate summary writing with a *Practice Passage* at a readability level that matches that of the lowest reader in the class.

Materials:
- A copy of the demonstration *Practice Passage* for each student.
- A copy of *Summary Paragraph Frame 1* or *Summary Paragraph Frame 2* (see *Appendix*) for each student.
- An overhead transparency of the demonstration *Practice Passage*.
- An overhead transparency of *Summary Paragraph Frame 1* or *Summary Paragraph Frame 2*.
- A transparency writing pen.

Procedure:
1. Distribute copies of the demonstration *Practice Passage* and *Summary Paragraph Frame 1* or *Summary Paragraph Frame 2* to students.
2. Introduce the summary paragraph frame and discuss the components of the frame.
3. Read the demonstration *Practice Passage* together with students.
4. Model filling in the components of the paragraph frame by thinking aloud.
5. Have students follow along and fill in their paragraph frame.
6. Using the completed paragraph frame, join students in writing summary paragraphs.

Summary Paragraph Frame 1

This passage was about _____. First, I learned _____. Next, I learned _____ . Finally, I learned _____.

Summary Paragraph Frame 2

Topic sentence (name the "who" or the "what"). Tell the most important thing about the "who" or the "what."

Example:

_____ is/was _____. One important fact is _____. Another important fact is _____. A final important fact is _____.

Conclusion: More Than Six Minutes a Day

One of the advantages of the *Six-Minute Solution Intermediate* fluency partner model is that students are able to increase their oral reading fluency in only six minutes of an instructional period. This curriculum's original grouping configuration is a partnership match based on instructional reading and fluency levels. By utilizing this configuration, the partnership is self-supporting—each partner's reading level and cwpm score mirror the other partner's. In this way, partnerships can function independently with little supervision.

However, there might be times when more than six minutes a day must be devoted to fluency practice, as in the following situations:

- On the first day of the week—when partnerships receive a new *Practice Passage*—more time will be required. Each student in the partnership silently reads the entire new *Practice Passage*. If any words are unknown, students consult first with their partners. If neither partner knows a word, the teacher supplies the correct pronunciation.
- Although the program can be easily implemented in a class of struggling readers, an individual fluency program may be more appropriate for some students. In these cases, additional time will be needed for fluency practice.
- Certain grouping configurations, such as guided reading groups, require more than six minutes a day.
- Incorporating additional comprehension activities and/or summary writing will require additional time.

The *Six-Minute Solution Intermediate* partnership fluency model works well if partners can be fairly evenly matched. However, some educational settings do not lend themselves to the partnership fluency model. If instructional levels of students are very diverse, it would not be appropriate to assign fluency partners.

Keep in mind that fluency practice is essential for *all* struggling readers. If a particular setting does not lend itself to the partnership model, *Six-Minute Solution Intermediate* may be adjusted to become an individualized fluency program. Refer to the "Individual Fluency Programs" section of *Chapter 2* for two individual fluency program options. As an individualized fluency program, the *Six-Minute Solution Intermediate* model may instead become the **Sixteen-Minute** *Solution Intermediate* model. However, the benefits of daily fluency practice will more than compensate for the additional time required.

SIX MINUTE

Assessments

Using the *Six-Minute Solution Intermediate* Assessment Passages

The six *Assessment Passages* included in *Six-Minute Solution Intermediate*—Levels 1–6 for first grade to sixth grade—were designed to serve several purposes, and they may be used in a variety of ways. Refer to *Chapter 1: Assessments* for additional information.

Using Assessment Passages to Assess Correct Words Per Minute (cwpm) and to Form Student Partnerships

1. **Select the *Assessment Passage* that matches the current grade level of the students being assessed.** For example, all students in a sixth-grade language arts class should be assessed on the same Level 6 *Assessment Passage*. The reading of *Assessment Passages* should be unpracticed, meaning that students should not silently read the passage before the fluency assessment is conducted.

   In the case of remedial or special education students who read significantly below their chronological grade level, select an *Assessment Passage* that is closer to their instructional level. For example, in a special education classroom for grades 4, 5, and 6 in which the majority of students read at the second-grade level, use the Level 2 *Assessment Passage* for assessment. **Note:** All students must read the same *Assessment Passage* so that partnerships may be evenly assigned. However, partnerships will read *Practice Passages* at their independent or instructional level.

2. **Make two copies of the selected *Assessment Passage*, and laminate them or insert them into plastic sleeves.** The assessor uses one copy to mark reading errors and stopping point with an erasable marking pen, and students read from the other copy. Tell students that they will be asked to individually read the selected *Assessment Passage* quickly and carefully for one minute.

3. **Set a timer for one minute, and tell the student to begin reading when he/she is ready.** Avoid saying, "Get ready, get set, go!" Rather, start the timer when the student begins reading. Mark the reading errors the student makes and supply any words the student can't read after a 3-second wait time. Mark any words supplied by you as errors. Student insertions and self-corrections are *not* counted as errors.

4. **At the end of one minute, stop the student, and mark the last word read.** Subtract the number of reading errors from the total number of words read to compute the correct words per minute (cwpm) rate for the student. Then, transfer the student's cwpm score to an *Initial Assessment Record* (see *Appendix*). Wipe off the markings on your copy of the *Assessment Passage*, and continue the one-minute timing procedure with the next student.

5. **To form fluency partnerships**, match each student's cwpm rate to within 10–15 words per minute of another student, with both students reading at the same-grade instructional level.

Using *Assessment Passages* to Assess Reading Instructional Level

Assessment Passages may also be used to ascertain a student's reading level on that particular grade-level's passage. Again, this should be an unpracticed reading for which the student has no opportunity to read before the assessment begins. **Note:** Since the rationale for this type of assessment is determining *accuracy*—not fluency—it is untimed.

The *Determining Reading Levels Chart* (see *Chapter 1*) should be referenced to decide whether or not students are reading the *Assessment Passage* at the independent level, instructional level, or frustration level. The independent level is the one at which a student can read a passage easily and without teacher assistance or instruction. The instructional level is the one at which a student can read a passage, but some teacher guidance and instruction are necessary for comprehension. The instructional level is the most important one to determine, since it is at this level that learning truly occurs. The frustration level is the one at which a student struggles to read a passage and little, if any, learning will occur.

In matching students for fluency partnerships, both students should be able to read the same grade-level *Assessment Passage* at an instructional level. Conduct the assessments as directed in steps 1–4 in the previous section, but do not time students. After each student reads the *Assessment Passage*, use the *Determining Reading Levels Chart* in *Chapter 1* to establish his/her reading level of the passage. **Note:** If it is quite apparent that the *Assessment Passage* is too difficult for a student to read, and the student is at his/her frustration level, stop the assessment immediately. Select a *Assessment Passage* that is at least two grade levels below the current passage, and begin the assessment again.

Using Assessment Passages for Pretest and Posttest Data Collection

Assessment Passages can be used as well to document fluency progress over time after conducting the *Six-Minute Solution Intermediate* program. Select the same *Assessment Passage* you used for the original baseline data collection, and have the initial fluency scores available for comparison. (This information would appear on the *Initial Assessment Record*.)

Conduct the one-minute timing assessment with individual students in the usual manner, and calculate their cwpm scores. Subtract the original cwpm from the new cwpm to determine the number of words gained per minute resulting from fluency practice. Share this reading progress with the student and the parents, using the *Fluency Assessment Report* (see *Appendix*).

Using Assessment Passages to Determine Progress in Reading Level for Making Instructional Decisions

Finally, *Assessment Passages* may be used not only to determine student progress in reading fluency but also to document reading level gains.

If a student's *Fluency Graph* confirms that he/she is reading consistently at or above grade-level, select the next level *Assessment Passage* and conduct an unpracticed fluency assessment. Use the *Determining Reading Levels Chart* in *Chapter 1* to ascertain an increase in the student's instructional reading level. If it has increased, assign a *Assessment Passage* at the new level.

Assessment Passages

Birds: Our Feathered Friends

0   There are thousands of different birds. Birds have two legs and two

12   wings. Some birds are very small. Others are large. Birds are the only

25   animals that have feathers. Feathers can be any color. They keep birds

37   warm and dry. Flight feathers are very smooth.

45   Most birds can fly. Birds can fly because they have very light

57   bones. Their strong muscles move the wings. The tail helps the bird

69   to steer in the sky. Different birds have different shaped wings. This

81   is because birds live in different places. Most birds live in trees. Other

94   birds live high in the hills. Some live on the ground. Some birds fly long

109   distances. They live one place in the summer. They live someplace else in

122   the winter.

124   Some birds cannot fly. They are too big. The biggest bird is

136   an ostrich. It can grow to be 8 feet tall and can weigh 300 pounds.

151   An ostrich has strong legs. It can run very fast. Some birds are good

165   swimmers. Penguins are birds that can swim. They can swim very fast.

177   They use their wings to swim.

183

Total Words Read _____

− Errors _____

= CWPM _____

Fish Facts

0   There are many kinds of fish. They come in many colors, shapes,

12   and sizes. Some fish are as small as tadpoles. Others are larger than

25   crocodiles. Some fish are thin, while others are fat.

34   All fish have three important things in common. They all live in

46   water. All fish have fins to control the direction of their movement. They

59   all use gills to get oxygen from the water.

68   Some fish live in the ocean. They are saltwater fish. Other fish live

81   in rivers and lakes. These fish are freshwater fish.

90   Fish are good swimmers. They propel themselves through the water

100   by moving their tails from side to side. Fish use their fins to steer. Some

115   fish have only one fin. But most fish have more than one fin.

128   Gills are water-breathing organs. They are located in the fish's

139   mouth. The fish takes in water through its mouth. The water goes

151   through gill slits. These help the fish to get oxygen from the water as it

166   passes through.

168

Total Words Read _____

− Errors _____

= CWPM _____

Reptiles: Cold-Blooded Animals

0	Reptiles have lived on earth for a long time. They have been here
13	for more than 300 million years. Reptiles are animals. They are cold-
25	blooded. This means that their body temperature changes. When it is
36	cold outside, reptiles are cold. When it is hot outside, reptiles are hot.
49	Reptiles eat 30 to 50 times less food than mammals. This is because they
63	do not have to burn fuel for energy. Reptiles have dry, scaly skin. Their
77	skin protects them from drying out.
83	There are many kinds of reptiles. More than 8,000 types of reptiles
95	live on earth. Reptiles live all over the world. Some reptiles live on land.
109	Others live in the water. Living reptiles fall into four classes. Turtles are
122	one class of reptiles. They are reptiles with a shell. Turtles are the oldest
136	living reptile group. Crocodiles are another class of reptiles. Alligators
146	are included in this group. Lizards are a type of reptile. Snakes are
159	reptiles, too.
161	

Total Words Read _____

– Errors _____

= CWPM _____

Marsupials

0	A marsupial is a type of mammal. Unlike other mammals,
10	marsupials have pouches. They carry their babies in their pouches. Most
21	of the marsupials in the world live in Australia.
30	Kangaroos are marsupials. They have strong back legs and can jump
41	long distances. Kangaroos have strong tails. Their tail is used for balance.
53	The red kangaroo can grow to be about seven feet tall. They can weigh
67	more than 200 pounds. They move fast. Sometimes, they travel at 40
79	miles per hour.
82	Another Australian marsupial is the koala bear. The koalas live in
93	trees. They have thick, gray fur, a black nose, and no tail. Koalas look
107	very cuddly. They eat only leaves from a gum tree. The leaves are juicy.
121	Koalas do not drink water.
126	Wombats are also marsupials. They are Australian rodents.
134	Wombats live in holes in the ground. They sleep during the day and come
148	out at night. Wombats' diet consists of grass and plant roots.
159	Opossums are the only marsupials that live outside Australia.
168	Opossums look like large rats. They have long faces and tails. Opossums
180	eat eggs, fruit, insects, and small animals. When they are scared, they
192	fall to the ground and pretend to be dead. This is how the term "playing
207	possum" originated.
209	

Total Words Read _____

– Errors _____

= CWPM _____

Insects

0	Insects belong to a huge group of animals. This group is called
12	arthropods. All arthropods have a hard outer coat called an exoskeleton.
23	This *exoskeleton* protects the soft insides of an arthropod's body.
33	An adult insect's body is divided into three sections: a head, a
45	thorax, and an abdomen. The insect's head contains mouthparts, eyes,
55	and antennae. The thorax is the middle part of an insect's body. Three
68	pairs of jointed legs are found on the thorax. Insects have six legs. Two
82	pairs of wings are also attached to the thorax. The abdomen is the bottom
96	part of an insect. It is the biggest part of the body.
108	Most insects undergo a change. This change is called a
118	*metamorphosis*. The metamorphosis has four stages: egg, larva, pupa,
127	and adult. Most insects lay eggs. Each egg then turns into a larva. After
141	several molts, the larva enters the pupa stage. During this stage, it does
154	not eat or move. When the pupa stage ends, the adult insect emerges.
167	There are thousands of insects in the world. More than 900,000
178	kinds have been found. That is more than three times as many other
191	animal types put together. Many more new insects are discovered every
202	year.
203	

Total Words Read _____

− Errors _____

= CWPM _____

Mammals: The Highest Animal Class

0	Mammals are the highest class of animals. There are about
10	5,000 living mammal species. Mammals have several characteristics in
19	common. All mammals are warm-blooded. That means that their body
30	temperature remains constant regardless of the temperature of their
39	environment. The majority of all mammals have bodies partially or
49	wholly covered with hair. Most female mammals give birth to live young.
61	They nourish their offspring with milk secreted by mammary glands.
71	Mammals have hearts with four chambers. They have three middle-ear
82	bones: the malleus, incus, and stapes.
88	Mammals have four kinds of diets. Herbivores are plant-eaters.
98	This group includes beavers, cows, horses, and pandas. Carnivores are
108	meat-eaters. Whales, dolphins, dogs, tigers, and lions fall into this group.
120	Omnivores eat plants and meat. Humans, raccoons, and some bears fall
131	into this category. Insectivores eat insects. Aardvarks and anteaters are
141	examples of insectivores.
144	There are many different kinds of mammals. The blue whale is the
156	largest of all mammals. African elephants are the largest land mammals.
167	In terms of speed, the cheetah is the fastest mammal, while the sloth
180	is the slowest. The giraffe is the tallest mammal. Pygmy shrews and
192	bumblebee bats are the smallest mammals. The striped skunk is the
203	smelliest mammal of all.
207	

Total Words Read _____

\- Errors _____

= CWPM _____

San Diego Quick Assessment of Reading Ability

Directions: This is an individually administered sight-word reading assessment. Because this is a measure of sight-word knowledge, students need to recognize the words very quickly. Give a copy of the Student Form to the student to read. Choose a word list that is two to three grade levels below the student's current grade level as the starting point. Ask the student to read each word aloud. Keep the student moving down the lists. Do not allow more than three to five seconds on any word. Rather, tell the student to go on to the next word. Mark the word skipped as incorrect. Stop the assessment when the student has missed three or more words in a list. Record the highest grade level for each of the three levels (independent, instructional, and frustration) in the Errors & Reading Levels table when testing is completed.

ERRORS & READING LEVELS

Student Name	Reading Level		
	Independent (1 error)	Instructional (2 errors)	Frustration (3+ errors)

San Diego Quick Assessment of Reading Ability

NAME: _____ DATE: _____

Record the highest grade level for each:

INDEPENDENT _____ INSTRUCTIONAL _____ FRUSTRATION _____

Preprimer		**Grade Three**		**Grade Seven**		**Grade Eleven**	
see	_____	city	_____	amber	_____	galore	_____
play		middle	_____	dominion	_____	rotunda	_____
me	_____	moment	_____	sundry	_____	capitalism	_____
at	_____	frightened	_____	capillary	_____	prevaricate	_____
run	_____	exclaimed	_____	impetuous	_____	visible	_____
go	_____	several	_____	blight	_____	exonerate	_____
and	_____	lonely	_____	wrest	_____	superannuate	_____
look	_____	drew	_____	enumerate	_____	luxuriate	_____
can	_____	since	_____	daunted	_____	piebald	_____
here	_____	straight	_____	condescend	_____	crunch	_____

Primer		**Grade Four**		**Grade Eight**	
you	_____	decided	_____	capacious	_____
come	_____	served	_____	limitation	_____
not	_____	amazed	_____	pretext	_____
with	_____	silent	_____	intrigue	_____
jump	_____	wrecked	_____	delusion	_____
help	_____	improved	_____	immaculate	_____
is	_____	certainly	_____	ascent	_____
work	_____	entered	_____	acrid	_____
are	_____	realized	_____	binocular	_____
this	_____	interrupted	_____	embankment	_____

Grade One		**Grade Five**		**Grade Nine**	
road	_____	scanty	_____	conscientious	_____
live	_____	business	_____	isolation	_____
thank	_____	develop	_____	molecule	_____
when	_____	considered	_____	ritual	_____
bigger	_____	discussed	_____	momentous	_____
how	_____	behaved	_____	vulnerable	_____
always	_____	splendid	_____	kinship	_____
night	_____	acquainted	_____	conservatism	_____
spring	_____	escaped	_____	jaunty	_____
today	_____	grim	_____	inventive	_____

Grade Two		**Grade Six**		**Grade Ten**	
our	_____	bridge	_____	zany	_____
please	_____	commercial	_____	jerkin	_____
myself	_____	abolish	_____	nausea	_____
town	_____	trucker	_____	gratuitous	_____
early	_____	apparatus	_____	linear	_____
send	_____	elementary	_____	inept	_____
wide	_____	comment	_____	legality	_____
believe	_____	necessity	_____	aspen	_____
quietly	_____	gallery	_____	amnesty	_____
carefully	_____	relativity	_____	barometer	_____

From "The Graded Word List: Quick Gauge of Reading Ability" by Margaret LaPray, Helen Ross, and Raman Royal, in *Journal of Reading, 12,* 305–307 (January, 1969) Copyright © by Margaret LaPray and the International Reading Association. All rights reserved. Reprinted with permission.

San Diego Quick Assessment of Reading Ability

see	exclaimed	daunted
play	several	condescend
me	lonely	capacious
at	drew	limitation
run	since	pretext
go	straight	intrigue
and	decided	delusion
look	served	immaculate
can	amazed	ascent
here	silent	acrid
you	wrecked	binocular
come	improved	embankment
not	certainly	conscientious
with	entered	isolation
jump	realized	molecule
help	interrupted	ritual
is	scanty	momentous
work	business	vulnerable
are	develop	kinship
this	considered	conservatism
road	discussed	jaunty
live	behaved	inventive
thank	splendid	zany
when	acquainted	jerkin
bigger	escaped	nausea
how	grim	gratuitous
always	bridge	linear
night	commercial	inept
spring	abolish	legality
today	trucker	aspen
our	apparatus	amnesty
please	elementary	barometer
myself	comment	galore
town	necessity	rotunda
early	gallery	capitalism
send	relativity	prevaricate
wide	amber	visible
believe	dominion	exonerate
quietly	sundry	superannuate
carefully	capillary	luxuriate
city	impetuous	piebald
middle	blight	crunch
moment	wrest	
frightened	enumerate	

SIX MINUTE

Fluency Building Sheets

Level 1 Practice Passages

All About Plants

0   There are many plants on our earth. Plants can be big. Plants can

13   be small. We can't even see some plants. They are too small. Plants need

27   many things to grow. They need sunlight. Other plants need a lot of

40   sunlight. Others need very little sunlight. Plants also need water to grow.

52   Just like sunlight, some plants need a lot of water. Other plants need very

66   little water. A cactus can live without a lot of water.

77   Plants also need food from the soil to grow. Plants use their roots

90   to get food and water from the soil. The roots also hold up the plant. The

106   leaves make food for the plant. They use the sun to make food. Stems

120   are different on plants. The stem holds up the leaves and flowers on the

134   plant. It also carries water and food to the plant. The stem of a tree is

150   hard and strong. The stem of a flower can bend easily. Plants have seeds

164   to grow new plants. Some seeds are very small. Other seeds are in fruit

178   that grow on the plants. Some plants have flowers. Other plants do not

191   have flowers. Plants give us many things. They are good to us.

203

Total Words Read _____

− Errors _____

= CWPM _____

Mexican Hat Dance

0	A fiesta is a party. People dress up to go to a fiesta. They wear
15	bright colors. Many people dance at fiestas. One dance is the Mexican Hat
28	Dance. It is a lot of fun. A big hat is put on the floor. It is a sombrero. It is
49	made of straw. It has a wide brim.
57	People dance around the hat. Each person has a partner. Partners
68	face each other. They hold hands. Each person jumps and taps their right
81	heel in front. Then they jump and tap their left heel in front. They clap
96	two times. Partners hook right elbows. They swing each other in a circle.
109	Then they change directions. The dance is repeated until the music stops.
121	

Total Words Read _____

− Errors _____

= CWPM _____

Cat Families: It's All Relative

0	Did you know that all cats are related? Small house cats and wild
13	lions belong to the same family. They have a lot of things in common. For
28	example, all cats have long claws. They use these claws to grip and tear.
42	Cats keep their claws sharp by scraping them on rough things like tree
55	trunks. Pet owners give house cats scratching posts to use. All cats walk
68	on their toes. Their heels do not touch the ground. Cats have five toes
82	on each front foot. But their back feet only have four toes. Small pads on
97	cats' feet help them to move quietly. Most cats hunt at night. They have
111	a good sense of smell, sharp hearing, and can see well at night. Cats are
126	graceful animals. They are able to climb and balance themselves very
137	well. Cats are able to run quickly and make great leaps.
148	Cats that live in homes are called house cats. Cats are not as
161	friendly as dogs. But they are neat and need less care than dogs. There
175	are two kinds of house cats. One kind has long hair and the other has
190	short hair. Pet cats should be given a warm, dry box for sleeping. They
204	need two or three meals each day.
211	House cats make very good pets for some people.
220	

Total Words Read _____

− Errors _____

= CWPM _____

Rome Becomes an Empire

0   The Romans wanted a big empire. The army was very big. Soldiers

12 signed up for twenty years. Each soldier did the job well. Some were

25 archers. There were spear throwers. Others were horse riders. The army

36 had many parts. Each part was called a legion. A legion had six thousand

50 men. There were nurses, cooks, and arrow makers. Often there were long

62 battles. They did not need to return to Rome for supplies.

73 The Romans built roads. This helped them to control the empire.

84 There were more than fifty thousand miles of roads. The roads were built

97 to last. The roads had three layers. First, the men dug the road. The bed

112 of the road was filled with rocks. They mixed gravel and concrete. This

125 was put on the rocks. Flat paving stones were on top. Stone curbs were

139 on each side. They dug drainage ditches. There was a ditch on each side

153 of the road. Many people used the roads. Farmers used the roads for

166 trade. The army used the roads to get places fast.

176 The Romans wanted to keep the empire. The empire spread to many

188 places. It was very big.

193

Total Words Read _____

- Errors _____

= CWPM _____

Flying Fish

0   Did you know that some fish can fly? It is true! They do not really

15   fly like birds. But some fish can glide through the air. These fish are

29   called flying fish. They have long fins on either side of their bodies. When

43   a flying fish leaves the water, it spreads its fins. The air catches under the

58   fins. The air under the fins helps the fish glide. Flying fish can glide at

73   speeds of 40 miles per hour. They can go as far as 30 meters before they

89   splash down.

91   The flying fish also has a special tail. Its tail is in two parts. Each

106   part of its tail can move very fast. Those two tail parts help the flying fish

122   to swim very fast. The tail also helps to propel the fish out of the water.

138   You may ask yourself, "Why would a fish want to fly?" The reason is that

153   the flying fish is trying to get away from a bigger fish. When a flying fish

169   is being chased, it swims fast to the top of the water. Then it leaps out of

186   the water. As it leaps, the flying fish spreads its fins and glides away from

201   danger.

202

Total Words Read _____

– Errors _____

= CWPM _____

Railroads in the West

0	Before railroads, it took a long time to go from New York to San
14	Diego. Most people used a horse and wagon to cross the U.S. Some
27	people sailed around Cape Horn. Either way, it took three months. People
39	wanted to travel faster.
43	The U.S. had no money to build the train tracks. So the U.S. gave
57	two groups land. Right-of-way land was for the train tracks. The U.S. also
72	gave large pieces of land for every mile of track that was laid. This land
87	could be sold. The groups sold some of the land. The groups used the
101	money to buy materials. Workers had to be paid.
110	The Union Pacific group started in Nebraska. They laid the tracks
121	toward the west. The Central Pacific group began on the West Coast. They
134	laid the tracks to the east.
140	Both groups worked hard. They had to cross rivers. Bridges were
151	built. There were tall mountains. The men had to dig tunnels. It was not
165	easy work. The tracks met in Utah. The last spike was made of gold. A
180	silver hammer was used. The track was finished.
188	Now people could cross the U.S. in one week. More people moved
200	to the West.
203	

Total Words Read _____

− Errors _____

= CWPM _____

Trees: Our Helpers

0	Trees help all of us. Trees give us wood. We use the wood to build
15	our houses. We have doors on our houses made from wood. The chairs
28	we sit on are made from wood. Our houses have many things made from
42	wood. Trees keep us dry if it is raining. Trees also keep us cool in the
58	shade with their leaves.
62	Paper is made from trees. Many other things come from trees. Fruits
74	such as apples and oranges grow on trees. Cherries and peaches come
86	from trees, too. Walnuts and almonds grow on trees. Maple syrup for
98	pancakes comes from maple trees. Birds live in trees. Many animals also
110	live in trees.
113	Trees help us when we are sick. Many medicines are made from
125	trees. When trees die, they still help us. They help to make new soil for
140	seeds to grow. They also become homes for animals such as rabbits. Bees
152	put their hives in fallen trees. Trees help the earth, too. The tree's leaves
166	work with the sun to make oxygen. Without oxygen, we could not live.
179	Trees are very important to us. Trees help us all in many, many ways. We
194	should take care of our trees because they take care of us.
205	

Total Words Read _____

− Errors _____

= CWPM _____

The Moon: Earth's Natural Satellite

0	On a clear night, the moon can be seen. The moon is a bright
14	object in the sky. Only the sun is brighter. The moon is thousands of
28	miles away. The moon is much smaller than the earth. The moon travels
41	around the earth. It takes about 27 days to make one orbit. Each night it
56	is in a different place in its trip around the earth. More or less light from
72	the sun gets to the moon. The moon reflects sunlight. Each night the
85	moon looks different. Sometimes it looks like a big ball. Other nights it
98	looks like a thin light. Sometimes there is no moon at all. It is a full moon
115	when the entire surface of the moon facing the sun reflects sunlight.
127	The moon is not like the earth. No one lives on the moon. It is
142	very rocky. There are no plants or animals. During the day it is very hot.
157	Sometimes it is two hundred degrees. At night, it is very cold. It can be
172	250 degrees below zero.
176	Men have visited the moon. They had to wear space suits. They did
189	not stay long. They put up a U.S. flag. Moon rocks were brought back
203	to Earth. There is not much on the moon. People have always enjoyed
216	looking at the moon at night. They probably always will.
226	

Total Words Read _____

– Errors _____

= CWPM _____

Stars and Stripes: The First American Flag

0   It is said that Betsy Ross made the first U.S. flag. It was called the

15   Stars and Stripes. It had thirteen rows of stripes. The top row was red.

29   The next row was white. The next row was red and so on. In the top left

46   was a field of blue. There were thirteen stars. Each star had five points.

60   One point was upward. They were arranged in a circle. At that time, there

74   were thirteen colonies. Each star was for a colony. The first flag was

87   raised on July 1, 1776.

92   When the U.S. became a nation, the stars stood for each state. As

105   the U.S. grew, a star was added for each state. At first, a stripe was also

121   added. One time the flag had fifteen stripes and fifteen stars. Then the

134   U.S. decided to keep the thirteen stripes. The stripes were for the thirteen

147   colonies. When a state joined the U.S., a new star was added. The order

161   of the stars was changed many times. Hawaii became a state in 1959. The

175   last star was added for Hawaii.

181   Now there are fifty stars on the flag. The flag still has thirteen

194   stripes. If another state joined the U.S., a star would be added.

206

Total Words Read _____

− Errors _____

= CWPM _____

Gifts from the Ancient Greeks

0   The ancient Greeks lived close to the sea. Many lived on islands.

12   The farmers grew crops all year. The winters were mild. It was sunny in

26   the summer. They grew grapes, olives, wheat, and barley. The Greeks had

38   many ships. They traded with others. To make it easy, they used coins.

51   The coins were made of gold and silver.

59   The Greeks had city-states. There was no king. The power was in

72   the hands of the citizens. There were rich and poor people. The men

85   citizens voted. They made the rules. When someone broke a rule, they

97   had a trial. The people served on juries. Most people lived in the city.

111   Some farmed land around the city. Sometimes they had wars. The wars

123   were over land. Some people moved. They made new city-states.

134   The Greeks liked to have fun. They also wanted to honor their

146   gods. Every four years they had sports events. There were foot races and

159   wrestling. They threw discs. The sports events were called the Olympics.

170   Two times each year they went to plays. The dramas were very good. The

184   plays told stories about gods and history. Most of the plays were very sad.

198   A few were very funny. They were always sad at the end. A jury voted for

214   the best play.

217   The Greeks had many good ideas. Many movies are based on their

229   stories. The name and dates are changed. People like to go to sports

242   events. Coins are used to buy and sell things. Citizens vote and make

255   rules.

256

Total Words Read _____

- Errors _____

= CWPM _____

The Roaring `20s: The Age of Jazz

0	After World War I, the U.S. was ready for change. People started
12	to change in the way they did things. They wanted to find new ways to
27	express themselves. Music was one way to enjoy life. The music that
39	most people in the U.S. liked was jazz. They saw jazz as a way to break
55	away from old rules. It was a way to be free.
66	Black people in the U.S. created jazz. It started in New Orleans. It
79	grew out of music called the blues. The blues was based on the hard life
94	of most blacks. The music told sad stories. It helped people cope with
107	hard times. Most of the black people who played jazz had no formal
120	schooling in music. Yet, they were great performers.
128	There was no right way to play jazz. It was about how people felt. It
143	was based on a theme or musical idea. The players chased a tune up and
158	down the scales as they played. This gave the player a sense of being free.
173	At the same time, young women wanted to be free of old ideas.
186	They cast out long, full dresses. They put on short skirts. They had
199	loose-fitting clothes. The young women cut their hair short. Women
210	wore makeup. They danced to jazz music. These women were called
221	"flappers."
222	Today women wear clothes they like. They cut their hair many
233	ways. People still like to listen to jazz.
241	

Total Words Read _____

- Errors _____

= CWPM _____

Hawaiian Islands

0   Captain Cook was the first white man to visit Hawaii. He landed in

13   the islands in 1778. The islands were very pretty. There was sun every

26   day. Palm trees grew there. There were flowers all year. Ships going to

39   and from Asia stopped in the islands. Sometimes sailors jumped ship.

50   They did not want to leave.

56   A king ruled Hawaii. Farmers from the U.S. moved to the islands.

68   They grew pineapples and sugar. The king let the U.S. build a navy base.

82   The king died. His sister became the queen. She was removed from the

95   throne. The islands became part of the U.S. The navy base grew larger.

108   More people moved to the islands. Hawaii became a state in 1959.

120   Many people like to visit the islands. They come by plane and ship.

133   The sun shines all year. There are lots of palm trees and flowers. Birds

147   live in the trees. The birds sing all of the time. People like to play in the

164   sun. They swim in the sea. A few like to surf. Many people play golf.

179   Some like to hike in the hills. Most like to listen to the music and watch

195   the dances. The islands are fun to visit.

203

Total Words Read _____

− Errors _____

= CWPM _____

Oil: Black Gold

0	Oil is sometimes called "black gold." Oil is used for many things. It
13	is worth a lot of money. Oil made some people very rich. At one time oil
29	was not worth much. People did not like oil on their land. It was dirty.
44	Oil smelled bad. Plants did not grow well near oil. That was two hundred
58	years ago.
60	The first oil well was in Pennsylvania. People used oil as a
72	medicine. This did not work well. Oil was also used to grease metal parts.
86	This made machines run smoother. When oil is heated, dirt and grime
98	go to the bottom. The oil at the top is called refined oil. People found
113	uses for refined oil. It was used for lamps and stoves. Oil was sold in the
129	grocery stores and door-to-door. People did not need to make candles
142	or buy whale oil. Gasoline is high-grade refined oil. About one hundred
155	years ago, people started to use gas for cars. Oil was found in the West.
170	People started to search for oil. They drilled wells. At first oil was shipped
184	east in barrels. Then they used railroad tank cars. Finally, pipelines were
196	laid. Oil is also shipped in big oil tankers.
205	Today there are many uses for oil. It is used to heat houses, for fuel,
220	and as a cleaner. Now people would like to find oil on their land. They
235	would be very rich.
239	

Total Words Read _____

− Errors _____

= CWPM _____

The Sun and Energy

0　　　　The sun is a star. It is a star like the thousands of stars seen at

16　　night. The sun is the closest star to earth. It is 93 million miles away.

31　　The sun is at the center of the solar system. It is much bigger than the

47　　earth. It is made of gas. The gas is on fire. In the center, there are many

64　　explosions. The sun is hotter than hot. The heat causes a lot of light.

78　　It takes about eight minutes for light to go from the sun to the earth.

93　　Animals and plants need the energy that comes from the sunlight.

104　　　　Light from the sun gives us energy. Plants need sunlight to grow.

116　　Trees grow tall. People cut down trees for the wood. When wood is

129　　burned, energy is released. Bugs and animals eat the plants. People eat

141　　plants and animals to give them energy. Some plants and animals die.

153　　They stay in the ground for millions of years. After a while, they turn into

168　　oil. Oil is used to run cars and trucks. The heat from the sun warms the

184　　air near the ground. The air gets warm and rises. This causes wind. Wind

198　　is a form of energy. The sunlight gives us many forms of energy.

211

Total Words Read _____

- Errors _____

= CWPM _____

Plants Are Alike and Different, Too!

0	There are so many plants on our earth. When we look at them,
13	they all seem so different from one another. Yet, all of these very different
27	plants are alike in some ways.
33	All plants need air, water, light, and minerals. Plants are alike in
45	other ways, too. All plants have some sort of roots. Some roots may be
59	close to the soil's surface. Some roots may go deeply down into the earth.
73	Some roots may even grow on top of the soil. But all plants have roots.
88	All plants have stems. The stems may look different from one
99	another. They may be short and narrow. They may be tall and thick.
112	There may be many stems on a plant, or very few stems. The stems on
127	trees are hard. The stems on roses have sharp thorns and are narrow. The
141	stems on daisies are short and bend easily. The stems are a part of all
156	plants. They may be different, but all plants have stems.
166	All plants have leaves. The leaves, just like the stems and roots,
178	are different from one another. Some leaves are large, like those on palm
191	trees. Some leaves are small and narrow. The spines on a cactus are
204	its leaves. The pine needles on a pine tree are its leaves. Just like roots
219	and stems, all plants have leaves, but they are very different from one
232	another.
233	

Total Words Read _____

− Errors _____

= CWPM _____

Gold Rush in California

0	In 1848, gold was found in California. It was found in a river.
13	People wanted to be rich. They wanted to find gold. Most of the people
27	lived in the East. People wanted to move west. They wanted to be
40	the first to get gold. There was a rush to find gold. Some people put
55	everything in wagons. Horses and oxen pulled the wagons. It was hard to
68	travel in wagons. It was a long trip. They had to cross rivers. The deserts
83	had no water. The mountains were tall. It took three months to get to
97	the gold fields. Some people came by ship. The ships sailed around Cape
110	Horn. Everyone wanted to get rich.
116	By 1850, many people lived in the West. People looked for gold in
129	the rivers. Some people dug mines. Mines were in the mountains and in
142	the deserts. A few people found gold. Some people opened stores. They
154	sold things to the miners. Some storeowners became very rich. Some
165	people farmed. They sold their goods to the miners. Soon there was not
178	much gold left. People found other jobs. Most people liked the West.
190	They liked the sunshine. They did not move back East.
200	

Total Words Read _____

– Errors _____

= CWPM _____

The Nile River in Ancient Egypt

0	The Nile River is in Egypt. It is the longest river in the world.
14	The Nile is four thousand miles long. The river flows north. Egypt gets
27	almost no rain. On both sides of the river, there is a desert. There are tall
43	mountains in Central Africa. This is where the river begins. Each year it
56	rains and the snow melts. The level of the Nile rises.
67	A long time ago, there were no dams on the Nile. Each year, the
81	level of the Nile rose. The water flowed over the banks of the river. There
96	were big floods. Black river mud covered the land. The mud was good
109	for growing crops. Farmers used the water for crops. They dug ditches to
122	move the water. Little dams were built in the ditches. Farmer saved the
135	water for the crops.
139	The river had many other uses. Boats sailed on the Nile. Animals
151	lived along the river. There were ducks, little birds, and fish. One river
179	plant was useful. Papyrus is reed. It is a tall, thin plant. The plant grows
194	wild by the river. It was used for boats, baskets, and shoes. The plant was
209	cut into thin layers. This made a kind of paper. The Nile River was very
224	useful.
225	

Total Words Read _____

− Errors _____

= CWPM _____

Log Cabins: Pioneer Homes

0   In the U.S., log cabins were home for many people. During the

12   1700s and the 1800s, many people lived in log cabins. Most of the log

26   cabins were on farms or in the woods. People built log cabins because

39   there were lots of trees.

44   A log cabin was simple to make. An ax was needed to make a log

59   cabin. The trees were cut down. The logs were notched. Then logs were

72   joined at the corners. The logs are put together to make a square room.

86   Log cabins were not big. They had one room. A chimney was at one end

101   of the room. The chimney was made of rocks. The rocks were piled up

115   high. Mud was put in the holes between the rocks. A family could make a

130   log cabin in a few days.

136   Log cabins were not big. They were only as long and wide as tall

150   trees. Some people made the log cabin bigger. They put boards in the

163   rafters. This made a loft. They used ladders to get to the loft. Children

177   slept in the loft. Some people built another log cabin room. Many people

190   liked to live in log cabins.

196

Total Words Read _____

− Errors _____

= CWPM _____

Eli Whitney and the Cotton Gin

0	Cotton is an important crop. It grows on a plant in pods. Fluffy
13	white fiber and black seeds are in the pod. It used to be hard to get the
30	seeds off the fiber. In 1793, Eli Whitney made the cotton gin. The gin
44	makes it easy to get the seeds off the fiber.
54	The cotton gin looks like a box. It is open at the top. There are little
70	slits down one side. Cotton fiber and seeds are placed in the box. There
84	is a roller outside the box. The roller is on one side of the box. Wire teeth
101	are around the roller. People can turn the roller. When the roller is turned
115	the teeth go into the box through the slits. The fiber in the box is caught
131	in the wire teeth. As the teeth come out of the box, they pull fibers out.
147	The seeds are wider than the slits. The seeds stay in the box. Another
161	roller turns the other way. It takes the fibers from the first roller. The first
176	roller turns back into the box. The first roller gets more fiber. Now it is
191	easy to get the seeds off the fiber.
199	The cotton fiber is made into thread. The thread is used to make
212	cloth. People like cotton clothes. Cotton clothes are cool in the summer.
224	They are easy to wash. There is a demand for lots of cotton. Many
238	farmers grow cotton.
241	

Total Words Read _____

— Errors _____

= CWPM _____

Alex Haley: Author

0   Alex was born in New York. When he was little, he moved. He lived

14   near his grandmother. She told stories. They were about their family. Alex

26   liked to hear them. One story was about Kunta. Kunta lived in Africa. He

40   came to the U.S. on a slave ship.

48   When Alex grew up, he went to sea. At sea, he wrote many stories.

62   He tried to sell his stories. At first, no one would buy them. After 8 years,

78   he sold a story.

82   Alex wanted to know if his family stories were true. So he went

95   to Africa. He talked to many people. The stories were true. Alex wrote

108   about his family. He wrote many stories. It took him 12 years. Alex put

122   the stories together. They became a book. The book was "Roots." It was

135   the story of Alex's roots. People liked the book. Stores sold lots of copies.

149   "Roots" became a TV show. It won many awards. The book made people

162   think. It made them think about their own roots.

171

Total Words Read _____

– Errors _____

= CWPM _____

Earth: Hometown Planet

0	The earth is one of the nine planets. It is the third planet from the
15	sun. It is also the fifth largest planet. As far as we know, Earth is the only
32	planet where there is life. There are many reasons for this. Earth is made
46	up of land and water. There is more water than land on Earth. More than
61	half of Earth is water. Humans need water to live. Earth is the only planet
76	where water is in liquid form. That is why there are oceans on Earth.
90	Oceans help keep the temperature stable. The greenhouse effect helps to
101	warm the earth. The earth is not too hot or cold for life. The earth's air
117	has oxygen. The earth's air also has carbon dioxide. Both are important
129	for life.
131	The earth is four to five billion years old. But the surface of the
145	earth is very young. That means that it has changed often since it was
159	formed. The earth is a very big planet. It is also the densest of all the
175	planets. The earth turns around in a circle. It turns once a day. The earth
190	goes around the sun. When the earth turns to the sun, it is day. When it
206	turns away from the sun, it is night.
214	

Total Words Read _____

\- Errors _____

= CWPM _____

Bruce Lee: Martial Arts Actor

0	Bruce Lee was born in the U.S. in 1940. His family then moved to
14	China. Bruce grew up in Hong Kong. His parents were actors. Bruce also
27	acted in movies. Life in Hong Kong was hard for Bruce. He learned Kung
41	Fu to defend himself.
45	Bruce moved back to the U.S. when he was 19. He finished high
58	school. Then he went to college. He became a Kung Fu master. Bruce
71	opened a Kung Fu school. Many students came to Bruce's school. They
83	wanted to learn from the best. Bruce showed them how to do two-finger
97	push-ups. He taught them how to break boards with one kick.
109	Bruce became famous. He starred on a TV show. He made action
121	movies. People loved to watch his movies. His most famous was "Enter
133	the Dragon."
135	Sadly, Bruce did not live long. He died suddenly in 1973. The cause
148	was brain swelling. Bruce had a short life. But his movies keep him alive
162	in the hearts of his fans.
168	

Total Words Read _____

- Errors _____

= CWPM _____

Nat King Cole: Unforgettable Singer

0   Nat King Cole was born in 1917. He came from a poor family. Nat

14   was one of 13 children. Nat's father was a minister. His mother taught

27   him to play the piano. Nat played for his father's church. He was a very

42   good piano player.

45   When he grew up, he played in a band. The band was the Nat King

60   Cole Trio. They played in small bars. One night, the owner of the bar

74   asked Nat to sing. Nat did not want to sing. But the owner said that he

90   would fire the band if Nat did not sing. So Nat sang a song. Everyone

105   liked how he sang. They liked his deep voice.

114   Nat became famous. His first hit song was based on one of his

127   father's sermons. It was "Straighten Up and Fly Right." Nat was the first

140   black man to have his own radio show. He was also the first black man to

156   have his own TV show.

161   People loved Nat's music. He sold many records. Nat became very

172   rich. He bought a fancy home in Los Angeles. Nat did not live to be very

188   old. He was a heavy smoker. This was bad for his health. He died of lung

204   cancer in 1965.

207   But, Nat's music lives on today. His daughter Natalie is also a

219   singer. She made a recording. In it, she blended her voice with Nat's.

232   New tapes of the Nat King Cole Trio were released. People still enjoy

245   listening to Nat's music.

249

Total Words Read _____

− Errors _____

= CWPM _____

The Secret of Silk

0	Silk is strong, beautiful cloth. Silk was first made in China. No one
13	else knew how to make silk. China guarded the secret. For thousands
25	of years people had to buy silk from China. China would not let people
39	come see how silk was made. China traded silk for gold, glass, and goods
53	from the West.
56	It takes lot of work to make silk. Silkworms are fed mulberry
68	leaves. After five weeks, each worm makes a cocoon. Workers gather
79	the cocoons. They boil water in big pots. The cocoons are put in the hot
94	water. This kills the worms. The hot water softens the cocoons. Workers
106	carefully unwind silk threads. The thread is very long. Each thread is very
119	thin. It can break easily. Thread from many cocoons is twisted together.
131	This makes one strong silk thread. This thread can be twisted with other
144	threads to make it stronger. The thread is washed. Silk is white. Most
157	silk is dyed. There are many different colors of silk thread. The thread is
171	made into cloth.
174	The silk is used to make many things. Most silk is used to make
188	clothes. Sometimes silk thread is used to make rugs. The rugs are made
201	of knotted silk threads. People like silk because it is beautiful and it lasts
215	a long time.
218	

Total Words Read _____

- Errors _____

= CWPM _____

Native American Homes

0   The first people to live in North America were Native Americans.

11   They lived in groups. Each group was a nation. They lived in many parts

25   of the land. Native Americans built homes based on where they lived.

37   The Inuit lived in cold places. They lived in the northern part of

50   North America. The Iniut built igloos. They used blocks of ice. The ice

63   was glued together with snow. Igloos were warm inside.

72   The Cherokee lived in the southeast part of the U.S. Their homes

84   were shaped like a circle. They were made from poles, trees, and mud.

97   The homes had thatch roofs. The Cherokee homes were cool in summer.

109   They were warm in winter.

114   The Sioux lived on the plains of the U.S. They lived in tents called

128   tipis. Tipis were made with poles. The poles were covered with animal

140   skins. Tipis could be put up or taken down quickly. When the Sioux

153   moved from place to place, they took their tipis with them.

164

Total Words Read _____

- Errors _____

= CWPM _____

Level 2 Practice Passages

The Panama Canal: A Sea Path

0   North and South America are joined by a little piece of land. Before

13   1900, it was hard to get from the East to the West Coast. Ships had to

29   sail around Cape Horn. It took three months to go from New York to San

44   Diego. People wanted a shorter trip.

50   The French started to dig a canal. It was hard work. Many workers

63   died of yellow fever. The French gave up. Doctors found a cure for yellow

77   fever. The U.S. made a deal to use the land in Panama. Men started to dig

93   the canal.

95   It took nine years to make the canal. It is 51 miles long. It goes

110   through two lakes. Workers cut a nine-mile path in the rock. The canal is

125   300 feet wide. The average depth is 120 feet. The canal was ready for use

140   in 1914. It took a third of the time to sail from the West to the East.

157   Parts of the canal are above sea level. At one place, it is 85 feet

172   above the sea. How can this be? The canal uses locks to move ships. A

187   lock is a water-filled space. The space is like a big room. There is no roof.

204   The room is made of cement. There is a door on each end of the lock.

220   One door of the lock opens. The water level is raised. A ship moves into

235   a lock. The other door opens. The ship moves out of the lock. The ship

250   sails into another lock. The water level is raised again. The ship is 85 feet

265   above sea level. The ship sails into the canal. The ship sails into another

279   lock. Water is let out of the lock. The ship is now lower. The canal has

295   three sets of locks.

299   Today many ships use the canal. The canal is very busy. Ships carry

312   many goods from one coast to the other. People take cruise ships through

325   the canal.

327

Total Words Read _____

− Errors _____

= CWPM _____

Mars: The Red Planet

0   Mars is one of the nine planets. It is the fourth planet from the sun.

15   Mars is the seventh largest planet. The planet Mars has a reddish color.

28   So people call it the Red Planet. It was named because of its color. The

43   month of March was named after the planet Mars. Mars was the name of

57   the god of war. The ancient Greeks worshiped Mars. He was also called

70   Ares.

71   Mars is the closest planet to Earth. When Mars is in the night sky,

85   it can be very bright. Then people can see Mars. They do not even need a

101   telescope.

102   Many spaceships have visited Mars. The first one to visit was in

114   1965. The last one was in 1997. The spaceships bring back clues about

127   Mars. People study the clues. They learn about Mars this way.

138   Mars is a small planet. It is also rocky. Mars is a very cold planet.

153   There is no water on Mars now. But there may have been water at one

168   time. There are clues that lakes or oceans may have been on Mars. People

182   think that there was water a very long time ago. They also think that the

197   water was there for a short time. Some people think that there was life

211   on Mars at one time. No one knows for sure. They must keep studying to

226   find out.

228

Total Words Read _____

− Errors _____

= CWPM _____

Maps: How to Read Them

0   A map is an important tool. It is not hard to learn to read a map.

16   There are four main directions on a map. They are north, east, south,

29   and west. The sun rises in the east. It sets in the west. It is easy to find

47   north and south. Point your right hand to the east. Point your left hand

61   to the west. You will be looking at the north. South will be at the back

77   of your head. On a map, the top is always north. The bottom is always

92   south. The right side is east and the left is west. To help people remember

107   the directions, there is usually a compass on the map with "N," "E,"

120   "S," and "W" at each of the four points. Each letter stands for one of the

136   directions.

137   On a world map, the land is usually brown, yellow, and green. The

150   brown areas stand for mountains. The yellow areas show the deserts.

161   Green is used to show low areas where many plants grow. The water

174   areas are blue. Across the middle is a line. This is the equator. This is

189   not a real line. It is put on the world map to show the middle of the

206   earth, where it is hot. In the north and south it is very cold. These areas

222   are usually white. Sometimes there are red dots on a world map. These

235   usually represent large cities. If there is a very big red dot, the city is very

251   big. If there is a smaller red dot, the city is smaller.

263   If you know a few simple facts, maps are easy to read. Maps are

277   very useful. People use them to find places and to get information.

289

Total Words Read _____

- Errors _____

= CWPM _____

Baseball: A National Sport

0   Many people like to play baseball. The game started in 1839 in New

13 York. A teacher, Mr. Doubleday, laid out the field. He made up the rules.

27 At first, players did not wear gloves. They caught the ball with their bare

41 hands. This hurt their hands. In 1875, players started to wear gloves. In

54 the beginning, catchers did not wear masks. Balls would hit them in the

67 face. One catcher made a wire mask. Soon all of the catchers had masks.

81 Now all players wear gloves. Catchers wear masks. They also wear knee

93 and chest pads.

96   Most towns had teams. Many boys and men joined the teams. Some

108 teams were very good. People liked to watch teams play the game. They

121 wanted their team to win. Some teams started to pay players. People

133 started to pay money to watch the game. This was in 1868. Soon there

147 were two major baseball leagues. The first World Series was in 1903.

159   Now baseball is played everywhere. Little boys and girls play on

170 town teams. Baseball is played in schools. Adults play the game for fun.

183 People still like to watch baseball. They pay to watch the pros play. There

197 are still two major leagues. Most big cities have a major league team.

210 Baseball is a national sport.

215

Total Words Read _____

- Errors _____

= CWPM _____

Henry Ford: Automobile Manufacturer

0   Many people think Henry Ford made the first auto. He did not.

12   There were autos since the 1890s. Each auto was made by hand. Only

25   rich people could own one. Mr. Ford had a dream. He wanted to make

39   a car for all the people. Mr. Ford wanted every family to own a car. He

55   wanted to make cars cheaply. Then a family could afford a car.

67   Mr. Ford made the Model T. It sold for $850. By 1916, he sold the

82   same car for $360. How did he do this? Mr. Ford used mass production.

96   He made many cars. They were all the same. Many workers put the

109   cars together. Each worker did one thing. One worker put on a top. Two

123   workers put on doors. Another put in a seat. The same model was made

137   each year. Year after year, it was the same car. The same car was made

152   for ten years. Everyone knew how to do the job well. There was a joke of

168   the day: You could have a Model T in any color you wanted as long as it

185   was black.

187   The profit on each car was small. Every family wanted a car. Mr.

200   Ford sold lots of cars. He became very rich. Henry Ford's dream came

213   true. Today many families can have a car. Some families have more than

226   one car.

228

Total Words Read _____

− Errors _____

= CWPM _____

The Model T: The Car That Changed America!

0   For thousands of years, it was hard for people to travel. Then came

13   the Model T car. The Model T was cheap. Nearly every family could own

27   the car. A new car cost $360. A used car could be $25 to $50. Cars freed

44   people. Cars let them travel more than ever before. They could live out

57   of town. Men and women could drive to work. Families visited places far

70   from home.

72   Cars had good and bad effects. Family trips were fun. People liked

84   to go sight-seeing. Often lots of people were in one car. Some people were

99   "back-seat drivers." Some were good drivers. Some were road hogs. A few

112   were bad drivers. By 1930 cars caused more than half of the accidental

125   deaths in the U.S.

129   Cars were good for business. Many people made cars. This was

140   good work. Steel was needed to make cars. More rubber was needed for

153   tires. Cars needed oil and gas to run. Gas stations opened all over the U.S.

168   Some people were needed to fix cars. Motels opened for people with cars.

181   Places for tourists to visit opened. More roads were built. Trucks carried

193   goods from place to place. It was easy for people to travel. Cars changed

207   the way of life.

211

Total Words Read _____

- Errors _____

= CWPM _____

Rosa Parks: Mother of the Civil Rights Movement

0	In 1955, some laws in the U.S. were not fair. All people were not
14	treated the same way. Black people did not have the same rights as
27	white people. In Alabama, they could not eat in the same places as white
41	people. They could not drink from the same water fountain. Black and
53	white children could not go to the same schools. White people could ride
66	in the front of the city bus. Black people had to ride in the back of the
83	bus. When black people got on the bus, they paid the driver. Then, they
97	had to get off the bus and go to the back door to get on. Sometimes, the
114	bus driver would leave a bus stop before black people got on. When the
128	bus was crowded, black people had to give up their seats to white people.
142	Rosa Parks was a black woman. She sewed for a living. Rosa rode
155	a city bus home from work every day. One day, Rosa sat down in a bus
171	seat. A white man got on the bus. He told Rosa to move. He wanted to
187	sit in her seat. Rosa was tired. She was tired from working long hours.
201	She was also tired of being treated unfairly. She told the man, "No." The
215	white man got mad. He called the bus driver. The bus driver told Rosa
229	to move. She would not leave her seat. The bus driver called the police.
243	They arrested Rosa. She was convicted. She had to pay a fine to get out
258	of jail.
260	People became angry at the way Rosa was treated. They decided not
272	to ride the city buses. This was called a *bus boycott*. It lasted 381 days.
287	Rosa's case went to the U.S. Supreme Court. The court agreed with Rosa.
300	The law was changed.
304	Rosa Parks was a hero to people of all races. Her peaceful protest
317	became a model for the civil rights movement in the U.S. When she died,
331	thousands of people of all races honored her. Rosa had made the world a
345	better place to live.
349	

Total Words Read _____

− Errors _____

= CWPM _____

Garter Snakes

0   Garter snakes make great pets. They live in many places. Garter

11   snakes live in gardens. They live near houses. They are often the first

24   snake a child sees. Children like to catch garter snakes. It is lucky that

38   garters are safe snakes. If someone comes near them, garters will hide. If

51   someone tries to fight, the garter will fight back. But garters never start

64   a fight. They will never attack people or pets first. Garter snakes live

77   between three and ten years.

82   Some people call garter snakes "garden snakes." Other people call

92   them grass snakes. Garter snakes are usually striped. Some garter snakes

103   have red or yellow stripes. Their background color is plain or checked.

115   Garter snakes are not very big. Full-grown garter snakes are two to three

129   feet in length. They are also very narrow in width. Because they are

142   small, garters are quick to heat up. They are also quick to cool down.

156   Garter snakes sleep in the ground during the winter. They come out of the

170   ground in the spring. Garter snakes like to bask in the sun during the day.

185   Garter snakes eat insects. They also eat worms and frogs. Since they

197   are small, they are agile. This makes it easier for them to catch their prey.

212   Garters use their sight mostly to hunt their prey, although they can also

225   "hear" vibrations in the ground. Garters hunt during the cooler part of

237   the day.

239

Total Words Read _____

– Errors _____

= CWPM _____

The Ancient Kingdom of Kush

0	Kush was once part of Egypt. It was on the southern part of the Nile
15	River. Egypt became weak. The army was not strong. Priests and nobles
27	fought with the kings. Kush rulers broke away from Egypt. This was in
40	671 B.C. Kush built a capital in Meroe.
48	Meroe was a good place for a city. It had iron ore and lots of wood.
64	Workers knew how to make pure metal from ore. Brick ovens were used
77	to heat the iron ore. Bellows were used to make wood fires very hot. Pure
92	iron was used to make tools and weapons. Iron spears and swords were
105	very strong. They were stronger than bronze weapons. There were also
116	many artists in Meroe. They made beautiful bowls, vases, and jewelry.
127	Meroe became a trade center. Traders came from all around. They wanted
139	iron and artworks. They traded fine cloth, glass, skins, gold, silver, and
151	ivory. Meroe was a great city.
157	In A.D. 350, a nearby army came to Meroe. They made war. The
170	people did not fight back. Some people were killed. Many became slaves.
182	A few ran away. The army took food and iron. The army set fire to reed
198	houses and brick buildings. The whole city burned down. No one came
210	back to the city. That was the end of Kush.
220	

Total Words Read _____

− Errors _____

= CWPM _____

Thomas Edison: An American Inventor

0   Thomas A. Edison is a well-known inventor in the U.S. His most

13   famous invention was the electric light bulb. He put thin wire inside an

26   airless glass globe. It was not like the lights used today. It did not have

41   a steady light. The light bulb flickered. But it worked for forty hours.

54   Soon the light bulb worked longer. People started to use light bulbs in

67   the house. They did not need to use lamp oil or candles. The bulbs were

82   safer. They did not need to use fire for light.

92   Edison had many good ideas. People liked the "talking machine."

102   This was the first record player. The first "record" was made from a thin

116   piece of tin. The tin covered a tube. The tube slipped over a pipe-like

131   part. Records were hollow tubes. The tubes were covered with wax. It

143   was years before records were flat and round.

151   He had other good ideas. At first, films did not have sound. The

164   words were printed at the bottom of the film. People read the words and

178   watched the actors at the same time. Edison made records to go with the

192   films. People could hear what the actors had to say. Today people use

205   things that Thomas A. Edison invented.

211

Total Words Read _____

- Errors _____

= CWPM _____

Boys and Girls Clubs: Great Places to Hang Out

0   The Boys and Girls Clubs started in 1860. At first, they were just

13   Boys Clubs. In Hartford, there were boys who roamed the streets. The

25   Boys Clubs were started to give these boys a safe place to go.

38   Many years later, in 1990, the name was changed. The Boys Club

50   became the Boys and Girls Club. Today, many kids are home alone after

63   school. They do not have adults to care for them. The Boys and Girls

77   Clubs can help these kids.

82   There are Boys and Girls Clubs in many U.S. cities. There are clubs

95   on Native American reservations, too. There are more than 3,000 clubs in

107   the U.S. More than 3 million boys and girls go to these clubs.

120   The clubs are open before school. They are also open after school.

132   The club staff helps kids with homework. The clubs also offer fun

144   things to do. There are games to play. The clubs have sports. Many have

158   computers. Boys and Girls Clubs have classes, too. The classes teach kids

170   skills they need to know to succeed in life. Boys and Girls Clubs are great

185   places to learn and grow.

190

Total Words Read _____

- Errors _____

= CWPM _____

The Food Chain: A Cycle of Life

0	The food chain is a cycle. Plants need sunlight, air, and water to
13	grow. Plants grow almost everywhere on earth. Animals eat living things.
24	Some eat plants. Some eat other animals. Many eat both plants and
36	animals. Animals, in turn, are food for even bigger animals. When big
48	animals die, smaller animals eat them. Some of the animal parts rot on
61	the ground. This makes nutrients for the ground. This helps the plants to
74	grow.
75	The food chain is very simple. Here is an example. A bear gets old
89	and dies. The body lies on the ground. The little bugs and flies find the
104	body. They eat the bear. One of the flies is caught in a spider web. The
120	spider eats the fly. Along comes a bigger insect. It eats the spider. The
134	insect rests on the lake water. A little fish snaps at the insect. The little
149	fish eats the insect. A bigger fish eats the little fish. A bear comes to the
165	lake and catches the big fish. The bear eats the big fish. The cycle starts
180	all over again. The food chain happens every day in many different ways.
193	Every part of the food chain is important.
201	

Total Words Read _____

− Errors _____

= CWPM _____

Rivers and Canals: Our Water Highways

0　　In the 1700s, going from one place to another was hard. The roads

13　were not good. The roads were more like trails. People had to walk, ride

27　horses, or use horses to pull wagons. Towns were far apart. It took a long

42　time to go from place to place. It was easier to use rivers to move people

58　and goods. Rivers became very busy. Rafts moved up and down the

70　rivers. Flour, grains, cotton, wheat, corn, and meat moved on the rafts.

82　Many people used rivers to move west. They wanted farms close to the

95　rivers. There were many towns along the rivers.

103　　The rivers and lakes were not connected. So people dug canals. The

115　longest canal was the Erie Canal. It was 363 miles long. It ran from the

130　Hudson River to Lake Erie. They started to dig the canal in 1819. It took

145　six years to dig the canal. Goods were placed on rafts. Mules pulled the

159　rafts. The mules walked along paths on the banks of the canals. A mule

173　could pull a load 50 times heavier than it could on any road. Now goods

188　and people could move easily.

193

Total Words Read _____

- Errors _____

= CWPM _____

Marco Polo: A World Traveler

0	Marco Polo was born in 1254. He lived in Venice. He was one of the
15	first people to travel to China. He was seventeen when he left on his trip.
30	He went with his father. It took three years to get to China. They used
45	camels. There were many stops along the way. They crossed mountains,
56	rivers, and deserts.
59	In China, Polo saw many new things. Colorful silk cloth was used
71	to make clothes. Food had many spices. The people ate rice and drank
84	tea. Life was well-ordered. The cities were large. Paper money was used.
97	Moveable print blocks were used to print on paper. Good records were
109	kept. They had fireworks. Kites flew in the sky. A compass was used
122	in travel. The Polos were away from home for twenty-four years. They
135	brought back gold, silver, diamonds, and rubies.
142	Marco Polo wrote a book. The book was about the many things he
155	saw and did in China. He told about life in China. At first people did not
171	believe him. Some people went to China. They found that Marco Polo
183	was right. Trade between China and Europe grew. It took a long time to
197	travel to China. Soon people wanted a faster way to travel. Men began to
211	sail to China.
214	

Total Words Read _____

\- Errors _____

= CWPM _____

The Great Wall: One of the World's Seven Wonders

0	The Great Wall of China is one of the Seven Wonders of the World.
14	The Great Wall is very big. It is in north China. The wall goes from east
30	to west. It goes over mountains, across grasslands, and through deserts.
41	The Great Wall is more than 3,000 miles long. It is about 40 feet tall and
57	15 feet wide. The top of the wall is more like a big road for horses and
74	people to walk on. Because the Great Wall is so big and long, it can be
90	seen from outer space
94	It took more than 2,000 years to build the Great Wall. It was built to
109	keep the enemies out of China. Along the wall are watchtowers. A long
122	time ago, soldiers and horses lived on the wall. There are big gates in the
137	wall. In times of peace, people could come and go from China.
149	There are hundreds of steps to the top of the wall. Today people can
163	climb to the top of the Great Wall. Many people come to visit the Great
178	Wall every year. They climb to the top of the wall. Some of them buy a
194	T-shirt that says, "I climbed to the top of the Great Wall." They are proud
209	that they were able to climb to the top of the wall.
221	

Total Words Read _____

\- Errors _____

= CWPM _____

Jim Thorpe: Athlete of the Century

0	Jim was born in 1888. He was a Native American. Jim was always
13	a great athlete. He rode horses at 3 years of age. By 5, he was a swimmer.
30	In high school, he played football. Later, Jim went to college. He played
43	semi-pro baseball. He was paid $60 a month.
52	In 1912, Jim went to the Olympics. The games were held in Sweden.
65	Jim won many gold medals. He won the pentathlon. It has five different
78	sports. Jim was first in four of them. Then he won the decathlon. It
92	has ten events. Jim was first in four of those. Jim came in second in
107	two more. He was third in the rest. He set a world's record. The king of
123	Sweden called him the best athlete in the world.
132	Olympic athletes are not supposed to be paid for playing sports.
143	Some people found out that Jim had been paid a little money to play
157	baseball. So, his gold medals were taken away. This made people angry.
169	Jim went on to play pro baseball. He also played pro football. He was a
184	star in both sports. People loved Jim. They even named a town after him.
198	Jim died in 1953. Thirty years later, his gold medals were given
210	back to his children.
214	

Total Words Read _____

- Errors _____

= CWPM _____

The Louisiana Purchase: A Good Deal

0   The Mississippi River valley is very large. In 1800, it belonged to

12   France. All of the rivers that feed into the Mississippi are part of the

26   valley. The people of the U.S. lived on the east side of the river. They

41   farmed the land. Rivers were used to move farm goods. They floated

53   wheat, lumber, tobacco, and cotton on log rafts. New Orleans is at the

66   end of the river. Farm goods were sold in New Orleans. The goods were

80   sent to the U.S. and other ports. New Orleans belonged to France. New

93   Orleans was a big city. People wanted New Orleans to be part of the U.S.

108   In 1802, France was in a long war. France was at war with England.

122   France wanted money for the army. The U.S. was going to give ten

135   million dollars for New Orleans. France offered to sell the whole valley.

147   Not just New Orleans. The U.S. took a chance. They offered five million.

160   France said, "No." The U.S. knew the river valley was very big. In the

174   west, it goes all of the way to the Rocky Mountains. In the north, it

189   goes almost to Canada. The U.S. made a final offer of 15 million. France

203   needed the money. They accepted the offer.

210   This was a good deal for the U.S. People could move west. There

223   was lots of land for the people to farm. The U.S. became much bigger.

237

Total Words Read _____

− Errors _____

= CWPM _____

Ben Franklin: Inventor and Statesman

0	Ben Franklin was born in Boston in 1706. His father was a soap and
14	candle maker. He had sixteen brothers and sisters. At ten, he started to
27	work in his father's shop. He worked for his father for two years. Then
41	he went to work for an older brother. Ben worked for nine years in his
56	brother's print shop. At the age of 17, he left.
66	Ben went to Philadelphia. He opened his own print shop. He
77	printed a newspaper and books. He wrote Poor Richard's Almanac. This
88	book was filled with advice. It had odd bits of wisdom. "Early to bed and
103	early to rise, makes a man healthy, wealthy, and wise." "God helps them
116	that help themselves." "One today is worth two tomorrows." "When the
127	well is dry, they know the worth of water." He printed a new book every
142	year. Many people bought his books. He became very rich.
152	Ben was an inventor. His cast-iron stove heated a room. Most of the
166	heat did not go up the chimney. Bifocal eyeglasses let people see near and
180	far. They did not need two pairs of glasses. He proved that lightning was
194	electricity. To do this he flew a kite in a storm. He made a lightning rod.
210	People put lightning rods on their houses. Lightning would strike the rod.
222	It would travel to the ground. The house would not burn. Ben became
235	famous.
236	Ben was a public servant. He helped to set up the first fire
249	department. He worked on the first library. He was the town postmaster.
261	He wanted to unite all of the colonies. He signed the Declaration of
274	Independence. Ben Franklin cared about the U.S.
281	

Total Words Read _____

- Errors _____

= CWPM _____

Weather: It's What's Outside That Counts

0	How do we tell the weather? We look outside. The weather is the
13	air around us. Weather can take many forms. Rain, snow, and wind are
26	forms of weather. Hurricanes and tornadoes are also forms of weather.
37	Many elements work together to make weather. There are three important
48	elements. They are heat, air, and water.
55	Heat comes from the sun to the earth. Without heat, there would
67	be no life. Heat travels in the form of light and energy. When it arrives,
82	it enters the blanket of air that surrounds the earth. This blanket of air
96	is called the atmosphere. Atmosphere has weight. It presses down on all
108	parts of the earth. This pressure is called air pressure. The earth's air is
122	full of air pressure. Some parts have low pressure. Warm air is lighter
135	than cold air. When there is warm, light air, there is lower air pressure.
149	Other parts of the earth have high air pressure. When the air is colder, the
164	pressure is higher.
167	Wind is made when air moves between low and high pressure
178	areas. When there is a big difference in pressure, the wind moves fast.
191	Sometimes this causes very strong winds. Strong winds cause hurricanes
201	and tornadoes
203	Water is also important. Our air is made up of many gases. One
216	kind of gas is water vapor. Water turns into water vapor when it is warm.
231	On warm days, there is more water vapor in the air. On cold days, there
246	is less water vapor. The amount of water vapor determines how humid
258	the air will be. When air rises, water vapor can turn into droplets. These
272	droplets can make clouds. Then clouds can cause water to fall from the
285	sky.
286	Weather is important. It affects our lives. If the weather is nice, we
299	like to be outside. We wear light clothes. If the weather is bad, we try to
315	stay inside. We wear thick, warm clothes. We can't control the weather.
327	But we need to pay attention to it.
335	

Total Words Read _____

− Errors _____

= CWPM _____

Guide Dogs: Helpful Pets

0   Most people think of dogs as great pets. But some dogs are more

13   than pets. They are guide dogs. Guide dogs help people in many ways.

26   Seeing Eye dogs help people who are blind. These dogs act as eyes for

40   their owners. Seeing Eye dogs help their owners travel from place to

52   place. Seeing Eye dogs ride on buses with their owners. They lead people

65   across busy streets. The dogs go in stores and restaurants with their

77   owners.

78   Hearing dogs help people who are deaf. These dogs alert their

89   owners to important sounds. Hearing dogs can be trained to listen for the

102 telephone ring. They might listen for the doorbell or alarm clock. They

114 can also listen for a baby's cry. The Hearing dog will nudge its owner

128 when it hears an important sound.

134   Other dogs are helpers for people in wheelchairs. These dogs help

145 with physical tasks. They might pick up dropped objects. They are trained

157 to flip light switches. These dogs are able to open drawers and doors.

170   Guide dogs help their owners to live full lives. With a guide dog,

183 owners don't have to rely on other people to help them. They can be

197 independent. Guide dogs are more than pets. They are lifelines for their

209 owners.

210

Total Words Read _____

- Errors _____

= CWPM _____

116   The Six-Minute Solution: A Reading Fluency Program (Intermediate Level)

Sharks: Amazing Fish

0   Sharks have lived in the oceans for millions of years. Sharks

11   were on earth before there were whales. They were on earth before the

24   dinosaurs.

25   Sharks are amazing fish. They have many teeth. In fact, sharks are

37   covered with teeth. Unlike other fish, sharks do not have bones. Most

49   fish have skeletons made of bone. But a shark skeleton is made of gristle.

63   Bony fish have skin that is covered with smooth scales. Sharks have skin

76   that is covered with denticles. Denticles are small, sharp teeth. They can

88   cut and scratch. Sharks have many rows of teeth. If a shark tooth falls

102   out, another tooth moves forward to take its place. This happens very

114   quickly. During its lifetime, a shark may have a thousand sets of teeth.

127   Many people think there is just one kind of shark. In fact, there are

141   at least 350 kinds of sharks. The largest shark is the whale shark. It is

156   as big as two elephants. The smallest shark is the cigar shark. It can fit

171   in a person's hand. The great white shark is known as "the man eater."

185   People are afraid of the great white shark. It sometimes attacks people in

198   water. The great white shark mostly eats large fish. It also eats seals and

212   otters.

213   There is no type of shark that naturally preys on humans. Only in

226   the last 100 years have there been reports of shark attacks on people. This

240   is because more people are going in the water. A person is more likely to

255   be killed in a car accident than to be attacked by a shark.

268

Total Words Read _____

- Errors _____

= CWPM _____

Roads and Highways

0   Until about 1850 there were no real roads in the U.S. Most towns

13   were near water. Roads were used to get things to docks. Rivers and

26   canals were used to carry things long distances. Most people traveled on

38   foot, on horses, or by horse-drawn wagons. Some people used trains and

51   boats. Roads were trails through the woods. The trails were narrow and

63   rutted. They were muddy when it rained. Snow piled up on the trails.

76   Trails were dusty in the summer. Sometimes the trails had logs across

88   them. The roads were not good.

94   In the 1900s, people began to own cars. People could not drive cars

107   on the trails. They wanted good roads. In 1909, there were over 190,000

120   miles of road with a hard surface. These roads were made of crushed

133   rock. They were not made of concrete. People wanted better roads.

144   By 1920, more people had cars. Cars saved time and work. People

156   did not want to wait for trains and boats. They wanted to go places that

171   trains and boats did not go to. People wanted to go lots of places in cars.

187   People wanted more roads.

191   When there were better roads, people started to use buses. Trucks

202   were a new way to carry things. By 1930, there were 640,000 miles of

216   roads with hard surfaces. People used roads more and more. Today there

228   are millions of miles of roads in the U.S.

237

Total Words Read _____

− Errors _____

= CWPM _____

The Mexican Flag: Green, White, and Red

0   The Mexican flag is a banner with three bands of color. Its colors

13   are green, white, and red. The green band is on the left side of the flag. It

30   stands for the earth. The white band is in the middle of the flag. It stands

46   for purity. The red band is on the right side of the flag. It is a symbol

63   of blood. It stands for the blood shed during battles. These battles took

76   place during Mexico's War for Independence.

82   There is an eagle inside the white band in the center of the flag.

96   The eagle is eating a rattlesnake. Its left claw is perched on a cactus.

110 There are green oak branches on the left below the eagle. These stand for

124 strength. There are laurel branches on the right below the eagle. These

136 stand for victory. The eagle is from an Aztec legend. The Aztecs were told

150 by their god of the sun to look for their promised land. They would know

165 the place when they found an eagle eating a snake while standing on a

179 cactus. The Aztecs found such a place in 1325. They built their homes on

193 land that is now Mexico City.

199

Total Words Read _____

- Errors _____

= CWPM _____

Harriet Tubman: Conductor of Freedom

0	Harriet was born in 1820. Her parents were slaves in Maryland.
11	That meant Harriet was a slave, too. Slaves were owned by a "master."
24	Even though she was just a child, Harriet had to work. Her job was to
39	take care of the master's baby. She had to keep the baby from crying at
54	night. If the baby cried, Harriet was whipped. Harriet hated being a slave.
67	She wanted to be free.
72	When she grew up, Harriet married John Tubman. He was a free
84	black man. But Harriet was still a slave. A few years later, Harriet became
98	worried that she was going to be sold. She decided to run away. She
112	escaped to the northern part of the U.S. There was no slavery in the
126	North. Harriet ended up in Pennsylvania. She got a job there and saved
139	her money.
141	Harriet wanted to help other slaves become free. It was dangerous
152	to help slaves escape. But Harriet was very brave. She went back to
165	Maryland 19 times to help the slaves there. She showed slaves how to
178	follow the Underground Railroad. This "railroad" was a group of homes.
189	They were called "safe houses." They were owned by people who wanted
201	to help the slaves. Slaves could stop to rest at the safe houses along the
216	way as they moved north.
221	Harriet Tubman helped 300 slaves become free. Harriet is an
231	American hero.
233	

Total Words Read _____

− Errors _____

= CWPM _____

Chinese Kite Flying: A National Pastime

0	Kites in China reflect culture. Kites have many shapes. Most of the
12	kites are made in the shape of animals. The kite shapes that most people
26	like are deer, tigers, birds, fish, and dragons. People in China think that
39	the animal shapes have meaning. Deer are good luck. The tiger, king
51	of the animals, is mighty and strong. Catfish are for more wealth in the
65	coming year. Dragons are wise and very important in China. Many kites
77	look like dragons. In China, there are many big and many small kites. Old
91	and young people fly kites.
96	In China people have flown kites for more than 2,400 years. The old
109	people teach the young people about kite culture. They show them how
121	to make the kites with paper and wood. Some little kites have one part.
135	Very big kites have many parts and shapes. The people paint the kites
148	with many colors. The kites are very pretty. Every day many people fly
161	kites in the sky.
165	People believe that kite flying is healthy. When someone is worn-
176	out and tired, or when they want to get out of the house, they go outside
192	and fly a kite. They watch their pretty kites go up in the sky. When
207	people fly kites, they can look at the sky, clouds, and trees. This makes
221	them feel good and happy. Many people in China like to fly kites.
234	

Total Words Read _____

– Errors _____

= CWPM _____

Level 3 Practice Passages

White, Brown, and Black: The Bear Facts

0   There are three types of bears in North America. They are the polar

13   bear, the brown bear, and the black bear. Canada and Alaska are the only

27   places where all three types of bears live.

35   Polar bears are marine mammals. They live in very cold climates

46   where there is ice and snow. Polar bears have hair that looks white. They

60   are the largest kind of bear. When they stand on their hind legs, polar

74   bears are between 8 and 10 feet tall. Polar bears can weigh between 600

88   and 1,400 pounds. They are meat eaters. They have special claws which

100 help them to hold onto the ice and catch seals. The ringed seal is the

115 polar bear's favorite meal!

119 Brown bears have different colors and names. Some brown bears

129 are dark brown. Other brown bears are blonder. All brown bears have

141 a hump above their shoulders. This hump is made of fat and muscle.

154 Brown bears who live on the coast are called brownies. Those who live in

168 the interior are grizzlies. Grizzlies are smaller and meaner than brownies.

179 Brown bears are 6 to 8 feet tall when standing on their hind legs. They

194 can weigh between 400 and 1,500 pounds. Brown bears eat a lot of

207 different things like bugs, fish, berries, and baby animals. They spend all

219 summer eating to store up fat for a winter nap.

229 Black bears are the smallest kind of bear. They are only 5 or 6 feet

244 when standing on their hind legs. Some black bears are a jet black color.

258 Others are lighter. Most black bears have brown noses and big ears. Black

271 bears weigh between 100 and 400 pounds. They have claws that are sharp

284 and curved. These special claws help them to climb trees.

294

Total Words Read _____

– Errors _____

= CWPM _____

Yangtze River

0	The Yangtze River is the longest river in China. It is the third
13	longest river in the world. It runs from the mountains in the West to
27	the flat land in the East by the China Sea. Over 700 rivers flow into the
43	Yangtze. The water in the river is brown. The river runs like a zigzag all
58	of the way from the mountains to the sea.
67	The Yangtze River is divided into three parts. In the upper part, the
80	river is small. There are many big rocks and waterfalls. The water moves
93	very fast. Boats cannot sail in the upper part.
102	In the middle part, the water flow is slower. Many boats sail on
115	the river. There are tall hills on both sides of the river. Sometimes only
129	one boat can sail at a time. There are lots of trees and flowers. It is very
146	pretty. There are many small towns and fishing villages built along the
158	river. In this part of the river, a dam is being built. It will be the world's
175	biggest dam. Then there will be no more floods.
184	In the lower part of the river, the river is wide. The water flow is
199	very slow. Many ships sail on the river. The land beside the river is flat.
214	There are many farms and big cities along the river.
224	The Yangtze River is a very important river in China. People have
236	lived and worked along the river for thousands of years.
246	

Total Words Read _____

- Errors _____

= CWPM _____

Is It a Solid, a Liquid, or a Gas?

0   Scientists tell us that all matter has three forms. All matter has some

13   weight or mass. All matter also takes up some space in our universe.

26   Atoms make up all matter. There are three forms of matter.

37   The first kind of matter is a solid. A solid has weight or mass, and it

53   takes up space. A solid is different from a liquid or a gas. A solid has its

70   own shape. Solids, such as wood, a glass, or a toy top, are one example

85   of matter. Solids are hard. They don't change their shapes. Some other

97   examples of solids are soft and bend easily. Shirts and modeling clay are

110   two examples of this kind of solid.

117   The second type of matter is a liquid. Water, milk, and honey are

130   examples of liquids. A liquid does not have a shape of its own. A liquid

145   takes the shape of whatever container it is in. If milk is in a tall glass,

161   then the milk is tall. If honey is on a spoon, then the honey takes the

177   shape of the spoon.

181   The third type of matter is a gas. A gas is like a liquid because it

197   takes the shape of its container. But a gas is different from a liquid in that

213   it fills the entire container. A gas may have color or a smell, but it may

229   not have either. We can't see the air, but we can feel it when the wind

245   blows. Matter is what makes up our universe, and it only takes three

258   forms. Those three forms make up everything in our world.

268

Total Words Read _____

− Errors _____

= CWPM _____

Sponges: Simple Animals

0   Many people think of a sponge as a kitchen tool. Kitchen sponges

12   are one kind of sponge. These sponges are man-made. Other types of

25   sponges are alive. These types of sponges are animals. They actually look

37   more like plants than animals. However, a sponge is the simplest form of

50   a multicellular animal. Most sponges live in the oceans of the world. A

63   few sponges live in fresh water. Sponges do not live on land.

75   There are two basic types of sponges: encrusting and freestanding.

85   Encrusting sponges look like moss. They cover the surface of rocks.

96   Freestanding sponges have more inner volume. They can grow into

106   strange shapes. They can become very big. The barrel sponge is a

118   freestanding sponge. It grows in the tropics. A whole person could fit

130   inside some barrel sponges. Tube sponges also grow in the tropics. They

142   come in many beautiful colors.

147   A sponge does not have a head or a mouth. Nor does a sponge have

162   arms or feet. So a sponge cannot move. It stays in one place for its whole

178   life. If a sponge is touched, it does not react. It lives on the bottom of

194   the ocean. A sponge attaches to something solid. It finds a place where

207   there is enough food. A sponge does not make its own food like a plant

222   does. That is one reason that the sponge is an animal. Sponges capture

233   food. A sponge eats tiny plants and animals that live in the water around

249   it. Sponges have a thin outside layer. Inside this outer layer is an open

263   space. The open space is called a pore. Tiny hairs move constantly in the

277   water. The hairs send food and water through the pores. Special cells in

290   the pores eat the tiny bits of food and organisms. The rest of the water

305   and food goes out the top of the sponge. Sponges are covered with pores.

319   No wonder that their scientific name means, "pore-bearing."

328

Total Words Read _____

- Errors _____

= CWPM _____

Camels: One Hump or Two?

0	Camels are funny looking mammals with humps on their backs.
10	Camels are large animals. They are seven or eight feet tall. They have
23	small heads but long, curved necks. Their legs are long, but their bodies
36	are heavy. Camels are used for riding or for carrying heavy loads.
48	There are two kinds of camels. Camels with one hump live in
60	Arabia, Asia, and North America. These camels have long legs and are
72	good for riding. One-hump camels can run 8 or 10 miles an hour. They
87	can travel 100 miles each day. Riding a camel is not like riding a horse.
102	First, a camel has to kneel down before the rider can get on its back.
117	These camels have hard pads on their knees and chest. The camel's feet
130	are wide, with two toes. This helps to keep them from sinking into the
144	sand. The camel moves its right legs together and then its left legs. Riding
158	on a camel is like rolling or swaying from side to side.
170	Two-hump camels live in Central Asia. They are used to cold
182	climates and rocky land. Camels with two humps have shorter legs with
194	hard soles on their feet. They are used as pack animals. These camels can
208	carry four- or five-hundred pounds on their backs. They can walk two or
222	three miles an hour.
226	

Total Words Read _____

– Errors _____

= CWPM _____

Seasons: Passages of Time

0   Our planet is always moving. Earth moves around the sun in a path.

13   This path is called an orbit. Each year, the earth orbits the sun. There is

28   an imaginary line that runs through the center of the earth. This line is

42   called an axis. The two points where the axis passes through the earth

55   are called poles. There is the North Pole and the South Pole. As the earth

70   moves around the sun, it spins on its axis. This spinning causes day and

84   night. The side of the earth that is pointed to the sun has daylight. The

99   side of the earth that is pointed away from the sun has darkness. The

113   days change as the earth orbits the sun. The length of the days changes.

127   The temperature changes.

130   There are four seasons: fall, winter, spring, and summer. The

140   seasons change because of the earth's axis and the earth's orbit. Each of

153   the earth's poles is turned toward the sun for part of the year. Each pole

168   is turned away from the sun for the other part of the year.

181   Fall begins in late September. The first day of fall is called the

194   fall equinox. During the fall equinox, the sun is just above the equator.

207   The day and the night are the same length. During the fall season,

220   temperatures drop more quickly.

224   Winter begins in December. The first day of winter is called the

236   winter solstice. It is the shortest day of the year. That means that there

250   are less hours of daylight than on any other day of the year. After

264   December 21, the days begin to get longer by a few minutes each day.

278   Spring begins around March 20. As in the fall season, there is an

291   equinox in the spring. That is when the day and the night are the same

306   length. After the spring equinox, the daylight hours get longer by a few

319   minutes every day. The temperatures start to get warmer.

328   Summer is the warmest season. It begins around June 21. The first

340   day of summer is called the summer solstice. It is the longest day of the

355   year. That means that there are more daylight hours on this day than on

369   any other day.

372

Total Words Read _____

\- Errors _____

= CWPM _____

Whales: Huge Sea Mammals

0	The whale is a sea mammal that breathes air but cannot live on
13	land. It is the largest known mammal. The whale is one of two kinds of
28	mammals that live in the water for their entire lives. Like all mammals,
41	whales are warm-blooded and nurse their young. There are many kinds
53	of whales. The largest whale is the blue whale. A blue whale can grow to
68	be about 94 feet long. That is the size of a 9-story building. The smallest
84	whale is a dwarf sperm whale. These whales only grow to be about eight-
98	feet long.
100	A whale looks like a very large fish. It has flukes in its tail, which
115	help it to swim through the water. Whales have flippers that are sort
128	of like the fingers and hands of mammals that live on land. The whale
142	is covered with smooth, glossy skin, which helps it to swim fast in the
156	water. Below the skin is a layer of fat called blubber that helps to keep
171	the whale warm. Because of this blubber, a whale does not need as much
185	hair or fur as a land mammal. In fact, adult whales have almost no hair.
200	Whales have large, broad heads, but very small eyes. Whales breathe
211	air through their lungs before diving underwater for fifteen or twenty
222	minutes at a time. While air is in the whale's lungs, it becomes warm and
237	moist. When this air is released through the whale's blowhole, it becomes
249	a kind of vapor. This is the called the spout. Each type of whale has its
265	own kind of spout. For example, the blue whale has a tall, thick spout
279	while the humpback whale's spout is low and round. Experienced whale
290	watchers can tell whales apart by their spouts.
298	

Total Words Read _____

− Errors _____

= CWPM _____

Terra-Cotta Warriors

0   The first emperor of China built a big tomb. When he died, he

13   wanted to be buried in his tomb. The tomb was very, very big. It was

28   made of wood. It covered more than five city blocks. The emperor had a

42   big army. He had more than 8,000 soldiers. He had more than 500 horses.

56   A clay model was made for each of his soldiers. Clay models were made

70   for the horses. The emperor put the clay soldiers and horses in the tomb.

84   He put bows, arrows, and spears in the tomb.

93   The emperor believed that the souls of the soldiers and horses

104 would go to the afterlife with him. The first emperor was not nice to his

119 people. He made them build his tomb and work on the Great Wall. The

133 people were not happy. When the emperor died, he was put in the tomb

147 with the clay soldiers and horses. Two years later, the poor farmers got

160 mad. They broke into the tomb. The farmers took the bows, arrows, and

173 spears. They knocked down the soldiers. The clay soldiers broke into

184 pieces. The poor farmers burned the tomb. Everyone forgot about the

195 tomb. Dirt covered the tomb. It became a little hill. People started to farm

209 on the hill.

212   Two thousand years later, in 1974, some farmers were digging a

223 well. They found some clay parts of the soldiers. They started to dig a pit.

238 In China, they are still digging in the pit to this day. They find parts of the

255 clay soldiers. Then they put each soldier back together. It will take many

268 years to dig up the soldier parts. It will take even longer to put all of the

285 soldiers together. There may even be more clay figures in the tomb of the

299 first emperor.

301

Total Words Read _____

- Errors _____

= CWPM _____

Bridges: An Important Beginning

0   Bridges are important. People have many reasons to build bridges.

10 Cave people built bridges with logs. They put logs across a stream. Then

23 they walked to the other side. People who lived in jungles made bridges

36 from vines. They twisted plant vines into ropes. They put two vine ropes

49 next to each other. Then they tied the vines to trees. Bridges helped

62 people to cross rivers. They could go to a better hunting ground. They

75 could go to trade with other people.

82 People all over the world build bridges. Bridges are made in many

94 ways. In China, bridges were made with houses on each end. Sometimes

106 there were places to eat on the bridges. These kinds of bridges were nice

120 for travelers. The Romans made beautiful stone bridges. Roman bridges

130 had rounded openings. These openings are called arches. Arch bridges

140 are still built today. In Persia, armies built bridges that floated. They used

153 small boats with a floor on top. Armies used floating bridges when they

166 wanted to cross water in a hurry. Floating bridges are called pontoon

178 bridges.

179 Not all bridges go over water. Some bridges go over land. Some

191 go over railroad tracks. Others go over buildings. Still others go over

203 highways. Early bridges were made of wood. Now they are made of steel

216 or concrete.

218

Total Words Read _____

– Errors _____

= CWPM _____

Jesse Owens: Olympic Athlete

0	Jesse was born in Alabama in 1913. His father was a sharecropper.
12	When he was 9, Jesse's family moved to Ohio. In high school, Jesse
25	tried out for the track team. Jesse ran the 100-yard dash. He was very
40	fast. Jesse ran it in just 9.4 seconds. His coach was amazed. Coach Riley
54	helped Jesse become a high school track and broad jump star.
65	Jesse went on to college in Ohio. He broke world records for
77	running and jumping. Jesse went to the Olympics in Germany in 1936.
89	Hitler was then the leader of Germany. He thought white Germans were
101	better than Jews. He also thought they were better than black people.
113	Jesse was African American. He won four gold medals at the Olympics.
125	This made Hitler mad. He did not congratulate Jesse.
134	Most other Germans liked Jesse. They admired his skills. One
144	German athlete helped Jesse at the Olympics. His name was Lutz Long.
156	Lutz gave Jesse advice. The advice helped Jesse to qualify for—and win—
169	the gold medal for broad jump. Jesse never forgot Lutz's friendship.
180	During his life, Jesse set seven world records. When he retired, he
192	gave speeches. He said that athletes should be honest. He told them to
205	live healthy lives.
208	Jesse Owens was not just a great athlete. He was a very good
221	person.
222	

Total Words Read _____

- Errors _____

= CWPM _____

The Right to Read

0   Reading is important. It is a useful skill. People who can read have
13   an easier time in life. They can read traffic signs, menus, and maps. They
27   can pass a test to get a driver's license. They can apply for a job. Reading
43   is also powerful. People who can read can learn about all kinds of things.

57   However, not everyone can read. Some experts study reading. They
67   say that one out of every six people in the world can't read. There are
82   many reasons for this problem. Some countries do not let girls go to
95   school. In those countries, many women cannot read. Other people live in
107   very poor countries. No one can afford to learn to read in these countries.
121   They are busy trying to find food to eat. Many countries are at war. Their
136   people are fighting to stay alive. They do not have time to learn to read.

151   In the U.S., there are many people who do not speak English. They
164   came from other countries. It is hard to come to a new country. It takes
179   time to learn the language well enough to read it. Other people have
192   learning problems. It is harder for them to learn to read.

203   The good news is that everyone can learn how to read. There
215   are special programs to teach people to read. One of the best ways to
229   become better at reading is to read every day. Countries want to show
242   their citizens how important it is to learn to read. Every September 8, we
256   celebrate International Literacy Day. Literacy is a word that means being
267   able to read, write, and speak.

273

Total Words Read _____

− Errors _____

= CWPM _____

A Mexican Fiesta

0   A fiesta is a party. Mexican people celebrate with a fiesta. A fiesta

13 can be held to honor a person. It can also be held to honor an event.

29 Some fiestas are simple ones. They may last only one day. Fiestas can

42 also be elaborate. They can last for a week or more.

53 Fiestas are colorful. Green, white, and red are used for decorations.

64 These are the colors of the Mexican flag. Flowers are also used. Fiestas

77 have lots of music. Mariachi bands usually play. There is much singing

89 and dancing. One kind of dance is the Mexican Hat Dance.

100 Fiestas have a lot of food. There are many kinds of spicy dishes.

113 People feast all day long. Some fiestas have parades. People dress up in

126 costumes. There may be fireworks. Sometimes, there are rodeos. Other

136 times, there may be bullfights.

141 One thing is for certain: Fiestas are FUN!

149

Total Words Read _____

\- Errors _____

= CWPM _____

134 The Six-Minute Solution: A Reading Fluency Program (Intermediate Level)

Helen Keller: Triumph Over Tragedy

0	Helen Keller was born on June 27, 1880. She was a healthy baby
13	at first. Then she got sick. She had a high fever. Helen almost died. The
28	fever went away after many days. But Helen was not the same. She was
42	now deaf and blind.
46	The next few years were very hard. Helen was angry. She cried
58	and threw things on the floor. She grabbed food off people's plates. Her
71	parents did not know what to do. They asked an expert for help. He was
86	Alexander Graham Bell. Bell had invented the telephone. But he also
97	worked with deaf children. Bell told Helen's parents to hire a special
109	teacher for Helen. Helen's parents wrote to a special school. It was the
122	Perkins School for the Blind. They asked for a special teacher to come
135	work with Helen.
138	On March 3, 1887, Annie Sullivan came to live at the Keller's home.
151	Annie told Helen's parents that Helen must learn to behave. She said that
164	it was not fair to let Helen act wild. The kind thing to do would be to
181	teach Helen. Annie showed Helen how to eat with a spoon and fork. Most
195	important of all, Annie taught Helen words by spelling them into her
207	hand. At first, Helen did not understand. Her teacher never gave up. One
220	day, Annie poured water over Helen's hand. Then she spelled the word
232	water into Helen's hand. Finally, Helen understood! She understood that
242	words had meaning. That day was the turning point for Helen. From then
255	on, she began to learn quickly. Helen learned to read using raised letters.
268	Later, she learned to read braille. Helen also learned to write. She used a
282	special typewriter. Annie Sullivan continued to help Helen. Helen Keller
292	went to college. The college was Radcliffe College in Boston. Helen was
304	the first deaf and blind person to earn a degree from Radcliffe. The story
318	of Helen Keller and her teacher, Annie Sullivan, is a famous one. Many
331	books, plays, and movies tell their story.
338	

Total Words Read _____

– Errors _____

= CWPM _____

The Birth of a River

0	Have you ever wondered how a river begins? A river gets its start
13	high in the mountains or in the hills. It begins as a very small stream.
28	The river may also get its start from a spring bubbling from beneath the
42	ground. The little stream begins to flow downward from its mountain
53	home. Other little streams join it. More and more water begins to flow
66	downward. Soon the little streams have joined to become a brook. The
78	brook continues to grow bigger. Then the brook becomes a river.
89	Some smaller rivers that join the big river are called its tributaries.
101	The ground that the river flows over is called the riverbed. The river's
114	banks are its left and right sides. As the river travels, it picks up small
129	stones, sticks, and soil. Where the river empties into a lake or a sea is its
145	mouth. The river drops what it is carrying at its mouth when it meets a
160	lake or the sea. All of the stones, sticks, and soil the river drops build up
176	to form land.
179	The land that is formed at the river's mouth is called its delta. The
193	river's delta has rich soil for farming. A river delta grows many crops.
206	It takes hundreds and hundreds of years to build up the river's delta.
219	Sometimes the river floods and takes soil from its delta. Other times it
232	just keeps on adding soil. This makes its delta even larger. All of the
246	small streams, brooks, and small rivers that empty into the big river form
259	the big river's basin. Some river basins are hundreds of miles wide.
271	

Total Words Read _____

− Errors _____

= CWPM _____

Dolores Huerta: Labor Leader

0	Dolores Huerta was born in 1930. She lived in a mining town in
13	New Mexico. Her parents divorced when she was three years old. Dolores
25	and her mother, Alicia, moved to California. They settled in the central
37	valley. There were many farms there. Farm workers picked crops. They
48	worked hard. Farm workers made little money. It was hard for them to
61	buy food and shoes.
65	Alicia owned a hotel. She was a generous woman. She let farm
77	workers and their families stay for free. Alicia taught her daughter to be
90	kind and caring.
93	Dolores went to college. She became a teacher. She felt sad for the
106	children of farm workers. Many of them came to school hungry. Some
118	needed shoes. Others had to work in the fields. Most of the children went
132	to many different schools.
136	Dolores left her job. She wanted to help the farm workers. Dolores
148	met a man named Cesar Chavez. He also worked hard to help farm
161	workers. Together, Dolores and Cesar started a union. It was the United
173	Farm Workers of America. Farm workers joined the union.
182	Sometimes, the union held a strike. That means that the farm
193	workers stopped working. They did not pick any more crops until their
205	changes were made. The FWA asked for the workers to be paid more
218	money. The grape farmers would not pay better wages. In 1965, the
230	workers went on strike. About 5,000 workers left their jobs. The strike
242	lasted five years. When it was over, the workers won. They would make
255	more money for their hard work.
261	Dolores did not quit when the strike was over. She spoke against
273	using pesticides on crops. The pesticides made the workers sick. She
284	kept fighting for farm worker rights. Dolores helped them become U.S.
295	citizens. She made sure that their children went to good schools. Dolores
307	has won many awards for helping farm workers to have better lives.
319	

Total Words Read _____

– Errors _____

= CWPM _____

Blackbeard: A Fierce Pirate

0   Blackbeard was one of the most hated pirates of all time. He

12   became a pirate around 1713. He is thought to have come from England.

25   His real name was Edward Teach. He had a long, black beard that

38   covered most of his face. He braided his long, black beard and tied the

52   braids with hemp. He also put hemp in his hair. Then he would light the

67   hemp during battles. Blackbeard looked like his face was circled with

78   fire. Many people were afraid of Blackbeard. When they saw him coming,

90   they would give him what he wanted. Then Blackbeard would let them

102   sail away. If people tried to fight Blackbeard, he would kill them. Even

115   Blackbeard's own men were afraid of him.

122   Blackbeard spent a lot of time off the coast of Virginia and the

135   Carolinas in 1717 and 1718. His ship was called Queen Anne's Revenge.

147   Blackbeard stole ships and held people for ransom. One day his ship

159   ran aground near Cape Fear. The governor of North Carolina pardoned

170   Blackbeard. But Blackbeard would not stop his pirate ways. Blackbeard

180   had captured more than 40 ships as a pirate. He had caused the death of

195   hundreds of people. Finally, the governor sent a ship to arrest Blackbeard.

207   There was a huge, bloody battle. Blackbeard put up a big fight but was

221   killed. He died with 5 bullets and more than 20 stab wounds in his body.

236

Total Words Read _____

− Errors _____

= CWPM _____

Beware of Bears

0   Bears! Many people are fascinated by them. After all, who can resist

12   a stuffed, cuddly teddy bear? Bear enclosures at zoos are often a popular

25   exhibit. Watching adorable bear cubs romp brings smiles and chuckles

35   from onlookers.

37   Bears in the wild are a different story. Bears are powerful animals

49   and can kill humans. If you are a camper or a hiker, it is important to

65   beware of bears. Bear country can be a dangerous place. Knowing some

77   bear essentials can help to keep you safe.

85   First of all, never, ever try to feed a bear. Bears love garbage and

99   are easily turned into junk-food addicts. They will then be attracted to

112 areas when people gather, such as a camping ground. National parks and

124 forests often have special "bear-proof" trash cans. Campers are told to

136 keep their food locked up and put up in a tree. Bears will destroy cars and

152 cabins in an attempt to get to a food source.

162 When in bear country, make noise to let the bears know that you

175 are around. Bears like to be alone. They do not like to be surprised by

190 people. Bears will usually stay away if they hear you coming.

201 Be alert when you are in bear country. Stay away from dense brush.

214 Use a flashlight at night. Be on the lookout for bear droppings. Do not

228 set up camp if you see signs of a bear. Be especially careful if you see

244 bear cubs. You can be sure that the mother bear is near. She might attack

259 to protect her cubs. If you happen to come across a bear, do not run!

274 Instead, back away very slowly. Use bear (pepper) spray only as a last

287 resort.

288

Total Words Read _____

– Errors _____

= CWPM _____

Sounds: Moving Waveforms

0	Sounds are a part of everyday life. Car horns beep. Dogs bark.
12	Children shout. Noisy jets roar across the sky. People whisper to one
24	another. There are hundreds of sounds made every day. It is easy for
37	people to tell them apart. But there are other sounds that cannot be heard
51	by people. These sounds are too high-pitched for the human ear. They are
65	called ultrasounds.
67	Sounds are produced by a certain type of motion. These motions
78	are called vibrations. Sound travels from a vibrating object to a human
90	ear. It does this by using a sound carrier. The sound carrier may be a
105	solid, liquid, or a gas. One way sound travels is through air. Sound waves
119	make the particles in the air move. One moving particle touches another
131	particle and makes that new particle move. Then that particle touches
142	the next particle and so on. If there is no sound carrier, no sound can be
158	heard.
159	The speed of sound depends upon how it is traveling. Sound travels
171	a little faster in warmer air than it does in colder air. However, sound
185	travels much faster in water than it does in air. It travels even faster in
200	solids such as steel or aluminum. The denser the sound carrier, the faster
213	the sound travels. The speed of sound is slower than the speed of light
227	though. That is why we hear thunder after we see lightning.
238	

Total Words Read _____

- Errors _____

= CWPM _____

Bones, Bones, Bones

0   Bones are alive! They are made of living tissue. Calcium and

11   phosphorous and bone cells make up bones. All of the bones in a body

25   make up the skeleton. An infant has over a hundred and forty more

38   bones than an adult. The baby has around three hundred and fifty

50   bones in its body. An adult has only two hundred and six bones. What

64   happened to over one hundred and forty bones? As a baby begins to grow

78   and develop, some of those bones grow together. This is called fusion.

90   Bones are very important. They give bodies their shape. Muscles

100   are attached to bones. The muscles allow the bones to give the body

113   movement. People are able to run and jump because of their bones and

126   muscles. Bones are also hard and strong. They protect the soft organs of

139   the body. The heart, lungs, and brain are soft organs. Bones provide a

152   protective cage around these important organs.

158   It is important to keep bones strong. One way to do this is to eat

173   green vegetables and drink milk. Green vegetables and milk have calcium

184   and phosphorous. These help keep bones strong. Strong bones help

194   bodies to stay healthy.

198

Total Words Read _____

- Errors _____

= CWPM _____

Caves: Underground Rooms

0   A cave is a hollow room found in the earth. There are many kinds

14   of caves. Caves are important to scientists who study early humanity.

25   Scientists can often find the signs of early life in caves. Cave people lived

39   in caves more than one hundred thousand years ago. The cave people

51   left paintings on cave walls. These paintings showed the types of animals

63   they hunted. Fossils of early plant and animal life have been discovered

75   in caves.

77   One type of cave is formed when water wears away soft rock under

90   the ground. Mammoth Cave in Kentucky is a famous United States cave.

102 Mammoth Cave is more than 200 miles long. Some of its rooms are over

116 fifty feet high. There are so many streams in Mammoth Cave that visitors

129 can travel in boats. Since the cave is dark, the fish that live there do not

145 have eyes. They do not need to see.

153   Another kind of cave is called a sea cave. This type of cave is

167 formed by ocean waves pounding against cliffs. A famous sea cave, called

179 Fingal's Cave, can be found in Scotland. Ice caves form when glaciers

191 melt and then freeze again. Austria is the home of a famous ice cave. An

206 ice cave called the Singing Cave can be found in Iceland. Another type of

220 cave is a lava cave. The lava of a volcano forms a lava cave.

234

Total Words Read _____

- Errors _____

= CWPM _____

Glaciers: Rivers of Ice

0	A river has a lot of water in it. Some rivers are long and wide.
15	Other rivers are short and narrow. One kind of river carries boats and
28	people and supplies to towns and cities along its banks. Another kind of
41	river has a lot of water in it. This river does not carry boats or people or
58	supplies. It does move, but it moves very, very slowly. This river is made
72	of ice, and it has a special name. This river of ice is called a glacier.
88	When snow falls in most places, it melts when the weather turns
100	warm. But there are some places that never get warm. The snow does
113	not melt. Year after year, the snow and ice sit on the tops of high, cold
129	mountains. After a time, the snow and ice become heavy and begin to
142	slip down the mountains. This glacier or river of ice may only move from
156	one to three feet per year. As the river of ice moves slowly down the
171	mountains, its bottom edge may begin to melt off. This melting is caused
184	because the bottom edge of the glacier reached lower, warmer valleys.
195	The glacier changes the soil it flows over as it moves slowly down the
209	mountains. Glaciers scrape the earth and move huge rocks and boulders
220	in their paths. They also move and push trees and anything else in their
234	paths.
235	

Total Words Read _____

- Errors _____

= CWPM _____

The Giraffe: World's Tallest Animal

0   The tallest animal in the world is the giraffe. A baby giraffe is

13   almost 6 feet tall when it is born. It can then grow to be almost 18 feet

30   tall! Because it is so tall, it takes a giraffe a long time to stand up. So, to

48   be safe, giraffes sleep standing up. Then, if predators come after them,

60   they are ready to run. Lions, hyenas, and wild dogs prey on giraffes.

73   Giraffes have to be careful when they rest or bend down to drink.

86   Sometimes, giraffes in a herd take turns resting or drinking. That way,

98   one giraffe is always on the lookout for danger. Giraffes have very good

111   eyesight. They can spot danger a long way away. Giraffes can run from

124   danger. In fact, they are fast runners. They can run up to 35 miles an

139   hour! Giraffes can even outrun most horses. Their speed helps them to

151   outrun their enemies. They also have strong hooves that they can use to

164   kick out an enemy.

168   Giraffes have long necks but make very little noise. Scientists used

179   to think that giraffes were mute. They now know that giraffes do make

192   noises. These noises are called infrasounds. These sounds cannot be

202   heard by humans. Giraffes also have long tongues. Their tongues are

213   between 18 and 21 inches long. Giraffe tongues are prehensile. That

224   means that the tongue is able to grab and hold on to objects. Giraffes

238   need a long neck and a special tongue in order to eat. The giraffe's

252   favorite food is the thorny leaf that grows on the acacia tree. Without a

266   long neck, the giraffe could not reach the tops of tall trees to eat their

281   tender leaves. Without the tongue and long lower lip, those same leaves

293   would be hard to pick off the tree tops.

302   The giraffe's coat is covered with yellow and brown spots. Its coat

314   helps the giraffe to blend in with trees and tall grasses in the wild. No

329   two giraffes have exactly the same pattern of spots on their coats. In the

343   wild, giraffes live together in herds of 5 to 45 animals. Giraffes are quiet,

357   peaceful animals that are favorites of children all over the world.

368

Total Words Read _____

– Errors _____

= CWPM _____

144   The Six-Minute Solution: A Reading Fluency Program (Intermediate Level)

The Sioux: Buffalo Hunters

0   The Sioux are a Native American tribe. Many years ago, they lived

12   in what is now North Dakota and South Dakota. The Sioux were buffalo

25   hunters. They did not live in one place. They moved to follow the buffalo.

39   The Sioux lived in tents called tipis. They took their tipis with them when

53   they moved. Whole villages traveled together.

59   The buffalo was very important to the Sioux. They used every part

71   of the buffalo. Many meals were made from buffalo meat. Buffalo skin

83   was used in two ways. One way was to tan it. Tanning made the skin soft.

99   Then it could be used like cloth. Another way to use buffalo skin was to

114   turn it into rawhide. Rawhide was as hard as leather. It could be used to

129   make drums or bags.

133   The Sioux slept on buffalo hides. Buffalo hair was woven into belts

145   or ropes. Buffalo bones were used to make tools and toys. A buffalo's

158   stomach could be made into a pot. The Sioux believed that the buffalo's

171   tongue was special. They kept it to use in tribal ceremonies. Even buffalo

184   droppings were saved. They were used for campfire fuel.

193

Total Words Read _____

- Errors _____

= CWPM _____

Cesar Chavez: Champion of Migrant Farm Workers

0   Cesar Chavez was born in 1927. He lived in Yuma, Arizona, with

12   his family. His grandfather had come to the U.S. from Mexico in 1880.

25   He hoped for a better life for his family. Cesar's father was a farmer. He

40   worked hard to grow crops on his own land. He also ran the general

54   store.

55   In 1937, the Chavez family did not have enough money to pay taxes

68   on their land. So they lost their farm. The family was forced to move. The

83   family became migrant farm workers. Migrant workers follow the crops.

93   They go from place to place. Farm owners hire these workers to pick ripe

107   fruit. Migrant farm work was hard. The farmers lived in shacks. They

119   did not have running water. Some migrant workers lived in their pick-

131   up trucks. Some children had to work and did not go to school. Other

145   children changed schools many times. Cesar Chavez went to more than

156   30 schools in nine years.

161   Most of the farm workers spoke only Spanish. The farm owners

172   spoke only English. It was hard for them to talk to each other. Cesar saw

187   that some farm owners did not treat the workers well. The farm owners

200   did not pay well. They did not give the workers a decent place to live.

215   Cesar grew up to be a leader of migrant farm workers. He helped

228   them to learn to read and write in English. He helped them to become

242   U.S. citizens. Cesar started a farm workers union. He led a strike against

255   the farm owners. A strike is refusing to work until people do what you

269   want. Cesar made the owners work with the union. Cesar used strikes

281   and boycotts to help the workers. A boycott is when people refuse to

294   buy something. The farm owners finally agreed to pay better wages. The

306   owners also gave workers better housing. Cesar Chavez fought very hard

317   to bring a better life to migrant farm workers.

326

Total Words Read _____

− Errors _____

= CWPM _____

Scott Joplin: Father of Ragtime Music

0   Scott was born in Texas in 1868. He came from a musical family.

13   His parents played music as a hobby. Scott's mother played the banjo. His

26   father played the fiddle. Not many black men made a living playing music

39   in those days. Scott's parents hoped things would be different for Scott.

51   Scott's mother cleaned houses for a living. She took Scott to work

63   with her. Scott played the piano in the houses where she worked. He

76   liked to play songs by Stephen Foster. Scott's mother worked hard to pay

89   for his piano lessons. In those days, there were not many schools for

102   black children. Scott did not go to school until he was a teenager. But he

117   worked very hard. Scott played the piano every day. When Scott was 17,

130   he left home to get a job. He played piano in St. Louis at the Silver Dollar

147   Saloon. When Scott was 28 years old, he went to college to study music.

161   Scott played a kind of music called ragtime. It had a bouncy rhythm.

174   Ragtime was first called "ragged time." People thought it sounded like a

186   piece of torn, ragged paper. Scott became friends with John Stark. John

198   was a white man. It was unusual at that time for a black man and a white

215   man to be friends. John helped Scott publish his music. They published

227   more than 50 songs. "Maple Leaf Rag" was the most famous. It was

240   published in 1899. "Maple Leaf Rag" was the first piece of sheet music to

254   sell 1 million copies.

258   Scott also wrote two operas. The first one was called "A Guest of

271   Honor." The original music score was lost. It has never been found. The

284   second opera was named "Treemonisha." It was performed only one time,

295   in 1915. Scott died two years later. He was buried in an unmarked grave.

309   Fifty-seven years after his death, "Treemonisha" was performed again.

319   Everyone who saw the opera loved it. It is considered to be the first

333   American opera. "Treemonisha" was awarded the Pulitzer Prize in 1976.

343   Today, Scott Joplin's grave has a headstone. It reads "American

353   Composer."

354

Total Words Read _____

− Errors _____

= CWPM _____

Level 4 Practice Passages

Wind: Friend or Foe?

0	Wind is moving air. The air around the earth is always moving.
12	That is because the earth is continually spinning. When the sun heats the
25	air, it becomes lighter. Lighter air moves more quickly. Lighter, hotter air
37	becomes strong wind. How hot or cold the air is determines how quickly
50	it moves. Winds are always blowing somewhere on the earth.
60	Wind can be a big help to us. There are many examples of how
74	wind is helpful. Wind power pumps water from wells deep in the earth.
87	Wind power also generates electricity. Windmills in Holland have kept
97	the seawater from flooding low areas of the small country. Wind helps
109	power sailboats and makes kites fly. Wind also cools us on hot, summer
122	days.
123	But the wind can also be harmful. Strong winds in storms can
135	damage buildings. Winds spinning in a tornado have destroyed parts of
146	towns and cities. They have also killed many people. Hurricane winds
157	form over warm waters. They blow into the land from the sea and cause
171	great property damage and loss of life. Wind that has been warmed by
184	forest fire becomes stronger. It blows the fire over larger areas of trees.
197	Forest fires and their winds cause many trees to burn and many animals,
210	houses, and people to be harmed.
216	We will always have wind because of the air surrounding our earth.
228	Sometimes the wind is helpful to us. But at other times, wind can be
242	harmful.
243	

Total Words Read _____

− Errors _____

= CWPM _____

The Giant Panda: The World's Best-Loved Animal

0	The giant panda bear is a favorite of many people. Giant pandas are
13	black and white animals. They are big and furry. They are cute and fun
27	to watch. Pandas live in China. They live in bamboo forests. The bamboo
40	forests grow in the mountains of southwest China.
48	The giant pandas eat bamboo. They only eat one kind of bamboo.
60	This type of bamboo can suddenly grow flowers. The bamboo flowers
71	for no reason at all. No one knows why or when the flowers will grow. It
87	can happen anytime. The bamboo may flower once every ten years. Or it
100	may go many more years without flowering. After the bamboo flowers,
111	it dies. This happens all at once. Then the bamboo forests all over China
125	die. This is very bad for the giant panda. It takes many months for the
140	bamboo to grow again. Without bamboo, the giant pandas have no food.
152	Many of the giant pandas die of hunger.
160	Only about 1,000 giant pandas live in the world. This is not a big
174	number. Pandas are in danger. They may become extinct. That means
185	that pandas would no longer exist. The next time the bamboo flowers,
197	many pandas may not survive. People want to help the giant pandas.
209	They study bamboo forests. They try to learn more about the giant panda.
222	The people of China set aside large areas of land. This land is to grow
237	bamboo for the giant pandas. No one can live in these areas. The Chinese
251	people hope that they can help the giant pandas. No one wants the panda
265	to become extinct.
268	

Total Words Read _____

− Errors _____

= CWPM _____

Blankets of Air Above Us

0   Blankets on our beds help keep us warm at night. Our earth has

13   blankets of air that do the same thing. In the atmosphere above us, there

27   are four blankets of air that help keep us warm and safe on Earth.

41   The first blanket of air closest to Earth is called the troposphere.

53   The troposphere is where we live. It contains the air we breathe and the

67   warmth we need. The troposphere has most of our weather in it. Seventy-

80   five percent of the atmosphere's total mass is found in this layer. It also

94   has most of the water vapor of the atmosphere. The seasons of the earth

108 occur in this first layer.

113 The second blanket of air in our atmosphere is the stratosphere. The

125 stratosphere has a very important part that protects us. That part is the

138 ozone layer. The ozone part of the stratosphere keeps the sun's harmful

150 rays away from the earth. The stratosphere does not have much moisture.

162 Therefore, it does not have many clouds. For that reason, airline pilots

174 like to fly in the stratosphere.

180 The third blanket of air is the coldest layer in the atmosphere. It is

194 called the mesosphere. Its name means "in between." The mesosphere

204 becomes colder as its altitude increases. There are many strong winds in

216 the mesosphere. These winds blow from west to east in the winter. In the

230 summer, they blow from east to west.

237 The last layer of air around our earth is called the thermosphere.

249 Its name means "warm place." It is the highest and the largest layer.

262 This layer is very hot. Its temperature can be thousands and thousands

274 of degrees. It is made up of gases. These gases have temperatures which

287 vary. At the top of the thermosphere is where space begins.

298 The atmosphere of our earth is made up of these four blankets of

311 air. Each one of them is important for life on Earth.

322

Total Words Read _____

- Errors _____

= CWPM _____

Super Waves

0	When people see waves on an ocean or on a lake, they may think of
15	surfboards and wave runners. They probably don't give much thought to
26	how strong those waves are. They also may not think about the changes
39	those waves are bringing about. Every wave that comes ashore brings
50	some change with it.
54	Winds start the waves. Winds that blow across the seas make the
66	waves. The waves move across the surface of the seas until they meet the
80	land or shoreline. When the waves meet the shoreline, they may change.
92	For example, if the winds are blowing strongly, the waves will be very
105	big. The big waves come crashing into the coast and bring a lot of power
120	with them. The powerful waves continually pound the rocks on the land
132	into small pieces. They do this again and again. The smaller pieces of
145	rock end up on the floor of the ocean. The waves also take dirt and sand
161	from one shore and move it to another shoreline. The waves and the
174	wind are constantly changing the shoreline. In one place, they remove
185	land and rocks. In another, they add to the land. The winds and the
199	waves they create are powerful change forces on our shores. People try to
212	build walls and barriers to stop them, but usually the wind and the waves
226	win the battle.
229	

Total Words Read _____

– Errors _____

= CWPM _____

Tigers: The Largest Cats

0	Tigers belong to the cat family. They are the biggest cats on earth.
13	Most tigers are brown with dark stripes. Their stomachs are whitish in
25	color. Tigers are endangered. That means that there are not many tigers
37	left in the world.
41	There are five kinds of tigers found in the world today. One kind
54	of tiger is the Bengal tiger. It can grow to be 12 feet long. The males can
71	weigh almost 500 pounds. Bengal tigers eat mostly deer and cattle. Most
83	Bengal tigers live in India. The white tiger is a kind of Bengal tiger. These
98	tigers have white fur with brown or reddish strips. Wild white tigers are
111	rare. None have been seen in the wild since the 1950s. Most white tigers
125	are in zoos.
128	The Siberian is the largest of all tigers. The male Siberian can weigh
141	as much as 660 pounds. Siberian tigers have pale orange fur. Their stripes
154	are brown. Siberian tigers live mostly in Russia. They eat elk and wild
167	boar. The Sumatran tiger only lives on the island of Sumatra. This island
180	is in Indonesia. The Sumatran tiger is the smallest of all tigers. The males
194	weigh only about 264 pounds. Sumatran tigers have coats that are darker
206	than other tigers. They have broad, black stripes. These stripes are close
218	together. Sometimes the stripes are doubled. The South China tiger is also
230	a small tiger. Only 20 to 30 of these tigers exist in the wild. The rest of
247	them live in zoos. Very little is known about these tigers. The Indochinese
260	tiger is another kind of tiger. It is smaller than the Bengal tiger. Its fur
275	is darker with short, narrow stripes. Many Indochinese tigers live in
286	Thailand.
287	

Total Words Read _____

− Errors _____

= CWPM _____

The Great Wall of China: The Longest Graveyard

0	The Great Wall of China is the longest structure ever built. It is more
14	than 4,000 miles long and can even be seen from outer space! An ancient
28	Chinese emperor ordered the wall built to keep out enemies. That was
40	more than two thousand years ago. The emperor's soldiers rounded up
51	people and marched them off to begin work on the Great Wall. The wall
65	was built completely by hand. It took tens of thousands of people to build
79	the Great Wall. The wall was made of stone, brick, and dirt. Watchtowers
92	and forts were added every one hundred yards. The Great Wall was built
105	to match China's landscape. It stretches east to west across deserts and
117	through mountains. The wall was built to be about 30 feet high. It was
131	also very thick. The base of the wall is about 25 feet thick. At the top,
147	it is about 15 feet thick. On top of the wall was a road where Chinese
163	soldiers traveled back and forth.
168	The Chinese workers had to work day and night. Most of them did
181	not have a choice. Some Chinese spent their entire lives working on the
194	Great Wall. If workers tried to run away or complain, they were buried
207	alive. If the Chinese did not work well, they were put to death. The Great
222	Wall of China is often called the "longest graveyard" because so many
234	people died while building the wall. The human cost of building this
246	great wall was tremendous.
250	

Total Words Read _____

− Errors _____

= CWPM _____

Water Bugs: Aquatic Insects

0   Many bugs that live in water are called water bugs. There are
12 several kinds of water bugs. Water boatman, backswimmers, and the
22 giant water bug are three kinds of water bugs. When water bugs are first
36 born, they live in the water. As they grow up, water bugs leave the water
51 to fly around at night. However, they spend their days in the water. The
65 giant water bug is the largest of the aquatic insects. It can be almost
79 3 inches in length. Most water bugs are good swimmers. The water
91 boatman got its name because its back legs were made to help it swim
105 in the water. When a water boatman swims, it looks like a man rowing
119 a boat. The water boatman is the most common kind of water bug. The
133 backswimmer looks like a water boatman. However, as the name implies,
144 backswimmers swim on their backs. The water boatman does not.

154 Water bugs eat other bugs and small fish. The water boatman eats
166 very small animals and plants found in mud. Backswimmers eat dead
177 animals that they find floating on water. Giant water bugs are able to
190 suck the juices from a frog. Many people do not care for water bugs.
204 Water bugs are pests. They like light and swimming pools. When people
216 are around water bugs, they can expect a big, painful bite!
227

Total Words Read _____

− Errors _____

= CWPM _____

The Moon: Is It Really Made of Green Cheese?

0　　There are many funny stories about the moon. Long ago, people

11　thought it was made of green cheese. They thought that because the

23　craters on the moon's surface looked like the holes found in certain

35　cheeses. But what are the facts about the moon?

44　　The moon is our closest neighbor. It does have tall mountains,

55　wide flat places, and deep craters just like earth. But the moon has no

69　atmosphere. It has no water. It also has no living things. It does have a

84　crust like the earth though. It also is very hot and is probably molten

98　deep inside. The moon has gravity like earth. However, earth's gravity

109　pull is six times greater than the moon's. No wonder astronauts on the

122　moon can leap as if they were the greatest jumpers ever seen.

134　　The moon experiences large temperature changes. During daytime,

142　its temperatures rise above 100 and at night they go below –100 degrees.

155　The temperature changes cause the moon's crust and rocks to crack and

167　break apart. Since there is no wind, the pieces of rock have changed over

181　time to a fine dust. This fine dust covers most of the moon's surface. The

196　craters or holes on the moon's surface are thought to have been made by

210　meteorites that crashed into it early in its history. Some of the craters are

224　very large, and others are quite small.

231　　Astronauts have brought back rocks from the moon that were much

242　older than the rocks here on earth. We still have much to learn about the

257　moon, but at least we know it's not made of green cheese!

269

Total Words Read _____

– Errors _____

= CWPM _____

Hummingbirds: Small and Fast

0	Hummingbirds are the smallest birds. Their average length is about
10	3 inches long. Sometimes people think they are large moths or butterflies.
22	Hummingbirds have short legs that have tiny, weak feet attached to them.
34	There are over 500 kinds of hummingbirds found in the United States.
46	Hummingbirds are mostly found in the eastern United States.
55	They are not found anywhere in Europe or Asia. These tiny birds fly so
69	fast their wings are a blur. They move their wings so fast that they can
84	even fly backwards or upside-down. Hummingbirds can also hover over
95	flowers. While they are hovering, they drink the flower's nectar using
106	their long bills and their long tongues. They fly so fast that they catch
120	insects in the air while they are flying. They also eat insects they find on
135	flowers.
136	Hummingbirds make their nests on leaves or twigs. They only lay
147	two tiny white eggs. These eggs are less than half-an-inch long. The
161	male hummingbird has nothing to do with building the nest. The male
173	does not help take care of the babies either. The female hummingbird is
186	the only caregiver. She takes care of the babies in the nest for about two
201	weeks. Then the young hummingbirds learn to fly and leave the nest for
214	good.
215	

Total Words Read _____

– Errors _____

= CWPM _____

The Koala: Is It a Bear?

0	The koala bear is a mammal found only in Australia. Koala is an
13	Aboriginal name meaning "no drink." The koala is not a bear. Koalas are
26	marsupials. That means they give birth to live young, then carry them in
39	a pouch until they are grown. The baby koala, like the baby kangaroo,
52	is called a "joey." The baby lives in the mother's pouch for about seven
66	months and then exits the pouch in the back. It continues to live on its
81	mother's back for another six months until it is fully grown.
92	The koala has a big, hairless nose and soft, thick, gray or brown
105	fur. The fur on its belly is white. The koala looks cuddly, but it has sharp,
121	curved claws and a strong grip. It lives in eucalyptus trees and eats the
135	young tender branches. Koalas get their liquids from the eucalyptus
145	leaves, so they do not drink water. They are nocturnal animals. That
157	means they sleep during the day and are active at night. Koalas only leave
171	their tree to go to another tree. This puts them at risk of being hit by cars
188	that cannot see them in the dark.
195	Koalas are an endangered species. People are working hard to save
206	them, but their numbers continue to decrease.
213	

Total Words Read _____

- Errors _____

= CWPM _____

Bats: Flying Creatures of the Night

0	Bats are small, furry animals that look like mice. Bats are the only
13	mammals that are able to fly. Bats have unusual body parts. The joint
26	bones of a bat's arm and hand are very long. There is a thin piece of skin
43	called a flying membrane between the last four digits of a bat's fingers.
56	This flying membrane looks like a webbed hand and is used as a wing.
70	Bats have a second piece of skin, or membrane, which connects their
82	hand and ankle joints. A third membrane stretches between the bat's
93	ankles and attaches to its tail. These pieces of skin stretch like an open
107	umbrella over the bones of the bat's arms and fingers. In order to fly, bats
122	use a type of motion called a flapping flight. A bat lifts and pushes itself
137	up by lowering its wings down and pushing them forward. The bat stays
150	in a horizontal position while it is flying. It almost looks like it is doing
165	the swimming breaststroke! Bats fly mostly at night. They are guided by
177	reflected sound waves. This navigation system is called echolocation. Bats
187	are able to send out supersonic sounds with a pitch higher than humans
200	can hear. When these sounds hit an object, they make an echo. The bats
214	hear the echo and change course so that they do not have a collision.
228	

Total Words Read _____

− Errors _____

= CWPM _____

Hero Street U.S.A.: Home to U.S. Veterans

0	Hero Street is in Silvis, Illinois. It is a town west of Chicago. Hero
14	Street received its name in 1968. It is named in honor of the many
28	residents of the street who have served in the U.S. military.
39	Hero Street used to be called 2nd Street. It was a short street on
53	the edge of town. The street was not even paved for many years. It was
68	muddy in the spring, icy in the winter, and dusty in the summer. In
82	the 1940s, large Hispanic families lived on 2nd Street. They had come
94	from Mexico many years before. 2nd Street was a special place to live.
107	Neighbors helped each other. Everyone was like one big family. It was
119	a close-knit neighborhood. At the front of the neighborhood was a big
132	slope. It was called Billy Goat Hill. The hill was a favorite place for
146	children to play.
149	The neighborhood was also patriotic. When wars came, many 2nd
159	Street residents enlisted. Eighty-seven men from 22 families on this street
171	fought in three wars. Many families sent more than one son. They fought
184	in World War II, the Korean War, and Vietnam. Eight men did not return.
198	In 1963, a Hispanic man was elected to the Silvis City Council. His
211	name was Joe Terronez. Joe wanted to honor the people of 2nd Street.
224	He helped pass laws to have the street paved and renamed to Hero Street.
238	Billy Goat Hill was turned into a park. A monument to the Hero Street
252	soldiers was built inside the park.
258	Today, people want to build a bigger monument on the hill. They
270	want to have all of the names and some information about each hero on
284	the monument. This is a big job. Many people are working together to
297	earn money to pay for the new monument.
305	

Total Words Read _____

\- Errors _____

\= CWPM _____

Gabriela Mistral:
Teacher and Nobel Prize-Winning Author

0   In 1889, Gabriela Mistral was born. She was born in Chile. Chile is

13   a country in South America. Gabriela was not the name she was given at

27   birth. She was named Lucila Godey Alcaya. Her mother was a teacher. As

40   a young child, Lucila loved to read. She also loved to write and to sing.

55   Lucila grew up to be a teacher like her mother. Lucila was not only

69   a teacher. She also was a writer. She wrote poems about nature. She also

83   wrote about people. Lucila wanted to try to publish her work. She was

96   afraid that the school officials would not like her work. Therefore, Lucila

108 did not want to use her own name. So she chose a pen name. A pen

124 name is a name that writers use only for their writing. They use their real

139 names for everything else. Lucila chose the name Gabriela Mistral as her

151 pen name.

153 Using her new name, Lucila won a poetry contest in Chile. Soon

165 she became famous as Gabriela Mistral. As a teacher, Gabriela worked

176 to improve schools in Chile and in Mexico. As a writer, she won the

190 Nobel Prize for Literature in 1945. The Nobel Prize is a very high honor.

204 Gabriela was the first Latin American writer to win the Nobel Prize.

216

Total Words Read _____

- Errors _____

= CWPM _____

Baboons: The Biggest Monkeys

0	Baboons are the biggest monkeys. They are sometimes called dog-
10	faced monkeys. This is because they have heads that resemble a dog's
22	muzzle. Baboons can be brown, black, or silver in color. They have long
35	arms and feet. Baboons are intelligent animals that are adaptable to their
47	environment. They are found primarily in Africa. Baboons can live to be
59	25 to 30 years old.
64	Baboons live in groups called troops. These troops are well-
74	organized. Each member has its place. Dominant males usually rule the
85	troop. They have two main jobs. The first job is to keep order within the
100	troop. Baboons do not always get along with each other and often fight
113	among themselves. The other job is to protect the troop from enemies.
125	Jungle cats, like leopards, are the baboon's greatest enemy. The male
136	baboons act as guards. They guard while the rest of the troop looks for
150	food. Baboons are often on the move, looking for food. They live mostly
163	on the ground. However, baboons are able to climb trees for safety. The
176	baby baboons travel by holding onto their mother's fur. As they get older,
189	the baby baboons ride on their mothers' backs.
197	Baboons eat insects, fruits, seed, reptiles, and rodents. Their favorite
207	food is the scorpion. Baboons have large pouches in their cheeks. These
219	pouches can hold almost as much food as their stomachs. They look
231	under rocks and bushes for food. Baboons also hunt along with herds of
244	other animals.
246	Baboons are social animals. One of their favorite activities is
256	grooming. Baboons engage in mutual grooming as a way of forming
267	social bonds. The grooming also helps to keep the baboons clean.
278	

Total Words Read _____

- Errors _____

= CWPM _____

Wilbur and Orville Wright: The Flying Brothers

0   Wilbur and Orville Wright were the first people to fly an airplane.

12   The brothers lived in Dayton, Ohio. They built bicycles for a living.

24   Wilbur and Orville loved to design and invent new bicycles. The brothers

36   opened their own bike shop in 1892.

43   As young boys, the brothers received a flying toy from their father.

55   They became fascinated by the idea of flying. Wilbur spent his spare time

68   reading many books about flying. He thought human flight was possible.

79   Soon the brothers began to build gliders as well as bicycles. Gliders are a

93   type of plane with no engine. The Wright brothers built three gliders in

106   all. With each new glider, they learned more and more about flying. They

119   collected data on wing design. Some of the data tables they created are

132   still used today.

135   In 1903, Wilbur and Orville Wright built an airplane. This airplane

146   was different from their gliders. This airplane had an engine to power

158   it. They named this airplane "The Flyer." The first flight of an airplane

171   was made on December 17, 1903. It took place near Kitty Hawk, North

184   Carolina. With Orville as the pilot, the plane flew 120 feet. That first flight

198   lasted only 12 seconds. The brothers continued to make flights with their

210   airplanes. Each time, they flew a longer time. Their fourth flight lasted

222   fifty-nine seconds. It flew for almost half a mile.

232   The Wright brothers' invention changed the world. For the first

242   time, people had access to places they had never before been able to

255   go. They could meet people in faraway places. The age of globalization

267   began. With air travel, people of different cultures could come together.

278   They could share ideas and values with one another.

287

Total Words Read _____

− Errors _____

= CWPM _____

Hurricanes: Harmful Storms

0	Hurricanes are violent storms. In fact, hurricanes are the most
10	destructive of all storms. Hurricane winds travel at speeds of at least 75
23	miles per hour. These storms are very large. They can measure from 300
36	to 500 miles in width. Their size and intensity makes them dangerous.
48	Hurricanes form in the late summer and early fall. They need moist
60	air and heat. As a result, hurricanes start over tropical seas. The process
73	begins when warm, moist air rises. Next, surrounding air flows toward
84	the rising air. Then water vapor from the warm air condenses. This
96	means that it turns into small drops of water. The drops of water form
110	clouds. Heat is given off during condensation. The air becomes warmer.
121	Thunderstorms develop, and the hurricane begins.
127	Hurricanes consist of spiraling winds. These winds spiral around a
137	low pressure area in the center of the storm. This area is called the "eye"
152	of the hurricane. Although winds rage around it, the eye of the hurricane
165	is calm. The sun may even be shining in the hurricane's eye.
177	Hurricanes die out when they no longer have moist air and heat.
189	This can happen if the hurricane moves over land. It can also happen if it
204	moves into a colder area. Some hurricanes last only a few hours. Others
217	can last as long as a couple of weeks. Hurricanes cannot be stopped.
230	However, they can be predicted. That way, people can be warned to get
243	out of the hurricane's path.
248	

Total Words Read _____

    - Errors _____

    = CWPM _____

Mexico: U.S. Neighbor

0 Mexico is a country. It is south of the U.S. Mexico is smaller than

14 the U.S. It is about one-fifth the size. Mexico has many land features. It

29 has mountains and deserts. There are rain forests and beaches.

39 Mexico has a mild climate. It does not get very cold, even in the

53 winter. Mexico has a dry season. The dry season lasts from October to

66 April. Mexico also has a rainy season. The rainy season lasts from May

79 until September.

81 Native Americans were the first people in Mexico. They lived there

92 in the 10th century. In the 1500s, the Spanish came to Mexico. They took

106 over the country. Spain ruled Mexico for more than 300 years. Mexico

118 was called New Spain. The Mexican people did not want Spain to rule

131 them. They went to war with Spain. The war lasted many years. Finally,

144 Mexico won the war. It became a free country in 1821.

155

Total Words Read _____

− Errors _____

= CWPM _____

The Five Oceans of the World

0   There are five oceans in the world. These five oceans are really just

13   one big ocean. The continents separate the oceans.

21   The Pacific Ocean is the largest. It covers almost half of the earth.

34   The Pacific is the deepest ocean. It is also the stormiest one. The Pacific

48   lies next to the west coast of North and South America. It is a warm

63   ocean.

64   The Atlantic Ocean is the second largest. It has the most coastline.

76   It also has the saltiest water. The Atlantic lies between Europe, Africa,

88   and the Americas. It borders the East Coast of the U.S. It extends between

102   the Arctic and Antarctic.

106   The Indian Ocean is the third largest. It is mostly south of the

119   equator. The Indian Ocean touches four continents.

126   The Arctic Ocean is sometimes called the North Polar Sea. Some

137   people consider this ocean to be part of the Atlantic. It is filled with ice. It

153   is the smallest of the world's oceans. It is also the shallowest. The Arctic

167   Ocean lies next to the state of Alaska.

175   The Antarctic Ocean is larger than the Arctic Ocean. It is sometimes

187   called the South Polar Sea. This ocean is made up of the southern

200   waters of three other oceans. The Antarctic surrounds the continent of

211   Antarctica. It is filled with ice just like the Arctic Ocean.

222

Total Words Read _____

− Errors _____

= CWPM _____

The London Bridge: From England to Arizona

0	The London Bridge has an interesting history. The first London
10	Bridge was built across the Thames River by the Romans in A.D. 43. It
24	was later rebuilt several times. These first London Bridges were made of
36	wood. Fire and floods caused these bridges to fall down. Finally, around
48	1176, a new London Bridge was built out of stone. It took 33 years to
63	build. People hoped that the new London Bridge would last forever.
74	Unfortunately, it did not. As the city of London grew, the bridge was too
88	narrow and small for the added traffic. Its granite and rock began to crack
102	and fall apart. The bridge was too old and had too many problems. By the
117	1960s, the London Bridge was starting to sink into the Thames River. The
130	people of London decided to build an entirely new London Bridge. They
142	put the old bridge up for sale.
149	An American named Robert McCulloch bought the old London
158	Bridge. He paid more than two million dollars for it. At the time, that
172	was the most money ever paid for an antique. The old London Bridge
185	was taken apart rock by rock. Each rock was numbered and packed in
198	order. The rocks were sent across the Atlantic Ocean to Arizona. There
210	the bridge was put back together again. The process took many years.
222	This "new" London Bridge was finished on October 10, 1971. It is in Lake
236	Havasu City, Arizona.
239	

Total Words Read _____

− Errors _____

= CWPM _____

The Hopi: Native Americans of the Southwest

0   Many hundreds of years ago, the Hopi lived in what is now Arizona.

13   These Native Americans were desert people. They lived on top of steep

25   hills with flat tops. These hills are called mesas. The Hopi built their

38   houses out of rocks covered with a plaster. The plaster was made of clay

52   and water. Then they joined their houses into villages. The Hopi villages

64   are called pueblos. When a Hopi man and woman married, they lived in

77   the woman's house. The Hopi women owned the houses in the pueblo.

89   The Hopi men had a special room that was underground. This room is

102   called a kiva. The Hopi men gathered in the kiva for special meetings.

115   Women were only allowed in the kiva on special occasions.

125   The Hopi grew beans and squash. Corn was their main food

136   though. The Hopi grew corn in many colors, not just yellow. Some of it

150   was red, blue, black, and purple. The Hopi women used the corn kernels

163   to make a kind of cornmeal pudding. Sometimes they added cactus plants

175   to the cornmeal to make it sweeter. Hopi women also used desert clay to

189   make colorful pottery.

192   The Hopi did not eat much meat. They did not hunt often because

205   there were not many animals in the desert. Occasionally, they ate turkey,

217   rabbit, antelope, or deer.

221   Today, many of the Hopi people still live in pueblos. They keep their

234   traditional ways. Other Hopi live a more modern American life.

244

Total Words Read _____

− Errors _____

= CWPM _____

Crispus Attucks: African American Patriot

0	Crispus Attucks was shot and killed in the Boston Massacre, which
11	happened in 1770. This event was thought to be the start of the American
25	Revolution.
26	Crispus was born a slave. As a young man, he ran away and
39	became a sailor. He worked on whaling ships. The ships sailed out of
52	Boston Harbor. When he was not sailing, Crispus worked as a rope
64	maker.
65	During this time in history, there were problems in Boston. The
76	American colonists were mad. They did not want to pay taxes to England.
89	So, the British sent soldiers to Boston. The American colonists did not
101	want British soldiers in their city. One night, some colonists began teasing
113	a British guard. They threw snowballs at him. They also threw sticks.
125	Other British soldiers came to help the guard. They aimed guns at the
138	crowd. People wanted to take the guns away from the soldiers.
149	Crispus took the lead. He led a group of white men toward the
162	British soldiers. Crispus lunged forward with a club. One soldier shot
173	and killed him. Then other shots rang out. Four white men were also
186	killed that night in the Boston Massacre. It was the start of the American
200	Revolution.
201	Crispus was not the only black man to fight the British. More than
214	5,000 black men fought for independence in the American Revolutionary
224	War. But Crispus was the first to die. Many believe he was a true martyr.
239	

Total Words Read _____

– Errors _____

= CWPM _____

The Azores: Portuguese Islands

0   The Azores are a group of nine islands. They are in the middle of

14   the Atlantic Ocean. The Azores are about 800 miles west of Portugal. The

27   islands belong to Portugal. The Azores were formed by volcanoes long

38   ago. They were once believed to be the lost continent of Atlantis.

50   Portuguese sailors discovered the Azores in 1427. By the middle

60   of the 15th century, farmers lived on the islands. They grew crops like

73   wheat and sugar. Many ships sailed the seas during this time. They were

86   on voyages of exploration. The Azores became a stopping place for ships.

98   Some ships were returning from Asia. Others came back from Africa. Still

110   others sailed from the Americas. Many ships carried treasure like gold

121   and jewels. Most ships stopped at the islands for food and water. The

134   Azores were soon an important port of call. In times of war, the Azores

148   were used for military bases. Spain occupied them during the period from

160   1580 to 1640. During the two World Wars, the Azores were used as naval

174   and air bases.

177   Today, farmers still make their home on the Azore islands. They

188   farm the rich soil of the islands. They grow many crops. Sugarcane, tea,

201   and pineapples are grown there. The farmers also raise cattle and sheep.

213   The islands' mountains have grasses for the animals to eat. Meat, cheese,

225   and butter are shipped to Portugal for sale.

233   Tourists like to visit the Azores. The islands are beautiful. They

244   have many mountains with steep cliffs. The hillsides are a brilliant green.

256   Many colorful flowers decorate the landscape. Deep lakes fill extinct

266   volcano craters. Life is calm and simple on the islands. The Azores may

279   be one of the few unspoiled spots left in the world.

290

Total Words Read _____

- Errors _____

= CWPM _____

Olympic Sports: An Ancient Beginning

0	The first Olympic games were held in 776 B.C. They ended about
12	eleven hundred years later in A.D. 393. The ancient Olympic games
23	were held once every four years to honor the Greek god Zeus. All war
37	in Greece was stopped during this time so the athletes could attend the
50	games safely.
52	The first games had only a foot race. As time went on, more games
66	were added. The games lasted about five days and were held in June
79	or July. The games tested skills and strength. On the first day, sacrifices
92	were held to the gods. On the second day, footraces were held. The most
106	famous was the 220-yard race. Only men were in the races. Women were
120	not allowed to watch the games because the runners did not wear clothes
133	during many of the events. There was one race in which the contestants
146	wore armor however. On other days, there were wrestling and boxing
157	matches.
158	The Olympic games were important in Greece. It was like a great
170	festival with much singing and dancing. The winners were given an olive
182	crown to wear on their heads and were invited to lots of parties. Olympic
196	winners were treated like movie and sports stars of today. Our modern
208	Olympic games began in 1896, just over one hundred years ago.
219	

Total Words Read _____

− Errors _____

= CWPM _____

Native North Americans: The First Settlers

0	Native Americans were the first people to live in what is now the
13	U.S. They were here thousands of years before Europeans came. The
24	Native Americans lived in groups. The groups were Native Nations. Each
35	group lived in its own way. Each nation had its own language. Each
48	had its own culture. Each nation had its own traditions. Many Native
60	Americans believed that land was sacred. It was like air or water. They
73	took care of their land. But, they did not think that land could be owned.
88	In the early 1600s, life changed for Native Americans. European
98	settlers came to North America. They began claiming land as their own.
110	They took any land that they wanted. Many Native American leaders
121	tried to protect their lands. They fought against the settlers. Other Native
133	American leaders tried to save their land by making treaties with the
145	Europeans. Some Native Americans helped the settlers.
152	By the late 1700s, life was very difficult for the Native Americans.
164	The settlers brought guns, alcohol, and disease to the native lands. Many
176	Native Americans died as a result. Others lost their land. They were
188	forced to live on reservations.
193	In spite of these problems, many Native Americans did not give
204	up. They took pride in their culture. Many kept up their traditional ways.
217	They continued to have hope.
222	

Total Words Read _____

− Errors _____

= CWPM _____

Sitting Bull and Crazy Horse: The Battle of the Little Bighorn

0	Sitting Bull and Crazy Horse led a famous battle against the U.S.
12	government. It was called the Battle of the Little Bighorn. Sitting Bull was
25	a Native American. He was a leader of the Lakota. He tried to save his
40	native land from settlers. Sitting Bull made an agreement with the U.S.
52	government in 1868. It was called the Fort Laramie Treaty. This treaty
64	gave the Black Hills to the Lakota.
71	In 1874, General George Custer found gold in the Black Hills. Then
83	the U.S. wanted the land back. They tried to buy it. But the Lakota did
98	not want to sell their land. U.S. soldiers moved onto the land. They told
112	the Lakota to move or fight. Many Native American groups were angry.
124	They joined together to fight for the land. Sitting Bull had a dream. He
138	saw soldiers falling into a valley. The Native American people saw the
150	dream as a sign that they would win.
158	Crazy Horse was also a leader of the Lakota. He was a brave
171	warrior. General Custer thought he and his troops could defeat the Native
183	American leaders. He was wrong. On June 25, 1876, he led troops into
196	the Little Bighorn River Valley. There was a fierce battle. The warriors led
209	by Sitting Bull and Crazy Horse won. It was the worst defeat ever suffered
223	by the U.S. government at the hands of Native Americans.
233	The victory was short-lived, though. From that time on, the
244	government pursued Sitting Bull and Crazy Horse. They were forced to
255	surrender to the U.S. in 1877.
261	

Total Words Read _____

- Errors _____

= CWPM _____

Level 5 Practice Passages

All About Seeds

0	Seeds are an important part of a plant. Seeds grow into new plants.
13	Some seeds are tiny and can hardly be seen at all. Other seeds are large
28	and stand out quite clearly, such as the pit in a peach or the seeds in a
45	watermelon. Each seed has a covering around it called a seed coat. It is
59	the seed coat that protects the seed inside it from any harm. Some seeds
73	have a hard protective shell around them, like the scales on the pinecone
86	that protect it. Other seeds are right outside in plain view, such as the
100	tiny seeds that are on the outside surface of the strawberry.
111	Each seed has the same two parts regardless of where the seeds
123	are located on a plant. The first part of the seed found inside the seed
138	coat is the tiny plant itself. Also within the protective seed coat is food
152	on which the tiny plant can feed. The seed does not start to grow until
167	the conditions are right for it. When the seed begins to grow, it is called
182	germination. For most seeds to begin germination, the right conditions
192	usually include warmth from the sun and water. When the seed begins
204	to grow, its roots begin to reach down in the soil to anchor it. Its stem
220	begins to grow up to form the plant and its leaves. While the seed is
235	growing, it feeds on the plant food that has been stored as part of the
250	seed and protected by the seed coat.
257	

Total Words Read _____

- Errors _____

= CWPM _____

Bones: Living Tissue

0   Some people do not realize that bones are alive. Bones are made

12   of living tissue. Calcium, phosphorous, and bone cells make up our

23   bones. Infants have about three hundred and fifty bones in their bodies.

35   However, an adult body contains only two hundred and six bones. That

47   means that an infant has over a hundred and forty more bones in its body

62   than an adult. The reason for this difference is bone fusion. As infants

75   begin to grow and develop, some of their bones fuse or grow together.

88   Every bone is covered with an outer layer. This layer consists of

100   compact bone and is very hard. Inside the outer layer of bone is a softer

115   bone. The inside layer is strong and spongy. Bone marrow is contained

127   within the bone. The bone marrow makes blood for the body. The largest

140   bone in the human body is the thighbone. Its length is related to the size

155   of the person. Its length is about one fourth of a person's height. The

169   smallest bones in the body are in the ear. There are three tiny ear bones

184   that are only three millimeters long.

190   Bones are very important. The hard bones of the body make up

202   a person's skeleton. The skeleton supports all the other systems in the

214   body. Without bones, bodies would not have shapes. A jellyfish is an

226   example of a body without a shape. Bones also protect the soft organs of

240   the body. They do this by forming a protective cage around organs such

253   as the heart, lungs, and brain. Damage to soft organs can cause serious

266   problems. Bones also work with muscles to allow bodies to move. It is

279   important to keep bones strong and healthy. One way to do this is to eat a

295   sufficient amount of green vegetables and dairy products. Another way is

306   to do plenty of weight-bearing exercise. Taking care of bones is important

319   to overall health.

322

Total Words Read _____

- Errors _____

= CWPM _____

Roadrunners: Full Speed Ahead!

0	Roadrunners are members of the cuckoo family. Their home is
10	in the desert. Roadrunners are black and white in color. They have a
23	distinct crest on the crowns of their heads. They also have long bills and
37	very long tails. Their legs are extremely powerful. Strong legs enable
48	roadrunners to run up to seventeen miles per hour. These birds can easily
61	outrun a horse.
64	Roadrunners need to be fast so they can catch their prey. They
76	feed almost entirely on other animals. These include insects, scorpions,
86	lizards, rodents, snakes, and other birds. They also chase grasshoppers.
96	If a grasshopper tries to escape, the roadrunner can jump three or four
109	feet into the air. The western roadrunner is famous for its ability to kill
123	rattlesnakes. It is one of the few animals that is able to do so. Because
138	of its lightning speed, the roadrunner can grab a rattlesnake by its tail.
151	The roadrunner swings the rattlesnake around like a whip. It slams the
163	rattlesnake's head into the ground until it is dead. The roadrunner then
175	proceeds to eat the snake. It is not able to swallow the whole snake at
190	one time though. So the roadrunner often keeps the snake dangling from
202	its mouth, eating an inch or two at a time.
212	Roadrunners rarely fly although they are able to do so. If it senses
225	danger, the roadrunner may take to its wings. However, it is hard to keep
239	its large body in the air for more than a few seconds. Consequently, the
253	roadrunner prefers to walk or run.
259	

Total Words Read _____

\- Errors _____

= CWPM _____

Plants on the Defensive

0	It seems strange that plants must defend themselves, but it is true.
12	Plants have enemies. Those enemies might be animals or insects who eat
24	plants. Other plant enemies are disease or molds that grow on plants and
37	kill them. Elements such as frost, fire, and strong winds are harmful to
50	plants. Plants have natural and interesting weapons to defend themselves
60	from enemies.
62	Poisons are one of the best ways for plants to defend themselves.
74	Many plants are poisonous when they are eaten. Plants like mountain
85	laurel make grazing animals sick. Certain mushrooms are extremely
94	deadly if they are eaten. Other plants have fruits, such as the nightshade
107	or pokeberry, that can cause illness and, in some cases, death. Some
119	plants poison livestock who may be grazing where they grow. The
130	animals learn to leave these plants alone. Other plants are poisonous to
142	the touch. Plants like poison oak and poison ivy cause skin itching.
154	Thorns, spines, and burrs protect other plants. Roses, cacti, and
164	berries have prickly ways of defending themselves. Other plants give
174	off an unpleasant smell or odor. Their bad odor discourages animals
185	from eating them. Some plants protect themselves from weather, fire,
195	and disease. The bark of many trees is a barrier against the weather and
209	insects. Desert plants have thick stems and few leaves. This helps them to
222	store water.
224	Plants may look harmless. However, they have many different ways
234	of protecting themselves. Some of these ways are quite deadly.
244	

Total Words Read _____

− Errors _____

= CWPM _____

Rome: A City Built on a Legend

0	A legend is a story about a person or a place. Although they are
14	entertaining, legends are not true stories. One famous legend is about
25	how the city of Rome was founded. In 753 B.C., as the legend goes, twin
40	brothers were the founders of Rome. The brothers' names were Romulus
51	and Remus. Their father was Mars, the Roman god of war. Their mother
64	was the daughter of King Numitor. The king's brother was jealous of the
77	baby boys. He did not want his nephews to inherit the throne. So the evil
92	uncle put the boys in a basket and set it to sail down the Tiber River. The
109	basket eventually washed ashore. Luckily for the boys, a friendly wolf
120	rescued them. This wolf took good care of the babies and even fed them
134	with her own milk. A kindly shepherd found the boys and raised them as
148	his own.
150	When the brothers grew up, they decided to build a city. They
162	wanted to honor the wolf that had rescued them as babies by dedicating
175	the city to her. They wanted their city to be a place where orphans
189	and homeless people could live. Unfortunately, the brothers got into
199	an argument over where they should build the city. They also argued
211	over which one of them would be the ruler of the city. In a fit of anger,
228	Romulus killed Remus. Romulus then built his city on Palatine Hill. That
240	was the spot where the wolf had found the twins. Romulus named the
253	city Rome after himself.
257	

Total Words Read _____

\- Errors _____

= CWPM _____

Pandas: Not All Black and White

0	"Black and white" and "cute and adorable" are words that come to
12	mind when most people hear the word "panda." These words describe
23	the giant panda. The giant panda is as big as a bear and indeed resembles
38	one. Giant pandas live in the mountains of central China. The Chinese
50	name for the giant panda literally means "white bear." Giant pandas are
62	about the same size as the American black bear. There are important
74	differences though. Giant pandas do not hibernate, nor are they able to
86	walk on their hind legs as black bears do. Pandas have strong teeth and
100	jaws that are useful for chewing bamboo. Giant pandas have unusual
111	front paws. There is a pad on each front paw. Giant pandas use these
125	pads like thumbs to pick up food and feed themselves. These "thumbs"
137	help the giant pandas to grab huge bamboo stalks. The giant panda is a
151	rare mammal. Giant pandas are small at birth. But by the time they are
165	one year old, they can weigh 60 pounds. In about five years, the giant
179	panda is full-grown and can weigh as much as 300 pounds!
191	Many people are surprised to learn that there is a lesser panda. The
204	lesser panda is different in appearance from the giant panda. The lesser
216	panda is considerably smaller, about the size of a house cat. Its body is
230	covered with long, thick rust-colored fur. The lesser panda has a white
243	face with dark strips from the eye to the corner of the mouth. The lesser
258	panda has a striped tail like a raccoon. However, both types of panda feed
272	on bamboo shoots, climb trees, and have friendly dispositions!
281	

Total Words Read _____

- Errors _____

= CWPM _____

Chopsticks: A Chinese Invention

0   Chopsticks were invented in China more than 5,000 years ago.

10   Long ago, food was chopped into little pieces so it would cook faster.

23   The faster food cooked, the more fuel it would save. Since food was

36   eaten in small pieces, there was no need for knives. Rather, chopsticks

48   were used to move food from the plate to the mouth. Confucius was a

62   Chinese philosopher. He was a vegetarian. It is believed that Confucius

73   did not like knives. Knives reminded him of the slaughterhouse. He

84   favored chopsticks. By A.D. 500, the use of chopsticks had spread to other

97   countries. The people in present day Vietnam, Korea, and Japan, as well

109   as China, use chopsticks today.

114   Chinese chopsticks are about 9 or 10 inches long. They are square

126   at the top, have a blunt end, and are thinner on the bottom. The Chinese

141   call them kuai-ai. This means "quick little fellows." Chopsticks have been

153   made of many materials. Bamboo is a popular choice since it is available

166   and inexpensive. Bamboo is also heat resistant. Other types of wood

177   such as sandalwood, cedar, and teak have also been used. Long ago, rich

190   people had chopsticks made from jade, gold, or silver. In the days of the

204   Chinese dynasty, silver chopsticks were used. People believed that silver

214   would turn black if it touched poisoned food. We know now that silver

227   will not react to poison. It sometimes changes color if it touches rotten

240   eggs, garlic, or onions.

244

Total Words Read _____

− Errors _____

= CWPM _____

A Rock Is a Rock. Or Is It?

0   All rocks might look alike, but they are quite different. Scientists

11   have identified three groups of rocks. Rocks are made of different kinds

23   of minerals. However, it is not the kinds of minerals they are made of that

38   determine what group they are in. How the rock was formed determines

50   its group. Deep down in the center of the earth, molten rock or magma

64   flows because it is so very hot. When some of this molten magma comes

78   closer to the earth's surface, it begins to cool and harden. This is how the

93   first type of rock is formed. Rocks that are formed from cooled magma are

107 called igneous rocks.

110   The earth is constantly moving beneath its surface with a great

121 deal of heat and pressure. When rock that already has been formed is

134 subjected to this heat and pressure, metamorphic rock is formed. The

145 earth takes one kind of rock and, because of heat and pressure, changes

158 it into another type of rock. The third type of rock also takes older rocks

173 and forms new rocks. When plants die, their remains form layers in

185 the earth. When animals die, their remains also form in layers. These

197 remains are worn down by weather and climate. Over time, the layers of

210 older rock, and plant and animal remains harden into the third type of

223 rock called sedimentary rock. The next time you see a rock, try to figure

237 out which type of rock it is: an igneous rock, a metamorphic rock, or a

252 sedimentary rock.

254

Total Words Read _____

− Errors _____

= CWPM _____

Totem Poles: Silent Storytellers

0	Totem poles are a beautiful, ancient art form. They also had an
12	important purpose. Long ago, written language did not exist. Many native
23	tribes relied on totem poles to tell a clan's history. In Alaska, natives
36	carved totem poles from huge cedar trees. They used animals in the
48	region to tell their stories. The raven was one of these animals. He can
62	be identified on the poles by his long, straight beak. The raven is thought
76	to be able to change into many forms. He is a symbol of God. The eagle
92	is another animal seen on totem poles. Unlike the raven, the eagle has
105	a curved beak. To the native Alaskans, the eagle was a symbol of peace
119	and friendship. The orca, or killer whale, was also carved on totem poles.
132	The killer whale could be identified by sharp teeth and a dorsal fin. Other
146	animals seen on Alaskan totem poles are the beaver, the bear, and the
159	wolf. The beaver has a long flat tail and two big front teeth. The wolf
174	can be distinguished from a bear on the totem pole by a longer nose and
189	sharper teeth.
191	Totem poles were painted with natural resources. For example,
200	native Alaskans used salmon eggs, minerals, and vegetables. The main
210	colors were black, white, and red-brown. Depending on the tribe, blue,
222	blue-green, and yellow were used as well. Totem poles often stood for 50
236	to 60 years. When a totem pole became rotten and fell to the ground, it
251	was either left to decay or used for firewood.
260	

Total Words Read _____

\- Errors _____

= CWPM _____

Bamboo: Useful Grass

0	Bamboo is a useful plant in many places in the world. It is a type
15	of grass that can grow to be very tall. Bamboo has stems that can reach
30	almost 120 feet tall. This kind of bamboo seems more like a tall tree
44	than a grass. Bamboo can be found in both the Eastern and Western
57	hemispheres. It grows best in warm, tropical climates. Some types of
68	bamboo can live in colder climates such as in Japan. They also grow in
82	parts of North and South America. A smaller type of bamboo, canebrakes,
94	grows in the southern United States swamplands.
101	The stem of the bamboo plant is the most useful part. Bamboo
113	stems are hollow, smooth, and very light in weight. They are sawed into
126	parts and used as building materials. The hollowness of the bamboo
137	stem is useful for making water drainpipes. Bamboo is also used to make
150	wind instruments, baskets, and containers. Some homes are decorated
159	with bamboo furniture. Bamboo is also used to make buckets, bridges,
170	fishing poles, and even paper. Some people even weave mats and rugs
182	from bamboo. In some parts of the world, bamboo seeds and new stems
195	are used for food. The shoots of some kinds of bamboo can be cooked
209	like asparagus spears. They can also be preserved in sugar or eaten
221	pickled. Cattle eat the leaves of the bamboo tree. As a building material,
234	decoration, and food source, bamboo is truly a useful plant.
244	

Total Words Read _____

– Errors _____

= CWPM _____

Paint: A Splash of Color

0	Paint has been used throughout history. In prehistoric times, people
10	painted on cave walls. While cave painting was decorative, it was also
22	used as a means of expression. Paint was later used to illustrate religious
35	books. Easel painting was created at the beginning of the Renaissance
46	Period.
47	Paint comes in many colors. It can be used as an expression of art
61	or to protect a surface like a wall. The color of paint is due to its pigment.
78	Pigment is a dry, colored powder that is mixed with a liquid. The liquid is
93	called the vehicle. Pigment is found on the bottom of a container of paint.
107	The vehicle, usually clear, can be seen at the top. The kind of vehicle
121	used is what makes paints different from one another.
130	Water paints rely on the caking of the pigment powder to make
142	it stick to a painted surface. Sometimes glue or paste is added to paint.
156	This helps improve the ability of the paint to adhere to a surface. Water
170	is added to latex paint to separate particles of latex rubber. The particles
183	stick together when the water evaporates. Latex paint can be washed out
195	of rollers and brushes with soap and water before it dries. If the paint
209	dries though, it is much harder to clean. Chemicals are needed to remove
222	it. Oil paints last longer and give more surface protection than other kinds
235	of paints. Linseed oil is used as the vehicle for oil paints. The linseed oil
250	works with oxygen to make a tough, waterproof seal. Oil paints are too
263	thick to apply with a brush, so thinner has to be used.
275	

Total Words Read _____

− Errors _____

= CWPM _____

Nessie: The Loch Ness Monster

0	Loch Ness is a big, deep lake in Scotland. It has many fish
13	swimming in it. But Loch Ness also has something else swimming in it.
26	According to local legend, there is a monster swimming in the lake. The
39	Loch Ness monster is nicknamed "Nessie." For hundreds of years, Nessie
50	has been the subject of various sightings. Nessie does not resemble any
62	other creature that has been sighted. People who have seen Nessie report
74	that the monster has a large body and a long neck. Scientists at first
88	did not believe that the Loch Ness monster existed. However, enough
99	evidence was gathered to prove that something unusual is in the lake!
111	A small team of scientists took sound and photographic equipment
121	to the lake. They lowered the equipment in the lake, looking for Nessie.
134	The team took pictures of what appeared to be two large creatures. The
147	creatures had large bodies and long necks. The creatures also appeared to
159	have eyes, a mouth, and stalks with nostrils at their ends. This first team
173	felt there might be as many as thirty Loch Ness monsters in the deep
187	lake. A larger scientific team began another search for Nessie. This team
199	had underwater television cameras with better sound equipment. The
208	first two tries were disappointing. The Loch Ness was dark and cloudy,
220	so not much could be seen. However, science has not given up on finding
234	Nessie. Perhaps one day the true secret of the Loch Ness monster will be
248	revealed!
249	

Total Words Read _____

− Errors _____

= CWPM _____

The Six-Minute Solution: A Reading Fluency Program (Intermediate Level)

Communities: Village, Towns, and Cities

0   A community is formed when people live together in one place.

11   There are basically three kinds of communities. There are villages, towns,

22   and cities. One of the most important differences between them is their

34   populations.

35   A village is the smallest community. Most villages are farming

45   communities. There might be one or two stores in a village. A village

58   does not have a police department or fire department. It must rely on the

72   closest town or city for those services. If a village has its own school, it is

88   small.

89   A town is larger than a village, but not as large as a city. A town

105   might be a suburb of a larger city. A town may have a few thousand

120   people living in it. It may have a downtown with a small shopping

133   area. Towns usually have a small police force and school system also.

145   Sometimes towns have their own hospitals.

151   Cities are the largest kind of community. They have always been

162   centers of activity. Some cities started as centers for religion. Other cities

174   started as centers of government. Cities may be financial centers. They

185   can also be manufacturing centers. Some cities are cultural centers. Cities

196   have many more people than towns. They have more services for their

208   citizens. Cities have their own fire and police departments. They have

219   hospitals and school systems. Cities have many types of housing available

230   and several shopping areas.

234   People choose to live in villages, towns, or cities for specific

245   reasons. One reason might be the types of jobs they have. Another reason

258   might be the needs of their families. Still others choose a place to live

272   based on the services available. People select to live in the community

284   that best suits their needs.

289

Total Words Read _____

− Errors _____

= CWPM _____

Glaciers: Nature's Bulldozers

0   The word "glacier" paints a vivid picture in the minds of most

12   people. The word "glacier" comes from French and Latin roots. "Glace" is

24   a French word meaning ice. The word can also refer to something coated

37   with a sugar glaze. It is not hard to imagine a glacier as "sugar-coated

52   ice."

53   A glacier could better be described as a river of ice. In fact, a

67   glacier is a huge, slow-moving mass of ice nestled between mountains.

79   Glaciers are formed when more snow falls than melts in the mountains.

91   As snowflakes fall, they are changed into snow. When more snow is

103 added, the old snow becomes compacted. That means that it becomes

114 smooth and rounded. Eventually, the old snow turns into ice. This cycle

126 occurs again and again until finally a solid mass of ice is created. The

140 ice becomes so thick that it overflows, slides downhill, and becomes a

152 glacier.

153 Glaciers are powerful forces of nature. As glaciers move downhill,

163 grinding their way to the sea, they flatten everything in their way.

175 Glaciers even pull small rocks along with them. These rocks scrape and

187 scratch the ground as they are pulled along. The rocks rub against one

200 another and eventually are ground into a fine dust-like powder which is

213 called glacial silt. Moving rocks and soil as they travel, glaciers sculpt the

226 landscape, carving mountain valleys or shaping peaks. It is easy to see

238 why glaciers are considered to be nature's bulldozers.

246

Total Words Read _____

- Errors _____

= CWPM _____

Break Dancing: High-Energy Moves

0   Break dancing is a popular acrobatic dance form. Its name is

11   associated with breaks in music. Break dancers dance to a break beat.

23   Disc jockeys create break beats by combining musical parts. They select

34   music with drum solos and rhythm. The music is looped together and

46   played again and again. Break dancers move their feet sideways and onto

58   their toes. They spin on their knees, hands, elbows, and even on their

71   heads. Many forms of break dancing include mock fight moves. Other

82   forms include pantomime.

85   Many people credit superstar James Brown with creating the first

95   break dancing moves. In 1969, when performing his big hit "Get On the

108   Good Foot," he danced around the stage. His "Good Foot" was a freestyle,

121   high-energy dance that included body drops and spins.

130   The "Good Foot" evolved into what is now called old-style breaking.

142   Old-style breaking was simpler in that it involved only the dancer's feet.

155   There were no handspins or backspins. But old-style breaking was very

167   challenging, too. It incorporated very fast, complicated leg moves. Other

177   moves were modeled after Kung Fu. This style was especially popular

188   with street gangs in New York's South Bronx. The best break dancer

200   was often the best fighter on the street. Break dancing contests started.

212   Breakers in street gangs would battle each other in dance contests.

223   New-style breaking took over in the early 1980s. New-style breaking

235   added a lot of acrobatic moves. Headspins and backspins were two of

247   these moves. Others were hand-glides and windmills. Break dancing has

258   evolved even more with music videos and rap music. It is popular all over

272   the world. International break dancing tournaments are held every year.

282

Total Words Read _____

    – Errors _____

    = CWPM _____

Martin Luther King: A Man of Peace

0   Martin Luther King, Jr. was a great African American leader. He

11   was born on January 15, 1929. When he was a boy, black people did not

26   have the same rights as white people. Black children and white children

38   went to different schools. They drank from different water faucets. They

49   ate in different restaurants. Separating black and white people was called

60   "segregation."

61   Martin Luther King grew up to become a minister. In 1954, he was

74   working in Montgomery, Alabama. He wanted to change the segregation

84   laws. In 1955, a black woman named Rosa Parks was riding a bus home

98   from work. The bus driver told her to give her seat to a white person.

113   Mrs. Parks refused. She was arrested and put in jail. This made the black

127   people in Montgomery very angry. They decided to boycott the buses

138   until the segregation laws were changed. Martin Luther King helped to

149   lead the protest. After one year, the unfair law was changed. Dr. King

162   believed in peaceful protest. He did not believe in violence. When Dr.

174   King gave a speech, many people came to listen. Dr. King is famous

187   for his "I Have a Dream" speech. In this speech, Dr. King talked about

201   a world where his children would not be judged by the color of their

215   skin. Martin Luther King was awarded the Nobel Peace Prize in 1964.

227   Unfortunately, this man of peace was shot and killed in 1968 at the age

241   of 39. He is honored every year in January when the nation celebrates his

255   birthday.

256

Total Words Read _____

- Errors _____

= CWPM _____

The Bald Eagle: America's National Bird

0	The bald eagle is America's national bird. It is the emblem or
12	symbol that stands for America. The bald eagle was chosen to represent
24	America on June 20, 1782. This was the date when the great seal of
38	America was adopted.
41	The bald eagle was chosen as America's emblem for many reasons.
52	The eagle represents the spirit of freedom. It soars high above the
64	mountains, living a life of freedom. It also stands for a long life. Wild
78	bald eagles can live as long as thirty years. Once an eagle is paired with
93	its mate, the pair will stay together until one of them dies. Pairs of eagles
108	build nests out of sticks on the tops of very tall trees. The bald eagle has
124	a majestic look as well. It is a big and powerful bird. It was named at a
141	time when the word bald meant white or streaked with white. So, the
154	bald eagle is not bald at all. Rather, the adult eagle's head is covered with
169	white feathers. Its tail is also white. The bald eagle's body and wings are
183	dark brown and its eyes, beak, and feet are yellow. The bald eagle was
197	also selected as America's symbol because it is the only eagle confined to
210	the North American continent.
214	One story suggests that during one of the first battles of the
226	Revolutionary War, bald eagles were circling above the fighting men. The
237	eagles were making shrieking cries. The patriots thought that the eagles
248	were encouraging them by crying for freedom!
255	

Total Words Read _____

− Errors _____

= CWPM _____

Are Giant Squids Really Giant?

0 In one scary movie, a giant squid attacks a diver. In another movie,

13 a giant squid even attacks a submarine and manages to move it around

26 underwater. Do these giant creatures exist only in Hollywood? Actually,

36 the giant squid really is a sea animal. The giant squid is large, but not as

52 large as it is portrayed in the movies.

60 Strangely enough, the giant squid is related to the small clam and

72 the small snail. A squid, a clam, and a snail all belong to the mollusk

87 family. The members of the mollusk family all have one thing in

99 common. They all have a hard shell. This hard shell is to protect their

113 soft bodies. A clam's shell surrounds its soft body and can be easily seen.

127 The snail's shell, too, is easily visible.

134 But where is the giant squid's shell? The shell that protects the

146 squid is inside its body. Instead of having one "foot" for movement like

159 the snail or clam, the squid's foot has been divided into eight tentacles.

172 Those tentacles have suckers for grabbing and holding food. The tentacles

183 can be as long as twenty-two feet. The squid's body can be over thirty

198 feet long. A large sea animal covered with tentacles reaching out to grab

211 food can be a frightening sight. No wonder Hollywood has used the giant

224 squid as a popular feature in horror movies.

232

Total Words Read _____

- Errors _____

= CWPM _____

Bessie Coleman: First Female African American Aviator

0	Bessie was born in Texas in 1896. Her parents were sharecroppers.
11	Bessie was one of 13 children. Bessie had to walk four miles each way
25	to school. She was smart and an outstanding math student. Bessie first
37	became interested in flying when she read about the air war during World
50	War I.
52	When she was 23, Bessie went to live with her brother in Chicago.
65	She listened to tales of soldiers returning from World War I. They told
78	stories of amazing flying adventures. Bessie learned that there were
88	women pilots in France. She decided that she wanted to become a pilot,
101	too. Very few American women had pilot's licenses in 1918. Bessie
112	applied to many American flight schools. Every one turned her down for
124	two reasons: she was a woman and she was black.
134	Bessie did not give up. She learned to speak French. Then Bessie
146	went to flight school in France. It took her seven months to learn to fly.
161	In 1921, Bessie earned an international pilot's license. She returned to
172	the U.S. and took up stunt flying. Bessie became a popular performer at
185	air shows. She became an advocate for other African Americans. Bessie
196	encouraged them to fly as well. She refused to perform at locations that
209	wouldn't allow other members of her race to attend.
218	Bessie's dream was to start a flight school of her own. Sadly, she
231	did not live to realize that dream. Bessie died in a plane crash in 1926
246	at the age of 30. Bessie Coleman is not forgotten, however. The Bessie
259	Coleman Aviator Club for women pilots of all races was started in
271	her honor. A network of Bessie Coleman Aero Clubs was also formed.
283	Every year on her birthday, groups of pilots fly over her grave to drop
297	flowers. Bessie Coleman Drive, near Chicago's O'Hare airport, bears her
307	name. The U.S. Postal Service issued a Bessie Coleman stamp. Bessie's
318	pioneering spirit lives on.
322	

Total Words Read _____

– Errors _____

= CWPM _____

The Metric System: Counting by Ten

0 More than two hundred years ago in France, a group of scientists
12 invented a new system of measurement. They wanted the new system to
24 be more exact than the old way of measuring. So the scientists figured out
38 the distance between the North Pole and the equator. Then they divided
50 this distance into ten million parts. Each part became one unit of length.
63 This unit was called a meter. It was named after the Greek word, meter,
77 that means to measure. The new system of measuring was named the
89 metric system. A meter is a little bit longer than a yard.

101 In the metric system, the other units for measuring and weighing
112 were based on the meter. The gram, a word that means "small weight,"
125 became the basic unit to measure weight. A gram is very small! It takes
139 28 grams to equal only one ounce. The liter, named after another Greek
152 word, became the basic unit for measuring the amount of liquid in a
165 container. A liter is equal to about 33 ounces. It is a little more than
180 a quart. Our system of measuring is a little confusing. We have many
193 different names and numbers that we have to remember. But in the
205 metric system, there are only a few names. And there is really only one
219 number: ten. The three main units in the metric system—the meter, the
232 gram, and the liter—are changed to larger or smaller units by multiplying
245 or dividing by ten.

249

Total Words Read _____

- Errors _____

= CWPM _____

Sacajawea: Native American Guide

0	Sacajawea was a Native American. She was the first woman to cross
12	the Rocky Mountains. Sacajawea was a guide for two famous explorers.
23	These explorers were Lewis and Clark. They were the first to explore the
36	U.S. west of the Mississippi River. Without Sacajawea's help, Lewis and
47	Clark may not have made it to the Pacific Ocean.
57	Sacajawea was born around 1788 in what is now Idaho. She was
69	from the Shoshone nation. Sacajawea was kidnapped when she was 12
80	by a warring nation. A few years later, she was sold to a French trapper
95	to be his wife. Sacajawea was only 16 when she met Lewis and Clark in
110	1804.
111	Sacajawea helped Lewis and Clark in many ways. First, she was
122	a helpful guide. She remembered trails from her childhood. Sacajawea
132	led the explorers in the right direction. Clark called her his pilot. She
145	knew the local plants and found food for them to eat. Second, Sacajawea
158	helped the explorers trade with the Shoshone for horses. The explorers
169	needed horses in order to cross the mountains. Third, Sacajawea's
179	presence kept the explorers safe from attacks by Native nations. She was
191	a mother and carried her baby on her back. Native American women
203	and children never traveled with war parties. The Native people they
214	met along the way knew that Lewis and Clark came in peace. Sacajawea
227	traveled with them for more than a year.
235	Lewis and Clark were grateful to Sacajawea. They named many
245	rivers and lakes after her. In 2000, the U.S. Mint made a coin in her
260	honor. It shows her carrying her son on her back.
270	

Total Words Read _____

− Errors _____

= CWPM _____

Volleyball: Up and Over

0   A man named William Morgan invented the game of volleyball

10   in 1895. Morgan was a physical education teacher in a Massachusetts

21   YMCA. He was interested in a game that would require less effort than

34   basketball. He also wanted a game in which opponents did not come into

47   physical contact.

49   Morgan designed a team game that consisted of the tapping of a ball

62   back and forth across a net. Morgan's game is one in which teams are on

77   opposite sides of the net. In volleyball, the players do not move around

90   too much. Once an indoor game, volleyball later became popular as an

102   outside game as well. It is played worldwide today.

111   Volleyball is played on a field or a court that is divided by a net.

126   There are six players on each team. Three of the players play in the front,

141   close to the net, and three play in the back. The volleyball is a rubber

156   ball covered in leather. To begin the game, the ball is served by the player

171   who stands at the right back of the volleyball court. The ball must go

185   over the net without first touching the ground, another player, or the net.

198   After the serve, the ball is tapped back and forth across the net by each

213   team until one team is unable to return a ball. The ball must be tapped or

229   batted by hand and may not be lifted or pushed. If the serving team fails

244   to serve fairly or fails to return a serve successfully, it loses the serve. If

259   the defending team fails to return a serve, then the serving team scores a

273   point. The game is won when one team scores fifteen points.

284

Total Words Read _____

- Errors _____

= CWPM _____

September 16: Mexican Independence Day

0   Mexican Independence Day is celebrated on September 16. For more

10   than 300 years, Mexico was part of the Spanish Empire. During that time,

23   Mexico was called New Spain. The Mexican people did not like being

35   ruled by Spain.

38   In New Spain, there was a caste system. It was based on race.

51   People were assigned to a caste level at birth. Those at the top of the

66   caste had a nice life. Those at the bottom did not.

77   Another reason was that Spain wanted money from New Spain.

87   Spain made New Spain pay taxes. Spain also took money from the New

100   Spain churches. A final reason was that New Spain had trouble feeding its

113   own people. There was a famine, and people were starving.

123   A Mexican priest started a revolt against Spanish rule. The priest's

134   name was Father Miguel Hidalgo. On September 16, 1810, he gave a

146   famous speech. It was called the "Cry of Dolores." The speech became

158   the Mexican battle cry for freedom. Hidalgo and his followers fought

169   against Spain. Father Hidalgo was captured. He was executed on July 31,

181   1811. His revolt failed. In spite of this, Miguel Hidalgo is known as the

195   father of Mexican independence.

199   Mexican Independence Day is celebrated on the anniversary of

208   the start of Father Hidalgo's revolt. The Mexican people finally achieved

219   freedom from Spain 11 years later in 1821.

227

Total Words Read _____

− Errors _____

= CWPM _____

Peter the Great: Russian Czar

0   Peter was born on May 30, 1672, in Moscow. When he was only 17

14   years old, he became the king of Russia. Russian kings were called czars.

27   At this time, Russia was a very backward country. Peter decided to travel

40   to Europe to learn how to make Russia a more modern country. He visited

54   countries like England and Holland. Peter brought back western ideas to

65   share with the Russian people. He introduced the European calendar and

76   alphabet to his countrymen. He also shared new ideas about government,

87   schools, and even clothes with the Russian people. Peter built a new city

100   in Russia and named it St. Petersburg. St. Petersburg was modeled after

112   some of the European cities Peter had visited. Peter the Great was also a

126   strong military leader. He was interested in ships. He even built his own

139   ship at the age of sixteen. A Russian navy was created during his reign.

153   He won land on the Baltic Sea so Russia would have a place to dock her

169   ships. Peter also made the Russian army stronger. Peter the Great was a

182   popular leader with young Russians. His popularity made it possible for

193   him to do what he wanted without being overthrown. Some historians

204   think that Peter the Great was a wonderful leader. They give him credit

217   for making Russia a more modern country.

224   Other historians do not think that Peter the Great was so great. They

237   point out that Peter was a cruel leader. He tried to control the Russian

251   Orthodox Church. He raided the church treasury. Peter forced the older

262   Russian men to cut off their beards against church wishes. He made the

275   men in his court dress like Europeans and smoke pipes. Peter forced

287   Russian serfs, or slaves, to work in factories. Nevertheless, Peter the Great

299   is considered a national hero in Russia. The many monuments that were

311   built to honor him are still maintained.

318

Total Words Read _____

− Errors _____

= CWPM _____

Chinese Railroad Workers: Men of Steel

0	In 1863, America was growing. It was becoming a large country.
11	Many people were moving west. There was a need for transportation
22	across the U.S. Two railroad companies started building one long railroad.
33	The Union Pacific started in the east, in Iowa. The Central Pacific started
46	in the west, in California. The two railroads then joined together as one
59	in Utah. They created the first coast-to-coast railroad system.
70	Building the railroad was hard work. It was also very dangerous.
81	Railroad track was laid across the Sierra Nevada Mountains in eastern
92	California. The mountains rose to 7,000 feet for more than 100 miles. The
105	workers had to blast their way through the mountains.
114	Chinese workers were hired to do the dangerous jobs that white
125	workers refused. The Chinese, though physically small, proved to be
135	strong and brave workers. They were lowered by baskets from the tops of
148	cliffs. While suspended in the air, the Chinese chipped away at the rock.
161	They used dynamite to make tunnels. Chinese workers dug ditches. They
173	dammed rivers. Hundreds of men died on the job.
181	In addition to the dangers of the job, workers had to endure poor
194	weather conditions. They worked in the extreme cold of the mountains.
205	They worked in the extreme heat of the deserts in California, Nevada, and
218	Utah. Chinese workers were not treated fairly. Other workers made fun
229	of the Chinese because they looked different. The Chinese workers were
240	paid less than white workers. They had to provide their own tents and
252	food.
253	In spite of the way they were treated, the Chinese worked hard and
266	never gave up. Without the efforts of 12,000 Chinese workers, the U.S.
278	transcontinental railroad may have never been built.
285	

Total Words Read _____

− Errors _____

= CWPM _____

Level 6 Practice Passages

Water: What Would We Do Without It?

0	Water is necessary for life. In fact, most living things are made of
13	water. Also, most living things need water to survive. Although the earth
25	is almost 70 percent water, most of the earth's water supply is frozen.
38	Much of the earth's water can be found at both the North Pole and the
53	South Pole. Water frozen in glaciers also contains a good deal of the
66	earth's water. Other water can be found in numerous lakes and rivers
78	throughout the world. Some of our earth's water supply is also found
90	underground and must be drilled for in water wells. Water is returned to
103	the earth by a cycle of precipitation followed by evaporation by the sun.
116	On average, people in the U.S. use about 100 gallons of water a
129	day. We use water as a part of our daily lives in numerous ways. We
144	drink it, bathe in it, and brush our teeth with it. We cook and clean with
160	water. Some of us swim in water or travel on it. Although we use water
175	over and over again, this does not mean we should take it for granted. It
190	is important that we conserve water in any way that we can. There are
204	many things we can do to save water. We should avoid letting water run
218	down the drain as we brush our teeth, wash our hands, or rinse dishes.
232	We can save more than 5 gallons a day by turning off the water when
247	brushing our teeth. We could rinse dishes in a sink partly filled with
260	clean water rather than under running water. Taking a quick shower
271	instead of a bath can save an average of 20 gallons of water. Checking
285	for and fixing dripping faucets and leaky toilets can save as much as 10
299	gallons of water per person a day. Outside, we can limit how much we
313	water plants and lawns. We can wash our cars with a bucket of soapy
327	water and stop the hose between rinses. Since water is necessary for our
340	survival, water conservation efforts should be taken seriously. Conserving
349	the earth's water supply is everyone's job.
356	

Total Words Read _____

– Errors _____

= CWPM _____

Granite: It's More Than Just a Rock

0	Granite is an unusual and unique kind of rock. However, granite
11	is also common and found in many places. Oftentimes, we may be
23	surrounded by granite. Mountains composed of granite stand out against
33	the sky. Many of the tallest buildings and famous statues in the United
46	States are made of granite. Granite is a special kind of rock called an
60	igneous rock. That means granite was once found in a hot liquid form
73	called magma in the middle of the earth. When the magma moved to
86	the earth's surface, it cooled and hardened. Some of that hardened rock
98	became granite.
100	The word "granite" was derived from a word meaning "grained."
110	Granite is a strong and rough rock. Granite is mostly made of two
123	minerals: feldspar and quartz. It is the quartz in granite that gives it its
137	sparkle. Granite must be polished to smooth out its rough surface. When
149	it is polished, it shines and displays beautiful colors. Various hues of
161	pink, red, brown, black, green, and even blue can be found in granite.
174	Because it is such a strong rock, granite is used on the walls and floors of
190	many buildings. Granite is the perfect choice for monuments and statues
201	because sun, wind, and other weather will not erode it.
211	To obtain the large pieces of granite necessary for buildings, the
222	sides of mountains are sliced off in large sheets. These sheets of granite
235	are subsequently cut into thinner slices and polished for decorative uses,
246	like walls and kitchen countertops. It is amazing to think that pieces of
259	tall, rough mountains can become the shiny, bright, colorful walls on
270	some of the nation's most beautiful buildings.
277	

Total Words Read _____

− Errors _____

= CWPM _____

The Road to Freedom: America's Journey

0	English people came to North America looking for a new life. They
12	found a new land with people living on it. These people were the Native
26	Americans. The English decided to live in America also. So they started
38	a colony in Virginia. They named it Jamestown. Jamestown was the first
50	permanent English colony. It was founded in 1607. Other English people
61	came to America, too. Some of these people were called Pilgrims. They
73	arrived on a ship called the Mayflower. The Pilgrims agreed to set up a
87	government. They promised to obey the laws of their government. This
98	agreement was the Mayflower Compact. It was signed on November 11,
109	1620.
110	Many other people came to America. Soon there were 13 colonies
121	of people. However, there were serious problems. The king of England
132	wanted the colonists to pay new taxes. The colonists did not want to pay
146	these taxes. By the 1760s, colonists were very angry with England. They
158	thought the taxes were unfair. They started to fight back. The colonists
170	stopped buying English products. On December 16, 1773, colonists led
180	a protest in Boston. They did not like a new tax on tea. So a group of
197	colonists dressed as Native Americans. They boarded an English ship.
207	Once on board, the colonists dumped tea into the harbor. This protest
219	was called the Boston Tea Party.
225	Soon after the Boston Tea Party, the colonists and England went to
237	war. This war was the American Revolution. The colonists won the war.
249	They won the right to be free from England's control. They were able
262	to have their own country. On July 4, 1776, the colonists declared their
275	independence from England. The Fourth of July is America's birthday. It
286	has been an important holiday for more than 200 years.
296	

Total Words Read _____

− Errors _____

= CWPM _____

The Great Lakes: North America's Freshwater Lakes

0	The Great Lakes are important natural resources. They make up the
11	largest system of fresh, surface water on earth. There are five great lakes,
24	which are bordered by Canada and seven U.S. states. Lake Superior is the
37	deepest and coldest lake. It has the most volume of water. It is shaped
51	like a wolf's head. The land around Lake Superior has many forests but
64	not many people live there.
69	Lake Michigan is the second largest lake. It is the only one that lies
83	within the boundaries of the United States. The northern part of Lake
95	Michigan drains into Green Bay. There are fisheries in Green Bay. There
107	are also waste products from paper mills. The southern part of Lake
119	Michigan has many people. The metropolitan areas of Milwaukee and
129	Chicago are located near Lake Michigan.
135	Lake Huron is the third largest lake. It is surrounded by sandy
147	shores. People like to visit it. There are summer cottages along the shores
160	of Lake Huron. Like Lake Michigan, Lake Huron also has a productive
172	fishery. Lake Erie is the smallest of the lakes in volume, as well as the
187	shallowest. Because it is shallow, Erie is also the warmest of the five
200	lakes. There are many city areas around the Lake Erie basin. The land
213	around Land Erie has fertile soil. Lake Erie is the lake most exposed to
227	the effects of city life and farming. From the air, Lakes Michigan, Huron,
240	and Erie resemble the shape of a mitten.
248	The smallest lake in terms of area is Lake Ontario. It is deeper than
262	its neighbor, Lake Erie, though. The cities of Toronto and Hamilton are
274	located around Lake Ontario. These five great lakes cover more than
285	94,000 square miles. They hold almost one-fifth of the world's supply
297	of fresh surface water. The United States obtains almost all of its fresh
310	water supply from the Great Lakes. North America's freshwater lakes are
321	important natural resources.
324	

Total Words Read _____

− Errors _____

= CWPM _____

Organizing Our Planet

0	Humans have always tried to organize the world in which they
11	live. Plants and animals have been named since the beginning of time.
23	Aristotle tried to organize the living world over 2,000 years ago. He
35	formed two groups. Living things were either plants or animals. He then
47	further grouped the animals by where they lived. There were animals that
59	lived on land, in the water, or in the air. He classified plants into three
74	groups. Plants, according to Aristotle, were trees, shrubs, or herbs.
84	Over time, many other ways to organize living things were tried.
95	They all failed because of language differences and lack of knowledge
106	about the plants and animals. For example, a starfish is not a fish. A
120	horseshoe crab should really be called a horseshoe spider. Depending on
131	where one lives, a mountain lion may also be called a puma or a cougar.
146	Finally, a Swedish scientist named Carl von Linne devised a
156	grouping system. He decided to use Latin to name the groups. Latin was
169	no longer used as an oral language, so it wouldn't change over time.
182	He liked Latin so much that he even changed his own name to a Latin
197	version of von Linne. His name became Carolus Linnaeus. Linnaeus
207	studied thousands and thousands of plants and animals. He decided to
218	group the plants and animals by their structures. His classification system
229	is used today by scientists all over the world to place plants and animals
243	into similar groups.
246	

Total Words Read _____

– Errors _____

= CWPM _____

Bats: Misunderstood Mammals

0	Bats are perhaps the most misunderstood of all the mammals. For
11	example, the expression "blind as a bat" is widely used. The supposition
23	that bats are blind is just one of the many misconceptions about these
36	flying mammals. In reality, bats are not blind at all. In fact, while all
50	bats can see, many bats can even see better than some people. There are
64	basically two kinds of bats—large and small. Mega bats have excellent
76	eyesight. Their large eyes enable them to see fruits and flowers in the
89	night. Smaller bats rely on echolocation while flying at night, but even
101	these bats are able to see. The echolocation assists them in finding
113	insects. Most bats have better night vision than day vision, however.
124	Many people think of bats as vampires that suck people's blood.
135	There are nearly 1,000 species of bats in the world. They live in almost
149	all areas of the world except for the very cold regions like Antarctica.
162	Only three species of bats, those living in Mexico and South America, eat
175	the blood of mammals and birds. Even these bats do not suck the blood.
189	Instead, they make a small bite in the animal's skin using their very
202	sharp teeth. They then lick up the blood. Bat saliva has a chemical that
216	prevents blood from clotting before the bat is finished eating. Scientists
227	are studying bats to see if this chemical could prevent human strokes
239	caused by blood clots.
243	Bats are important to humans in other ways. They pollinate trees
254	and flowers and spread seeds so that plants grow in other areas. Bats can
268	eat half of their weight in insects each night. Therefore, they are very
281	effective controllers of pests who harm crops and spread disease. These
292	misunderstood mammals are actually very valuable creatures.
299	

Total Words Read _____

- Errors _____

= CWPM _____

The Printing Press

0	Imagine having to copy an entire book by hand. That's what people
12	had to do before the printing press was invented. Books sometimes took
24	years to copy. They were very rare and extremely expensive. Monks spent
36	their entire lives just making one copy of the Bible.
46	In the early fifteenth century, a German named Johann Gutenberg
57	had a wonderful idea. He thought of a way to print books instead of
71	copying them by hand. Gutenberg took small blocks of wood and made
83	them all the same size. He then took each block of wood and carved one
98	letter of the alphabet on it. When Gutenberg wanted to print a word, he
112	would line up the blocks with the letters that would spell that word. He
126	would spread ink on each of the letters and then press them down on a
141	piece of parchment paper. He could use the same alphabet letter blocks
153	over and over again, as he strung the blocks together to make words. This
167	method still took a great deal of time, but then Gutenberg thought of a
181	way to design a machine that would print an entire page at one time.
195	Gutenberg invented that printing machine, called the printing press,
204	in 1448. He printed three hundred Bibles in Latin, the language of the
217	church at the time. Forty of those 300 Bibles still exist today. They are
231	called the Gutenberg Bibles, and they are worth millions and millions of
243	dollars. The next time you pick up a book to read, imagine how long it
258	would take to print just one page if you had to line up blocks of wood
274	letters before it could be printed.
280	

Total Words Read _____

− Errors _____

= CWPM _____

Klondike Gold Rush: A Tale of Two Trails

0	Between 1896 and 1900, nearly 100,000 people rushed to Alaska
10	and the Yukon Territory. The reason? Gold, of course! The word that
22	gold had been discovered in the Yukon River traveled quickly across the
34	United States. People from all walks of life set out to find their fortune.
48	Unfortunately, gold-seeking was a dangerous undertaking. It is estimated
58	that only 40,000 of the 100,000 actually made the trip to the Dawson gold
72	fields. Once there, only 10 percent of them found gold.
82	Gold seekers had two choices to get to the Dawson Chilkoot and
94	the White Pass. The Chilkoot Pass was too steep for horses, so men who
108	could not afford horses often took this trail. The Canadian Mounties
119	required that each miner bring a year's worth of supplies. A year's worth
132	of supplies could weigh as much as one ton. Without these supplies,
144	miners were not allowed to cross. Consequently, gold seekers had to strap
156	heavy packs on their backs and drag loaded dog sleds and canoes as they
170	hiked along. It took the men many backbreaking trips over the pass to
183	haul their supplies. Once over the pass, miners had to build boats and
196	travel down rushing rapids to finally reach the gold fields. Many men
208	turned back along the way.
213	The White Pass trail was the other route to the gold fields. Since
226	the White Pass was not as steep as the Chilkoot Pass trail, pack animals
240	were allowed on this trail. Sadly, the trail proved to be too much for these
255	animals to bear. Three thousand animals died and were abandoned along
266	this trail. The White Pass became known as Dead Horse Trail.
277	

Total Words Read _____

− Errors _____

= CWPM _____

Cells: Basic Units of Life

0   Cells are considered to be the basic units of life itself. All living

13   things are made up of cells. A tree is made up of cells, as is an alligator.

30   Some living things only have one cell, such as bacteria. Other living

42   things, such as humans, have trillions of cells in their bodies.

53   It wasn't until the early 1600s that the existence of cells was

65   discovered. An English scientist, Robert Hooke, built an early microscope.

75   He placed a thin slice of a piece of cork under the microscope, magnified

89   it, and made observations. Imagine his surprise when he saw many small

101   squares in the cork. Robert Hooke thought the small squares resembled

112   the tiny rooms in which monks lived. Robert Hooke named his discovery

124   after these rooms, which were called cells.

131   As microscopes improved, scientists made important discoveries

138   about cells. They observed that there are many kinds of cells and that

151   these cells are very complicated. Scientists discovered that all cells do

162   not look alike. Many cells apparently specialize in performing a certain

173   kind of function. These cells have shapes that help them do their jobs.

186   For example, muscle cells are elongated. These cells have the ability to

198   expand and contract. Narrow white blood cells have a rounded shape.

209   Their shape assists them in better flowing through veins. Cells that make

221   up the eye are sensitive to light, as is the eye itself.

233   Microscopes have greatly improved, so much so that Robert Hooke

243   would not believe his eyes if he looked through one today. Scientists'

255   knowledge of cells and their functions have advanced considerably as

265   well. Scientists are continually studying and discovering more each

274   day about cells. One important area of research on cells is how to stop

288   dangerous cells, such as cancer cells, from growing. What started with

299   Robert Hooke and a slice of cork is ongoing, with the health and well-

313   being of humankind as the ultimate goal.

320

Total Words Read _____

– Errors _____

= CWPM _____

Salmon: Uphill Fighters

0   The salmon is the state fish of Alaska. Named after Greek words

12   meaning "hook" and "nose," salmon are sometimes called the Greek gods

23   of the sea. Salmon contain Omega 3, considered by some to be a miracle

37   ingredient. Omega 3 reportedly helps to reduce the risk of heart attack.

49   Many people consider salmon to be a delicious tasting fish as well. It is a

64   popular choice on many restaurant menus, in grocery stores, and in fish

76   markets. Consequently, commercial fishermen catch millions of salmon

84   each year.

86   As part of their natural life cycle, wild salmon have but one purpose

99   in life. Their only goal is to spawn, or reproduce. Once a salmon has

113   spawned, it dies. Salmon are on the move from the time they are born.

127   Most wild salmon are born in gravel beds in streams or lakes. Recently

140   hatched salmon, called fry, travel far and wide on a quest to find salt

154   water. As they travel, salmon must dodge bigger fish to avoid being eaten.

167   After a period of one to seven years of adventure, a salmon's natural

180   instinct tells it that it is time to return home. Salmon will bravely fight

194   many obstacles as they embark on their trip. Frequently, they battle

205   water currents, swimming upstream to reach the spawning beds where

215   they were born. They then lay and fertilize their eggs. Once that job is

229   completed, the salmon dies. This journey back to their birthplace for the

241   purpose of reproduction is called the salmon run.

249

Total Words Read _____

− Errors _____

= CWPM _____

The Constitution:
America's Most Important Document

0	The Constitution is an official plan. It is very important. The
11	Constitution tells how our country should be run. This important plan
22	was written in 1787. The first meeting, or convention, was held on May
35	25. James Madison was a leader at the convention. He was in favor of
49	a strong national government. He worked very hard and took detailed
60	notes. James Madison is known as the father of the Constitution.
71	Delegates from the 13 states attended the convention. They tried
81	to decide how to elect members of Congress. Some delegates liked the
93	Virginia Plan. This plan said that states with more people should have
105	more members in Congress. Other delegates liked the New Jersey plan.
116	This plan said that all states should have the same number of members
129	in Congress. The delegates decided to compromise. They came up with
140	a plan that created two law-making groups. These law-making groups
152	were called houses. One house would elect delegates based on how many
164	people lived in each state. The other house would elect two delegates
176	from each state regardless of the size of the state. On September 17,
189	1787, thirty-nine of the fifty-five delegates signed the Constitution.
200	Later, changes were made to the Constitution. These changes are called
211	amendments to the Constitution. The first ten amendments to the
221	Constitution are called the Bill of Rights. In 1791, the Bill of Rights was
235	added to the Constitution. Over the next 215 years, other changes were
247	made to the Constitution. Our current Constitution has 27 amendments.
257	

Total Words Read _____

- Errors _____

= CWPM _____

Leonardo da Vinci

0   Leonardo da Vinci was a famous painter. He lived a long time ago

13   during the Italian Renaissance. This was a period of time between 1300

25   and 1500. Wealthy people and church leaders hired artists. They wanted

36   the artists to paint pictures and make statutes. Da Vinci was one of the

50   greatest artists of the Italian Renaissance.

56   Leonardo da Vinci painted two very famous paintings. One is

66   called the Mona Lisa. The Mona Lisa is a picture of a woman. She has

81   a mysterious smile. People wonder why she is smiling and what she is

94   thinking. The other painting is called The Last Supper. This painting

105 is a picture of Jesus Christ and his 12 disciples. Da Vinci painted it on

120 a church wall in Italy. These two paintings by Leonardo da Vinci are

133 probably two of the most famous in the entire world.

143 Although famous as a painter, Da Vinci was also a scientist and an

156 inventor. He studied the human body and how it worked. Da Vinci then

169 made detailed drawings showing how muscles are attached to bones. Da

180 Vinci was fascinated by machines and how they work. Da Vinci invented

192 many machines. For example, he made a flying machine out of wood,

204 cloth, and feathers. It had wings that flapped like a bird. Da Vinci also is

219 credited with inventing military weapons. Leonardo da Vinci was truly a

230 man of many talents.

234

Total Words Read _____

- Errors _____

= CWPM _____

All That Glitters Might Be Gold

0	Gold is a valuable metal. For thousands of years, it has been valued
13	for its beautiful yellow color. It also has been valued for its shine and
27	glitter.
28	Gold can be melted and molded into many different shapes. Gold is
40	used to make beautiful jewelry, coins for various countries, crosses and
51	statues for churches, and, in some cultures, teeth. Gold has been found
63	in many countries all over the world. The Egyptians filled the pharaohs'
75	pyramids with it. The Incas of Peru and the Aztecs of Mexico were
88	experts in using the gold they mined for jewelry and religious statues.
100	In 1848, gold was found at Sutter's Mill in California. Heavy bars
112	of gold were sent by stagecoach and steamship from California. When
123	people in other parts of the United States saw this gold, they rushed to
137	California, hoping to get rich. These people were called the "forty-niners"
149	because that was the year they started to arrive in California. Gold was
162	found in rushing rivers by prospectors panning for it. Sluice boxes were
174	built on the banks of rivers. The prospectors shoveled the river rock and
187	sand into the sluice box. Water was poured through the sluice box. Gold,
200	which is very heavy, sunk to the bottom of the box while the lighter river
215	rock and sand washed out. Gold has also been found deep in mines.
228	Prospectors found valuable veins of gold in quartz rock deep in the
240	earth and mined the quartz. The quartz rock was crushed and the gold
253	removed from it.
256	The quest of gold has been the cause of both positive and negative
269	events. The search for this valuable metal caused wars, murders, and
280	whole civilizations to be wiped out. On the other hand, the search for
293	gold led explorers to discover and settle new lands and allowed for the
306	creation of beautiful works of art.
312	

Total Words Read _____

- Errors _____

= CWPM _____

Zeus: Father of the Greek Gods

0   Gods were important in the ancient Greek religion. The Greeks

10   believed that their gods lived in families and that each god or goddess

23   had a certain kind of power. They also thought that each of the gods had

38   a distinct personality. Sacred places called sanctuaries were built by the

49   Greeks to honor their gods. Greeks prayed to different gods for different

61   reasons. They also made sacrifices to the gods as a way to please them.

75   Zeus, the god of the sky and of the weather, was also considered

88   the father of all the Greek gods. The Greeks believed that Zeus was the

102   absolute master of all the Greeks, other gods, and perhaps the universe.

114   The Olympic games were actually created to honor Zeus. The games were

126   named after the highest mountain in Greece, Mount Olympus. Ancient

136   Greeks pictured Zeus sitting in a golden throne on top of Mount Olympus.

149   The Greeks believed that Zeus would take pleasure from watching

159   athletes compete in the Olympic games. All Greeks, regardless of where

170   they lived, worshiped Zeus and the other gods in his family. Zeus's wife,

183   Hera, was known as the goddess of marriage. His brother, Poseidon, was

195   the god of the sea. Zeus himself was thought to control the weather. In

209   the Greek people's minds, thunder and lighting occurred as a punishment

220   when Zeus was very angry. One of Zeus's sons, Apollo, was the god of

234   light and health. It was believed that Apollo was responsible for the sun

247   rising and setting each day. The ancient Greeks explained many of the

259   wonders of nature by attributing them to the behavior and personalities

270   of the Greek gods.

274

Total Words Read _____

- Errors _____

= CWPM _____

King Salmon and Friends

0   If you are a fish eater, chances are good that you have eaten

13   salmon. Salmon are a popular and plentiful fish. In Alaska alone, more

25   than 173 million salmon were commercially harvested last year.

34   King salmon are the largest and best-known type of salmon. King

46   salmon average between 20 and 40 pounds but can grow to be much

59   larger. In 1949, a king salmon weighing 126 pounds was caught in a fish

73   trap near Petersburg, Alaska. Ranging from California's Monterey Bay to

83   the Chukchi Sea near Russia, king salmon spend one to seven years in

96   the ocean. Then they, like all salmon, head for their freshwater homes to

109 reproduce or spawn. Once that job is completed, the salmon die. Thus,

121 the natural life cycle of the salmon comes to an end.

132 In addition to the king salmon, there are four other types of salmon.

145 The coho or silver salmon weighs 8 to 12 pounds on average. The

158 coho is an active salmon—leaping and jumping out of the water when

171 hooked by a fisherman. The sockeye salmon is small, weighing only 4

183 to 8 pounds. The sockeye is sleek and silver-looking when in the ocean.

197 Once it returns home to spawn, the sockeye salmon turns red. Humpback

209 salmon are the smallest of the Pacific salmon, weighing on average 3 to 4

223 pounds. The males develop their humpbacks when spawning. They also

233 change color—turning brown to black. The females turn an olive green

245 color. The fifth type of salmon is the chum. These salmon range from the

259 Sacramento River in California to the Mackenzie River in Canada. Chums

270 are the preferred choice of the Alaskan sled dog. Many stores in Alaska

283 sell smoked chum salmon in dog treat packages!

291

Total Words Read _____

− Errors _____

= CWPM _____

Alexander Graham Bell: Telephone Inventor

0   Alexander Graham Bell invented the telephone in 1876. Bell's father

10   was a teacher of people who were deaf. Alexander became interested in

22   speech and hearing problems. He grew up to become a teacher of the

35   deaf like his father. One of his students later became his wife.

47   Alexander wanted to make speech visible for the deaf. He tried to

59   find a way to record sound vibrations. He worked with another inventor

71   named Thomas Watson. They tried different ways of sending messages.

81   By accident, they found a way to have sound carried by electrical current.

94   After that, it was only a matter of time before they found a way to

109 transmit human sound along a wire.

115   Bell went to the Centennial Exposition of 1876 in Philadelphia. He

126 presented his invention to the public. It was very well received. People

138 could now talk to one another across great distances. Bell continued to

150 improve the telephone. Telephone service companies were organized

158 in England and in the United States. Bell became wealthy and famous.

170 But he never forgot about helping the deaf. If it had not been for Bell's

185 interest in deafness, the telephone would not have been invented. Bell

196 used his own money to set up a fund to study deafness. He was in

211 favor of teaching deaf people to use language instead of signs. Bell was

224 opposed to keeping people who were deaf separate. Many of his methods

236 were used in schools for people who were deaf. Alexander Graham Bell

248 is well-known as the inventor of the telephone. However, he was also an

262 advocate for people who are deaf.

268

Total Words Read _____

− Errors _____

= CWPM _____

Estevanico and the Seven Cities of Gold

0	Native Americans tell many stories about black men who came
10	from faraway places. The story of Estevanico, or "Little Seven," is a
22	popular one.
24	Estevanico was born in Africa in the early 1500s. He was one of the
38	early explorers of the southwestern U.S. Estevanico was a Muslim slave.
49	He sailed with his master and a crew to the New World in 1527. They
64	were looking for gold. The trip was very hard. They were shipwrecked at
77	what is now Tampa Bay, Florida. Estevanico and the crew members then
89	made their own rafts. They sailed west toward Mexico on five rafts. Three
102	of the rafts sank along the way. The other two rafts landed at Galveston
116	Island near what is now Texas.
122	After a very harsh winter, only 15 of 80 men were still alive. They
136	headed west on foot, walking along the Colorado River. By 1533, only
148	Estevanico and three other crew members had survived. Along the way,
159	they were helped by some native tribes but enslaved by others.
170	In 1534, Estevanico and the three other men were living with a
182	native tribe in inland Texas. They became medicine men. Soon, they were
194	known as healers of the sick. Estevanico carried a medicine rattle as a
207	good luck symbol. He was gifted in learning languages. Soon, he spoke
219	several native dialects. The natives called Estevanico and his friends
229	"Children of the Sun" because they traveled from east to west. They were
242	the first non-natives to travel in this part of the Southwest.
254	Thousands of natives took turns guiding Estevanico and his friends
264	on their journey to Mexico City. They arrived in July 1536. The Spanish
277	governor asked them to join a northern expedition. Only Estevanico
287	agreed to go. His job was to be a scout. The purpose of the trip was to
304	look for the mythical "Seven Cities of Cibola."
312	While exploring, these men discovered what is now Arizona and
322	New Mexico. This was 45 years after Columbus had arrived on the shores
335	of the New World. In these new lands, Estevanico found a village with
348	many buildings. The buildings were made of stone and were many tiers
361	high. Estevanico thought he had found the seven cities of gold, but he
373	had not. He had stumbled onto a pueblo belonging to a Zuni tribe. The
387	Zuni did not trust him. Estevanico and most of his native followers were
400	killed on the spot.
404	

Total Words Read _____

- Errors _____

= CWPM _____

The Thermometer: A Measure of Many Things

0 — Is it cold or hot outside today? We often rely on a thermometer to

14 — let us know the temperature. Temperature is a measure of how hot or cold

28 — something is. Many factors influence the outside temperature. At certain

38 — times of the year, the sun is closer to our part of the earth. During these

54 — times, the sun warms the earth, and the temperature is higher. At other

67 — times of the year, our part of the earth is tilted away from the sun. Then

83 — the temperature is colder. Cloud cover can also influence temperature. If

94 — there are few clouds, the temperature is higher. Being close to water is

107 — another factor. The air near the water is cooler than inland air. Air high

121 — up in the mountains is cooler than desert air. Winds affect temperature as

134 — well. When strong winds blow, they usually help cool the air. However, if

147 — there is a strong wind blowing in from the hot desert, it will warm up the

163 — air.

164 — Meteorologists are people who study the weather. They use

173 — thermometers to measure the outside air. But there are other kinds

184 — of thermometers as well. Thermometers are also used to determine

194 — a person's body temperature. Human beings have a normal body

204 — temperature of 98.6 degrees Fahrenheit. Variations from this body

213 — temperature can mean that a person is ill. Chemists may use

224 — thermometers to check the temperature of a scientific solution. The

234 — temperature of the solution can make a difference in a scientist's

245 — research findings. Chefs and bakers use thermometers in their work.

255 — Meat thermometers indicate whether food is cooked well enough to eat.

266 — Candy thermometers are used to help pastry chefs create perfect sweets.

277 — Thermometers measure many kinds of things!

283

Total Words Read _____

- Errors _____

= CWPM _____

Rap Music: Its Historical Beat

0   Rap is a popular musical form. Its roots are in West Africa.

12   Thousands of native tribes celebrated rituals and ceremonies. They

21   celebrated with pounding drumbeats, chanting, and dancing. Beginning

29   in the late 1400s, African slaves were brought to America. They made up

42   their own music with the rhythms they remembered from their homeland.

53   Almost 500 years later, rap began in New York. It started in the

66   South Bronx, with teenagers talking in rhyme to the rhythm of a beat. In

80   the early 1970s, rap was first known as hip-hop. Rhythms and melodies

93   from existing music were mixed with poems.

100   Early rap was first a street art. Its tales reflected life in the inner

114   cities of New York. Rapping was a popular addition to neighborhood

125   block parties. Clubs began featuring rap music. Rap became popular with

136   black teens in New York, Philadelphia, and Washington, D.C.

145   In September 1979, "Rapper's Delight" was released by the Sugarhill

155   Gang. It was very successful. Record companies became interested in this

166   new sound. As a result, rap music gained a wider audience. It became

179   popular not only in the U.S. but also across the world's oceans, as people

193   starting tuning in to this new sound.

200   Not everyone became a rap fan, however. Critics were concerned

210   about rap lyrics. Many of these lyrics reflected the hardships of inner-city

223   life and other harsh topics. Supporters argue that rap music has helped to

236   bridge gaps among cultures. No one can deny that rap is a very popular

250   form of music. It continues to grow and attract new fans.

261

Total Words Read _____

− Errors _____

= CWPM _____

Balance of Power: Three Branches of Government

0	The makers of the United States Constitution did not want to
11	give too much power to one group. They were afraid that it would be
25	dangerous for the country. The lawmakers decided to divide the jobs
36	of the government. They created three branches of government. Article
46	I of the Constitution created the first branch. The first branch is the
59	Legislative Branch. The legislative branch is the Congress. Congress
68	makes the laws of the nation. It also handles money. Congress is
80	responsible for making the money, borrowing money, and collecting
89	taxes. It is also in charge of the military.
98	The second branch was created as Article II of the Constitution. It is
111	the Executive Branch. The Executive Branch is the President of the United
123	States. The president is responsible for making sure laws are carried out.
135	He is able to put laws into effect by signing them. He can also veto laws
151	he does not like. The president is the commander-in-chief of the nation's
165	armed forces. He appoints people to important positions and makes
175	treaties with other countries.
179	Article III of the Constitution created the third branch of the
190	government. This third branch is the Judicial Branch. The Judicial Branch
201	is the Supreme Court and other national courts. The Judicial Branch is
213	responsible for explaining what laws mean. This branch decides if current
224	laws passed by Congress follow the intention of the Constitution.
234	

Total Words Read _____

- Errors _____

= CWPM _____

Maria Tallchief: Prima Ballerina

0	Maria was born in Oklahoma. Her father was chief of the Osage
12	tribe. Maria's mother was Scottish-Irish. From the time she was a little
25	girl, Maria loved to sing and dance. She started taking dance lessons
37	when she was only four years old. She also took piano lessons.
49	After high school, Maria went to New York City. She wanted to
61	work as a ballerina. She danced so well that she was hired right away.
75	Her first job was with the Ballet Russe de Monte Carlo. Soon after, she
89	met George Balanchine. He was a famous choreographer from Russia.
99	Choreographers design dances by matching dance steps to music.
108	In 1948, George became the artistic director of the New York City
120	Ballet. He created special ballets for Maria. One of the most famous was
133	a version of Igor Stravinsky's "Firebird." In this ballet, Maria danced the
145	part of a magical bird. Maria had many other famous roles as well. She
159	was queen of the swans in the ballet "Swan Lake." In the "Nutcracker"
172	ballet, Maria danced the part of the Sugar Plum Fairy. At the age of
186	35, Maria became the prima, or first, ballerina for the American Ballet
198	Theatre.
199	Maria Tallchief is recognized as one of the most accomplished
209	ballerinas in America. The state of Oklahoma honored her as "Woman
220	of Two Worlds." Not only was she a gifted ballerina, she was also a
234	promoter of Native American culture and contributions to the arts.
244	

Total Words Read _____

− Errors _____

= CWPM _____

Sequoya: Inventor of the Cherokee Alphabet

0   Sequoya was born in Loudon Country, Tennessee, in about 1760.

10   He was a member of the Cherokee tribe. As a young man, Sequoya

23   became a silversmith. His job was to make objects and jewelry from

35   silver. Sequoya traded his jewelry with the new settlers who had come to

48   his land. Sequoya had never learned how to read. He became interested

60   in how the settlers used marks on paper to record what they said. The

74   Cherokees called these marks "talking leaves." It became apparent to

84   Sequoya that being able to read and write was important. He realized that

97   the Cherokees had no way to do this. As a result, he decided to create a

113   Cherokee alphabet.

115   Sequoya worked for more than 10 years. He matched 85 Cherokee

126   syllables to a written symbol. Finally, the Cherokee alphabet was

136   finished. Sequoya's alphabet was easy to learn. Using this system, most

147   Cherokees learned to read and write in one week's time! Soon thousands

159   of Cherokees were literate. They were able to read the articles Sequoya

171   wrote about their history. The Cherokees made written laws. They also

182   developed a constitution. In the 1827, the Cherokee nation was formed.

193   They adopted English as their second language. Their first newspaper

203   was published in 1828. It was called the Cherokee Phoenix. Without

214   Sequoya's invention, none of this would have been possible. Sequoya is

225   honored in California's Sequoia National Park. The giant redwood trees

235   are named after him.

239

Total Words Read _____

− Errors _____

= CWPM _____

222   The Six-Minute Solution: A Reading Fluency Program (Intermediate Level)

Cinco de Mayo: A Celebration of Spirit

0   Cinco de Mayo is the 5th of May. It is a national holiday in Mexico.

15   It is second only to Mexican Independence Day.

23   On May 5, 1862, there was a famous battle. It was the Battle of

37   Puebla. A group of Mexican peasants fought against a French army. The

49   Mexican fighters were outnumbered. Also, they were poorly armed. But

59   they fought bravely and fiercely. The Mexicans won the battle in spite of

72   overwhelming odds. It was a triumph of a few over many.

83   This victory was very important to Mexicans. Cinco de Mayo is a

95   celebration of spirit. It is a symbol of freedom and liberty. It honors those

109   who fight for what they believe in against all odds.

119   People of Mexican descent everywhere celebrate Cinco de Mayo.

128   There are parades in many Mexican and American towns. There are also

140   speeches. Sometimes, the Battle of Puebla is reenacted. Cinco de Mayo is

152   a chance to celebrate Hispanic culture in general. It is also an opportunity

165   to celebrate the friendship between the U.S. and Mexico.

174

Total Words Read _____

− Errors _____

= CWPM _____

George Washington: America's First President

0   George Washington was born in Virginia on February 22, 1732. At

11   that time, Virginia was a colony of England. When George grew up, he

24   joined the Virginia army. He was a good soldier. Soon he became the

37   leader of the army. There were problems in the colonies. Many of the

50   people did not want to belong to England anymore. They felt that the

63   king of England did not treat them fairly. The king made the colonists pay

77   unfair taxes. The king did not want to give the colonies their freedom. So

91   they went to war. This war was called the Revolutionary War. It was also

105 called the War for Independence. George Washington was the leader of

116 the American army in this war. He was a good leader and helped America

130 to win the war.

134   After the war, the colonies became a new country. This country was

146 the United States of America. Americans wanted George Washington to be

157 the leader of the country. He was elected to be the first president in 1789.

172 George Washington was one of the best loved presidents in American

183 history. He is celebrated in many ways. For example, our nation's capital,

195 Washington, D.C., was named after George Washington. The famous

204 Washington Monument was built to honor George Washington. This tall,

214 pointed building is more than 555 feet high. People can go to the top of

229 the monument. They are able to look over the entire city of Washington,

242 D.C. George Washington's face is on our quarters and dollar bills. George

254 Washington's birthday is celebrated as a national holiday.

262

Total Words Read _____

- Errors _____

= CWPM _____

224   The Six-Minute Solution: A Reading Fluency Program (Intermediate Level)

The Cherokee Nation

0	The Cherokee homeland was the Appalachian Mountains. This
8	land is in the southeastern part of the U.S. The Cherokee lived there for
22	thousands of years. Then European settlers began to arrive.
31	In 1540, a Spanish explorer came to Cherokee land. His name was
43	Hernando de Soto. He was looking for gold. He and his men brought
56	diseases from Europe. These diseases killed many Cherokee. By the
66	1700s, many other European settlers had arrived. American colonists had
76	taken over Cherokee lands. The Cherokee tried to protect their homeland.
87	They signed a treaty with England. They fought with the British against
99	the colonists. The fight became the Revolutionary War. The colonists won
110	the war.
112	When Andrew Jackson became U.S. president in 1830, he declared
122	war on the Cherokee. He suggested the Indian Removal Bill. The U.S.
134	Congress made the bill law. It became legal for the U.S. to remove
147	the Cherokee and other Native Americans from their homelands. The
157	Cherokee were forced to march to what is now Oklahoma. There was
169	little food or water along the way. More than 4,000 Cherokee died on this
183	march. It came to be known as the "Trail of Tears."
194	The Cherokee suffered many hardships. In spite of these difficulties,
204	their culture has survived. Some Cherokee were able to move back to
216	their homeland. Others stayed in Oklahoma and made it their new home.
228	Today, there are three Cherokee reservations with more than 137,000
238	members.
239	

Total Words Read _____

− Errors _____

= CWPM _____

Automatic Word Lists

The *Automatic Word Lists* contain the most frequently encountered sight words in reading texts (Carroll, Davies, & Richman, 1971). These lists can be used to build fluency at the single-word level and to increase sight-word recognition. Struggling readers will benefit from additional fluency timings that focus on these high-frequency words.

Students who are reading fewer than 40 cwpm may need to work three to five times per week with *Automatic Word Lists* instead of *Grade-Level Practice Passages* during the timed fluency practices.

During small-group instruction, use *Automatic Word Lists* to provide additional fluency practice with single words.

Determining Which Automatic Word List to Use

To determine which *Automatic Word List* a student should use for practice, begin with *Set 1* and move sequentially through the sets. Time the student for one minute on each set, beginning with *Set 1*. When the student reads fewer than 60 cwpm, stop. This is the set the student should use to begin building sight-word fluency. Have the student practice with the set until he or she reads 60 cwpm on two subsequent timings. Then, move on to the next set.

Determining CWPM

To determine a student's cwpm on *Automatic Word Lists*, follow these steps:
1. Use the word-count numbers on the left side of the set to quickly determine the total number of words read.
2. Count the number of words that were errors.
3. Subtract the number of error words from the total number of words read.

Automatic Word List

0	the	of	and	to	a
5	in	that	is	was	he
10	for	it	with	as	his
15	on	be	at	by	I
20	this	had	not	are	but
25	the	of	and	to	a
30	in	that	is	was	he
35	for	it	with	as	his
40	on	be	at	by	I
45	this	had	not	are	but
50	the	of	and	to	a
55	in	that	is	was	he
60	for	it	with	as	his
65	on	be	at	by	I
70	this	had	not	are	but
75					

Total Words Read _____

\- Errors _____

= CWPM _____

Automatic Word List

0	from	or	have	an	they
5	which	one	you	were	her
10	all	she	there	would	their
15	we	him	been	has	when
20	who	will	more	no	if
25	from	or	have	an	they
30	which	one	you	were	her
35	all	she	there	would	their
40	we	him	been	has	when
45	who	will	more	no	if
50	from	or	have	an	they
55	which	one	you	were	her
60	all	she	there	would	their
65	we	him	been	has	when
70	who	will	more	no	if
75					

Total Words Read _____

\- Errors _____

\= CWPM _____

Automatic Word List

0	out	so	said	what	up
5	its	about	into	than	them
10	can	only	other	new	some
15	time	could	these	two	may
20	then	do	first	any	my
25	out	so	said	what	up
30	its	about	into	than	them
35	can	only	other	new	some
40	time	could	these	two	may
45	then	do	first	any	my
50	out	so	said	what	up
55	its	about	into	than	them
60	can	only	other	new	some
65	time	could	these	two	may
70	then	do	first	any	my
75					

Total Words Read _____

− Errors _____

= CWPM _____

Automatic Word List

0	now	such	like	our	over
5	man	me	even	most	made
10	after	also	did	many	before
15	must	through	back	years	where
20	much	your	way	well	down
25	now	such	like	our	over
30	man	me	even	most	made
35	after	also	did	many	before
40	must	through	back	years	where
45	much	your	way	well	down
50	now	such	like	our	over
55	man	me	even	most	made
60	after	also	did	many	before
65	must	through	back	years	where
70	much	your	way	well	down
75					

Total Words Read _____

– Errors _____

= CWPM _____

Automatic Word List

0	should	because	each	just	those
5	people	Mr.	how	too	little
10	us	state	good	very	make
15	world	still	see	own	men
20	work	long	here	get	both
25	should	because	each	just	those
30	people	Mr.	how	too	little
35	us	state	good	very	make
40	world	still	see	own	men
45	work	long	here	get	both
50	should	because	each	just	those
55	people	Mr.	how	too	little
60	us	state	good	very	make
65	world	still	see	own	men
70	work	long	here	get	both
75					

Total Words Read _____

− Errors _____

= CWPM _____

Automatic Word List

0	between	life	being	under	never
5	day	same	another	know	year
10	while	last	might	great	old
15	off	come	since	go	against
20	came	right	states	used	take
25	between	life	being	under	never
30	day	same	another	know	year
35	while	last	might	great	old
40	off	come	since	go	against
45	came	right	states	used	take
50	between	life	being	under	never
55	day	same	another	know	year
60	while	last	might	great	old
65	off	come	since	go	against
70	came	right	states	used	take
75					

Total Words Read _____

− Errors _____

= CWPM _____

Automatic Word List

0	three	himself	few	house	use
5	during	without	again	place	American
10	around	however	home	small	found
15	Mrs.	thought	went	say	part
20	once	high	general	upon	school
25	three	himself	few	house	use
30	during	without	again	place	American
35	around	however	home	small	found
40	Mrs.	thought	went	say	part
45	once	high	general	upon	school
50	three	himself	few	house	use
55	during	without	again	place	American
60	around	however	home	small	found
65	Mrs.	thought	went	say	part
70	once	high	general	upon	school
75					

Total Words Read _____

− Errors _____

= CWPM _____

Automatic Word List

0	every	don't	does	got	united
5	left	number	course	war	until
10	always	away	something	fact	water
15	though	less	public	put	think
20	almost	hand	enough	far	look
25	every	don't	does	got	united
30	left	number	course	war	until
35	always	away	something	fact	water
40	though	less	public	put	think
45	almost	hand	enough	far	look
50	every	don't	does	got	united
55	left	number	course	war	until
60	always	away	something	fact	water
65	though	less	public	put	think
70	almost	hand	enough	far	look
75					

Total Words Read _____

− Errors _____

= CWPM _____

The Six-Minute Solution: A Reading Fluency Program (Intermediate Level)

Automatic Word List

0	head	yet	government	system	set
5	better	told	nothing	night	end
10	why	didn't	know	eyes	find
15	going	look	asked	later	point
20	knew	city	next	program	business
25	head	yet	government	system	set
30	better	told	nothing	night	end
35	why	didn't	know	eyes	find
40	going	look	asked	later	point
45	knew	city	next	program	business
50	head	yet	government	system	set
55	better	told	nothing	night	end
60	why	didn't	know	eyes	find
65	going	look	asked	later	point
70	knew	city	next	program	business
75					

Total Words Read _____

− Errors _____

= CWPM _____

Automatic Word List

0	give	group	toward	days	young
5	let	room	president	side	social
10	present	given	several	order	national
15	second	possible	rather	per	face
20	among	form	important	often	things
25	give	group	toward	days	young
30	let	room	president	side	social
35	present	given	several	order	national
40	second	possible	rather	per	face
45	among	form	important	often	things
50	give	group	toward	days	young
55	let	room	president	side	social
60	present	given	several	order	national
65	second	possible	rather	per	face
70	among	form	important	often	things
75					

Total Words Read _____

− Errors _____

= CWPM _____

Automatic Word List

0	looked	early	white	John	case
5	become	large	need	big	four
10	within	fell	children	along	say
15	best	church	ever	least	power
20	development	thing	light	seemed	family
25	looked	early	white	John	case
30	become	large	need	big	four
35	within	fell	children	along	say
40	best	church	ever	least	power
45	development	thing	light	seemed	family
50	looked	early	white	John	case
55	become	large	need	big	four
60	within	fell	children	along	say
65	best	church	ever	least	power
70	development	thing	light	seemed	family
75					

Total Words Read _____

\- Errors _____

= CWPM _____

Automatic Word List

0	interest	want	members	others	mind
5	country	area	done	turned	although
10	open	God	service	problem	certain
15	kind	different	thus	began	door
20	help	means	sense	whole	matter
25	interest	want	members	others	mind
30	country	area	done	turned	although
35	open	God	service	problem	certain
40	kind	different	thus	began	door
45	help	means	sense	whole	matter
50	interest	want	members	others	mind
55	country	area	done	turned	although
60	open	God	service	problem	certain
65	kind	different	thus	began	door
70	help	means	sense	whole	matter
75					

Total Words Read _____

\- Errors _____

= CWPM _____

Automatic Word List

0	perhaps	itself	York	it's	times
5	law	human	line	above	name
10	example	action	company	hands	local
15	show	whether	five	history	gave
20	today	either	act	feet	across
25	perhaps	itself	York	it's	times
30	law	human	line	above	name
35	example	action	company	hands	local
40	show	whether	five	history	gave
45	today	either	act	feet	across
50	perhaps	itself	York	it's	times
55	law	human	line	above	name
60	example	action	company	hands	local
65	show	whether	five	history	gave
70	today	either	act	feet	across
75					

Total Words Read _____

\- Errors _____

\= CWPM _____

Automatic Word List

0	taken	past	quite	anything	seen
5	having	death	week	experience	body
10	word	half	really	field	am
15	car	words	already	themselves	I'm
20	information	tell	together	college	shall
25	taken	past	quite	anything	seen
30	having	death	week	experience	body
35	word	half	really	field	am
40	car	words	already	themselves	I'm
45	information	tell	together	college	shall
50	taken	past	quite	anything	seen
55	having	death	week	experience	body
60	word	half	really	field	am
65	car	words	already	themselves	I'm
70	information	tell	together	college	shall
75					

Total Words Read _____

– Errors _____

= CWPM _____

Automatic Word List

0	money	period	held	keep	sure
5	real	probably	free	seems	political
10	cannot	behind	Miss	question	air
15	office	making	brought	whose	special
20	major	heard	problems	federal	became
25	money	period	held	keep	sure
30	real	probably	free	seems	political
35	cannot	behind	Miss	question	air
40	office	making	brought	whose	special
45	major	heard	problems	federal	became
50	money	period	held	keep	sure
55	real	probably	free	seems	political
60	cannot	behind	Miss	question	air
65	office	making	brought	whose	special
70	major	heard	problems	federal	became
75					

Total Words Read _____

– Errors _____

= CWPM _____

Automatic Word List

0	study	ago	moment	available	known
5	result	street	economic	boy	position
10	reason	change	south	board	individual
15	job	areas	society	west	close
20	turn	love	community	true	court
25	study	ago	moment	available	known
30	result	street	economic	boy	position
35	reason	change	south	board	individual
40	job	areas	society	west	close
45	turn	love	community	true	court
50	study	ago	moment	available	known
55	result	street	economic	boy	position
60	reason	change	south	board	individual
65	job	areas	society	west	close
70	turn	love	community	true	court
75					

Total Words Read _____

− Errors _____

= CWPM _____

Automatic Word List

0	force	full	course	seem	wife
5	future	age	wanted	department	voice
10	center	woman	control	common	policy
15	necessary	following	front	sometimes	six
20	girl	clear	further	land	run
25	force	full	course	seem	wife
30	future	age	wanted	department	voice
35	center	woman	control	common	policy
40	necessary	following	front	sometimes	six
45	girl	clear	further	land	run
50	force	full	course	seem	wife
55	future	age	wanted	department	voice
60	center	woman	control	common	policy
65	necessary	following	front	sometimes	six
70	girl	clear	further	land	run
75					

Total Words Read _____

− Errors _____

= CWPM _____

Automatic Word List

0	students	provide	feel	party	able
5	mother	music	education	university	child
10	effect	level	stood	military	town
15	short	morning	total	outside	rate
20	figure	class	art	century	Washington
25	students	provide	feel	party	able
30	mother	music	education	university	child
35	effect	level	stood	military	town
40	short	morning	total	outside	rate
45	figure	class	art	century	Washington
50	students	provide	feel	party	able
55	mother	music	education	university	child
60	effect	level	stood	military	town
65	short	morning	total	outside	rate
70	figure	class	art	century	Washington
75					

Total Words Read _____

\- Errors _____

= CWPM _____

Automatic Word List

0	north	usually	plan	leave	therefore
5	evidence	too	million	sound	black
10	strong	hard	various	says	believe
15	type	value	play	surface	soon
20	mean	near	lines	table	peace
25	north	usually	plan	leave	therefore
30	evidence	too	million	sound	black
35	strong	hard	various	says	believe
40	type	value	play	surface	soon
45	mean	near	lines	table	peace
50	north	usually	plan	leave	therefore
55	evidence	too	million	sound	black
60	strong	hard	various	says	believe
65	type	value	play	surface	soon
70	mean	near	lines	table	peace
75					

Total Words Read _____

− Errors _____

= CWPM _____

Automatic Word List

0	modern	tax	road	red	book
5	personal	process	situation	minutes	increases
10	schools	idea	English	alone	women
15	gone	nor	living	months	America
20	started	longer	Dr.	cut	finally
25	modern	tax	road	red	book
30	personal	process	situation	minutes	increases
35	schools	idea	English	alone	women
40	gone	nor	living	months	America
45	started	longer	Dr.	cut	finally
50	modern	tax	road	red	book
55	personal	process	situation	minutes	increases
60	schools	idea	English	alone	women
65	gone	nor	living	months	America
70	started	longer	Dr.	cut	finally
75					

Total Words Read _____

– Errors _____

= CWPM _____

Automatic Word List

0	third	secretary	nature	private	section
5	greater	call	fire	expected	needed
10	that's	kept	ground	view	values
15	everything	pressure	dark	basis	space
20	east	father	required	union	spirit
25	third	secretary	nature	private	section
30	greater	call	fire	expected	needed
35	that's	kept	ground	view	values
40	everything	pressure	dark	basis	space
45	east	father	required	union	spirit
50	third	secretary	nature	private	section
55	greater	call	fire	expected	needed
60	that's	kept	ground	view	values
65	everything	pressure	dark	basis	space
70	east	father	required	union	spirit
75					

Total Words Read _____

– Errors _____

= CWPM _____

Automatic Word List

0	except	complete	wrote	I'll	moved
5	support	return	conditions	recent	attention
10	late	particular	nations	hope	live
15	costs	else	brown	taking	couldn't
20	hours	person	forces	beyond	report
25	except	complete	wrote	I'll	moved
30	support	return	conditions	recent	attention
35	late	particular	nations	hope	live
40	costs	else	brown	taking	couldn't
45	hours	person	forces	beyond	report
50	except	complete	wrote	I'll	moved
55	support	return	conditions	recent	attention
60	late	particular	nations	hope	live
65	costs	else	brown	taking	couldn't
70	hours	person	forces	beyond	report
75					

Total Words Read _____

– Errors _____

= CWPM _____

 The Six-Minute Solution: A Reading Fluency Program (Intermediate Level)

Automatic Word List

0	coming	inside	dead	low	stage
5	material	read	instead	lost	St.
10	heart	looking	miles	data	added
15	pay	amount	followed	feeling	single
20	makes	research	including	basic	hundred
25	coming	inside	dead	low	stage
30	material	read	instead	lost	St.
35	heart	looking	miles	data	added
40	pay	amount	followed	feeling	single
45	makes	research	including	basic	hundred
50	coming	inside	dead	low	stage
55	material	read	instead	lost	St.
60	heart	looking	miles	data	added
65	pay	amount	followed	feeling	single
70	makes	research	including	basic	hundred
75					

Total Words Read _____

– Errors _____

= CWPM _____

Automatic Word List

0	move	industry	cold	developed	tried
5	simply	hold	can't	reached	committee
10	island	defense	equipment	son	actually
15	shown	religious	ten	river	getting
20	central	beginning	sort	received	doing
25	move	industry	cold	developed	tried
30	simply	hold	can't	reached	committee
35	island	defense	equipment	son	actually
40	shown	religious	ten	river	getting
45	central	beginning	sort	received	doing
50	move	industry	cold	developed	tried
55	simply	hold	can't	reached	committee
60	island	defense	equipment	son	actually
65	shown	religious	ten	river	getting
70	central	beginning	sort	received	doing
75					

Total Words Read _____

− Errors _____

= CWPM _____

Automatic Word List

0	terms	trying	friends	rest	medical
5	care	especially	picture	indeed	administration
10	fine	subject	higher	difficult	simple
15	range	building	wall	meeting	walked
20	cent	floor	foreign	bring	similar
25	terms	trying	friends	rest	medical
30	care	especially	picture	indeed	administration
35	fine	subject	higher	difficult	simple
40	range	building	wall	meeting	walked
45	cent	floor	foreign	bring	similar
50	terms	trying	friends	rest	medical
55	care	especially	picture	indeed	administration
60	fine	subject	higher	difficult	simple
65	range	building	wall	meeting	walked
70	cent	floor	foreign	bring	similar
75					

Total Words Read _____

\- Errors _____

= CWPM _____

Vowels/Vowel Combinations (ay, ai, au, aw, a_e, ar)

0	ay	ai	au	aw	a_e
5	ar	aw	ay	a_e	au
10	aw	ay	ai	au	ar
15	au	ai	ar	a_e	ay
20	ai	aw	a_e	ar	ay
25	ay	ai	au	aw	a_e
30	ar	aw	ay	a_e	au
35	aw	ay	ai	au	ar
40	au	ai	ar	a_e	ay
45	ai	aw	a_e	ar	ay
50	ar	ai	a_e	aw	au
55	au	aw	a_e	ai	ar
60					

Vowels/Vowel Combinations (ay, ai, au, aw, a_e, ar) With Words

0	delay	tray	gray	away	spray
5	plain	snail	paint	praise	wait
10	haul	launch	author	cause	taught
15	yawn	hawk	lawn	straw	awful
20	late	came	grade	space	save
25	party	harm	charge	shark	garden
30	yarn	gate	raw	sauce	train
35	play	plate	scarf	Spain	barn
40	haunt	march	bait	railway	draw
45	inflate	crawl	relay	crate	state
50	August	artist	audience	shawl	trail
55	thaw	display	quake	brain	caught
60					

Vowels/Vowel Combinations (er, ee, ea, oi, oy, or)

0	er	ee	ea	oi	oy
5	or	oy	er	oi	ea
10	ee	or	oi	er	oy
15	ea	oi	ee	oy	or
20	oi	ee	or	er	oy
25	oy	er	oi	ee	ea
30	er	ee	ea	oi	oy
35	or	oy	er	oi	ea
40	ee	or	oi	er	oy
45	ea	oi	ee	oy	or
50	oi	ee	or	er	oy
55	oy	er	oi	ee	ea
60					

Vowels/Vowel Combinations (er, ee, ea, oi, oy, or) With Words

0	stern	nerve	clerk	germ	herb
5	steer	green	fleet	redeem	wheel
10	peach	wreath	cleat	feast	clean
15	noise	coin	spoil	moist	point
20	enjoy	annoy	ploy	destroy	boy
25	born	cork	storm	report	word
30	joint	stork	cheek	employ	teacher
35	spoil	concern	yearn	serve	beet
40	adverb	join	chord	merge	speech
45	heave	sleek	avoid	toys	perch
50	choice	breeze	please	porch	smear
55	score	person	cowboy	sirloin	hoist
60					

Vowels/Vowel Combinations (ir, ur, oa, ou, ow)

0	ir	ur	oa	ou	ow
5	ow	ir	ou	ur	oa
10	ou	oa	ir	ow	ur
15	ur	ow	ur	ir	ou
20	oa	ou	ow	ur	ir
25	ir	ur	oa	ou	ow
30	ow	ir	ou	ur	oa
35	ou	oa	ir	ow	ur
40	ur	ow	ur	ir	ou
45	oa	ou	ow	ur	ir
50	ir	ur	oa	ou	ow
55	ow	ir	ou	ur	oa
60					

Vowels/Vowel Combinations (ir, ur, oa, ou, ow) With Words

0	bird	shirt	circle	squirt	first
5	burn	return	sunburn	unhurt	suburb
10	coach	railroad	foam	coast	float
15	mouth	hound	shout	noun	count
20	prowl	gown	brown	powder	tower
25	down	curve	twirl	burst	croak
30	broach	firm	hurt	pound	drown
35	churn	nurse	boast	chirp	soak
40	owl	mount	church	charcoal	roast
45	throat	disturb	power	purple	flower
50	growl	circus	third	load	curl
55	firm	urge	south	crown	grown
60					

Vowels/Vowel Combinations oo (as in "moon"), oo (as in "look"), a_e, i_e, o_e, u_e

0	oo	a_e	oo	i_e	u_e
5	i_e	oo	u_e	oo	a_e
10	o_e	oo	i_e	a_e	u_e
15	oo	u_e	a_e	oo	i_e
20	a_e	i_e	oo	o_e	u_e
25	u_e	a_e	oo	i_e	o_e
30	oo	a_e	oo	i_e	u_e
35	i_e	oo	u_e	oo	a_e
40	o_e	oo	i_e	a_e	u_e
45	oo	u_e	a_e	oo	i_e
50	a_e	i_e	oo	o_e	u_e
55	u_e	a_e	oo	i_e	o_e
60					

Vowels/Vowel Combinations oo (as in "moon"), oo (as in "look"), a_e, i_e, o_e, u_e With Words

0	moon	smooth	troop	school	proof
5	book	wooden	good	stood	shook
10	cape	trade	place	stage	brake
15	bribe	pride	knife	smile	mine
20	note	stone	choke	those	hope
25	cube	muse	cute	fuse	mule
30	zoom	tribe	mute	shade	clove
35	took	good	fool	graze	yule
40	cone	brook	robe	bride	shade
45	wood	mood	wrote	wise	dome
50	lone	grape	while	fuse	spool
55	shore	flute	wore	while	stood
60					

Prefixes (un-, re-, in-, im-, il-, dis-)

0	un	re	in	im	il
5	il	un	dis	in	im
10	dis	il	im	in	re
15	re	in	un	im	il
20	im	un	in	re	dis
25	in	dis	re	un	il
30	un	re	in	im	il
35	il	un	dis	in	im
40	dis	il	im	in	re
45	re	in	un	im	il
50	im	un	in	re	dis
55	in	dis	re	un	il
60					

Prefixes (un-, re-, in-, im-, il-, dis-) With Words

0	unable	unclip	uncap	unclear	unstuck
5	refill	restate	rewind	repaid	reuse
10	indoors	insane	insight	indirect	inept
15	impure	improper	immature	impolite	imperfect
20	illegal	illiterate	illiteracy	illegible	illegally
25	disable	dislike	disturb	disgrace	distrust
30	unable	unclip	uncap	unclear	unstuck
35	refill	restate	rewind	repaid	reuse
40	indoors	insane	insight	indirect	inept
45	impure	improper	immature	impolite	imperfect
50	illegal	illiterate	illiteracy	illegible	illegally
55	disable	dislike	disturb	disgrace	distrust
60					

Prefixes (en-, em-, non-, over-, mis-)

0	en	em	non	over	mis
5	mis	over	non	em	en
10	non	en	mis	over	em
15	over	non	en	mis	em
20	em	mis	non	en	over
25	non	en	over	em	mis
30	en	em	non	over	mis
35	mis	over	non	em	en
40	non	en	mis	over	em
45	over	non	en	mis	em
50	em	mis	non	en	over
55	non	en	over	em	mis
60					

Prefixes (en-, em-, non-, over-, mis-) With Words

0	enable	encode	enclose	enforce	enlarge
5	employ	embark	embattle	embroil	embed
10	nonfiction	nonstop	nonslip	nonliving	nondrip
15	overact	overfill	overpay	overdo	overload
20	mislead	misorder	misname	misread	mistreat
25	enable	encode	enclose	enforce	enlarge
30	employ	embark	embattle	embroil	embed
35	nonfiction	nonstop	nonslip	nonliving	nondrip
40	overact	overfill	overpay	overdo	overload
45	mislead	misorder	misname	misread	mistreat
50	enable	encode	enclose	enforce	enlarge
55	employ	embark	embattle	embroil	embed
60					

Prefixes (sub-, pre-, inter-, fore-, de-)

0	sub	pre	inter	fore	de
5	de	fore	inter	pre	sub
10	inter	sub	fore	de	pre
15	pre	inter	de	sub	fore
20	fore	sub	de	inter	pre
25	de	pre	inter	fore	sub
30	sub	pre	inter	fore	de
35	de	fore	inter	pre	sub
40	inter	sub	fore	de	pre
45	pre	inter	de	sub	fore
50	fore	sub	de	inter	pre
55	de	pre	inter	fore	sub
60					

Prefixes (sub-, pre-, inter-, fore-, de-) With Words

0	subgroup	subclass	submarine	subway	submerge
5	precut	preplan	preheat	prejudge	pretrial
10	interact	interlock	intermix	intersect	interstate
15	forearm	forego	forewarn	foreground	forecast
20	deface	defrost	derail	deflate	dethrone
25	subgroup	subclass	submarine	subway	submerge
30	precut	preplan	preheat	prejudge	pretrial
35	interact	interlock	intermix	intersect	interstate
40	forearm	forego	forewarn	foreground	forecast
45	deface	defrost	derail	deflate	dethrone
50	subgroup	subclass	submarine	subway	submerge
55	precut	preplan	preheat	prejudge	pretrial
60					

Prefixes (trans-, super-, semi-, anti-, mid-)

0	trans	super	semi	anti	mid
5	semi	trans	anti	mid	super
10	mid	anti	semi	super	trans
15	super	mid	trans	semi	anti
20	anti	semi	mid	trans	super
25	semi	mid	super	anti	trans
30	trans	super	semi	anti	mid
35	semi	trans	anti	mid	super
40	mid	anti	semi	super	trans
45	super	mid	trans	semi	anti
50	anti	semi	mid	trans	super
55	semi	mid	super	anti	trans
60					

Prefixes (trans-, super-, semi-, anti-, mid-) With Words

0	transfer	transmit	transfix	transplant	transcript
5	superman	superpower	supervise	supersede	superstar
10	semifinal	semidry	semipro	semiskilled	semiautomatic
15	antigravity	antidote	antisocial	antibacterial	antitrust
20	midday	midnight	midweek	midwinter	midrange
25	transfer	transmit	transfix	transplant	transcript
30	superman	superpower	supervise	supersede	superstar
35	semifinal	semidry	semipro	semiskilled	semiautomatic
40	antigravity	antidote	antisocial	antibacterial	antitrust
45	midday	midnight	midweek	midwinter	midrange
50	transfer	transmit	transfix	transplant	transcript
55	superman	superpower	supervise	supersede	superstar
60					

Prefixes (under-, ex-, be-, pro-, com-)

0	under	ex	be	pro	com
5	com	pro	be	ex	under
10	ex	under	pro	com	be
15	pro	ex	be	under	com
20	under	ex	be	pro	com
25	com	pro	be	ex	under
30	ex	under	pro	com	be
35	pro	ex	be	under	com
40	com	pro	be	ex	under
45	ex	under	pro	com	be
50	pro	ex	be	under	com
55	com	pro	be	ex	under
60					

Prefixes (under-, ex-, be-, pro-, com-) With Words

0	undercut	underage	undersea	undergo	underfoot
5	explode	explore	expend	expel	export
10	become	becalm	bedeck	bedazzle	bedevil
15	proclaim	prolong	project	propel	program
20	combine	combustion	command	commence	commit
25	undercut	underage	undersea	undergo	underfoot
30	explode	explore	expend	expel	export
35	become	becalm	bedeck	bedazzle	bedevil
40	proclaim	prolong	project	propel	program
45	combine	combustion	command	commence	commit
50	undercut	underage	undersea	undergo	underfoot
55	explode	explore	expend	expel	export
60					

Suffixes (-ed, -ing, -ly, -er, -or)

0	ed	ing	ly	er	or
5	or	er	ly	ing	ed
10	ly	ed	er	or	ing
15	ing	or	ed	ly	er
20	er	ly	or	ed	ing
25	ed	ing	ly	er	or
30	or	er	ly	ing	ed
35	ly	ed	er	or	ing
40	ing	or	ed	ly	er
45	er	ly	or	ed	ing
50	ed	ing	ly	er	or
55	or	er	ly	ing	ed
60					

Suffixes (-ed, -ing, -ly, -er, -or) With Words

0	caved	chimed	jammed	smiled	used
5	fixing	matching	saying	wishing	floating
10	softly	quietly	nicely	loudly	quickly
15	banker	flier	painter	teacher	farmer
20	actor	sailor	visitor	governor	senator
25	caved	chimed	jammed	smiled	used
30	fixing	matching	saying	wishing	floating
35	softly	quietly	nicely	loudly	quickly
40	banker	flier	painter	teacher	farmer
45	actor	sailor	visitor	governor	senator
50	caved	chimed	jammed	smiled	used
55	fixing	matching	saying	wishing	floating
60					

Suffixes (-ion, -tion, -ible, -able, -al)

0	ion	tion	ible	able	al
5	al	able	tion	ible	ion
10	tion	ible	al	ion	able
15	ible	al	able	tion	ion
20	able	ion	ible	al	tion
25	ion	tion	ible	able	al
30	al	able	tion	ible	ion
35	tion	ible	al	ion	able
40	ible	al	able	tion	ion
45	able	ion	ible	al	tion
50	ion	tion	ible	able	al
55	al	able	tion	ible	ion
60					

Suffixes (-ion, -tion, -ible, -able, -al) With Words

0	passion	occasion	concussion	diversion	profusion
5	competion	description	attention	action	adoption
10	edible	horrible	possible	visible	digestible
15	readable	durable	agreeable	noticeable	capable
20	bifocal	clinical	chemical	criminal	general
25	passion	occasion	concussion	diversion	profusion
30	competion	description	attention	action	adoption
35	edible	horrible	possible	visible	digestible
40	readable	durable	agreeable	noticeable	capable
45	bifocal	clinical	chemical	criminal	general
50	passion	occasion	concussion	diversion	profusion
55	competion	description	attention	action	adoption
60					

Suffixes (-ation, -ition, -ial, -y, -ness)

0	ation	ition	ial	y	ness
5	ness	y	ition	ial	ation
10	y	ition	ial	ation	ition
15	ition	ial	y	ness	ation
20	ial	ation	ness	ition	y
25	ation	ition	ial	y	ness
30	ness	y	ition	ial	ation
35	y	ition	ial	ation	ition
40	ition	ial	y	ness	ation
45	ial	ation	ness	ition	y
50	ation	ition	ial	y	ness
55	ness	y	ition	ial	ation
60					

Suffixes (-ation, -ition, -ial, -y, -ness) With Words

0 application	admiration	quotation	relation	creation
5 ambition	definition	audition	condition	exhibition
10 financial	artificial	crucial	judicial	essential
15 editorial	territorial	ceremonial	industrial	memorial
20 bloody	frosty	itchy	stormy	tricky
25 dampness	kindness	happiness	shyness	nearness
30 application	admiration	quotation	relation	creation
35 ambition	definition	audition	condition	exhibition
40 financial	artificial	crucial	judicial	essential
45 editorial	territorial	ceremonial	industrial	memorial
50 bloody	frosty	itchy	stormy	tricky
55 dampness	kindness	happiness	shyness	nearness
60				

Suffixes (-ity, -ty, -ment, -ic, -ous)

0	ity	ty	ment	ic	ous
5	ous	ic	ty	ment	ity
10	ic	ous	ity	ty	ment
15	ty	ment	ic	ous	ity
20	ment	ity	ous	ty	ic
25	ity	ty	ment	ic	ous
30	ous	ic	ty	ment	ity
35	ic	ous	ity	ty	ment
40	ty	ment	ic	ous	ity
45	ment	ity	ous	ty	ic
50	ity	ty	ment	ic	ous
55	ous	ic	ty	ment	ity
60					

Suffixes (-ity, -ty, -ment, -ic, -ous) With Words

0	unity	agility	falsity	necessity	humidity
5	honesty	specialty	safety	loyalty	amnesty
10	agreement	payment	treatment	pavement	statement
15	civic	volcanic	artistic	magnetic	heroic
20	fabulous	numerous	enormous	vigorous	gorgeous
25	unity	agility	falsity	necessity	humidity
30	honesty	specialty	safety	loyalty	amnesty
35	agreement	payment	treatment	pavement	statement
40	civic	volcanic	artistic	magnetic	heroic
45	fabulous	numerous	enormous	vigorous	monstrous
50	unity	agility	falsity	necessity	humidity
55	honesty	specialty	safety	loyalty	amnesty
60					

Suffixes (-eous, -ious, -en, -er, -ive)

0	eous	ious	en	er	ive
5	ive	er	ious	en	eous
10	en	eous	ive	ious	er
15	ious	ive	er	ive	eous
20	er	en	eous	ious	ive
25	eous	ious	en	er	ive
30	ive	er	ious	en	eous
35	en	eous	ive	ious	er
40	ious	ive	er	ive	eous
45	er	en	eous	ious	ive
50	eous	ious	en	er	ive
55	ive	er	ious	en	eous
60					

Suffixes (-eous, -ious, -en, -er, -ive) With Words

0	gorgeous	nauseous	spontaneous	courteous	erroneous
5	cautious	curious	delicious	furious	nutritious
10	broken	glisten	quicken	thicken	darken
15	shorter	higher	deeper	warmer	narrower
20	adoptive	captive	massive	inactive	incentive
25	gorgeous	nauseous	spontaneous	courteous	erroneous
30	cautious	curious	delicious	furious	nutritious
35	broken	glisten	quicken	thicken	darken
40	shorter	higher	deeper	warmer	narrower
45	adoptive	captive	massive	inactive	incentive
50	gorgeous	nauseous	spontaneous	courteous	erroneous
55	cautious	curious	delicious	furious	nutritious
60					

Suffixes (-ative, -itive, -ful, -less, -est)

0	ative	itive	ful	less	est
5	est	less	ful	itive	ative
10	ful	ative	less	itive	est
15	less	itive	ful	est	ative
20	ative	itive	ful	less	est
25	est	less	ful	itive	ative
30	ful	ative	less	itive	est
35	less	itive	ful	est	ative
40	ative	itive	ful	less	est
45	est	less	ful	itive	ative
50	ful	ative	less	itive	est
55	less	itive	ful	est	ative
60					

Suffixes (-ative, -itive, -ful, -less, -est) With Words

0	comparative	conservative	informative	narrative	talkative
5	competitive	primitive	sensitive	definitive	fugitive
10	cheerful	colorful	healthful	thoughtful	peaceful
15	timeless	doubtless	cloudless	worthless	fearless
20	warmest	smoothest	fullest	brightest	poorest
25	comparative	conservative	informative	narrative	talkative
30	competitive	primitive	sensitive	definitive	fugitive
35	cheerful	colorful	healthful	thoughtful	peaceful
40	timeless	doubtless	cloudless	worthless	fearless
45	warmest	smoothest	fullest	brightest	poorest
50	comparative	conservative	informative	narrative	talkative
55	competitive	primitive	sensitive	definitive	fugitive
60					

SIX MINUTE

Appendix

Q1. **Is the classroom noise level distracting when so many students are reading aloud at the same time?**

ANSWER: Although teachers are initially concerned about the noise level, they usually find that if students are well trained in partnership behavior (i.e., "lean in and whisper"), noise level is not an issue. Partnerships are usually reading different passages, so there is little or no echo-reading.

The noise level does not bother most students because they are being raised in a multisensory world. However, if the noise is distracting to a sensitive student, that partnership could read in a corner of the room or outside the classroom door.

Q2. **What happens when one partner is absent?**

ANSWER: For the occasional absence, there are several options:

Option 1—The teacher or an instructional aide could substitute for the absent partner. If two different partnerships have an absent partner, the teacher can listen to one student read for one minute and then go to the other partnership and listen to that student read for the second minute. The solo partners would whisper-read to themselves during the second timing.

Option 2—Temporary partners could be assigned just for the day based on attendance. For example, if two partnerships were reading passages at the same readability level and each had an absent partner for the day, a temporary partnership could be formed.

Option 3—Students from a neighboring classroom could be assigned to substitute for an absent partner.

Q3. **What do you do in the case of a permanent odd number of (e.g., 27) students assigned to one class or period?**

ANSWER: The teacher could assign some students to a triad rather than a partnership. Three students whose fluency and reading levels closely match would be selected to form a triad. Partner 1 (the strongest reader) and Partner 2a (the next-strongest reader) will read on the first day with Partner 2b monitoring. On the second day, Partners 2a and 2b will read and Partner 1 will monitor. On the third day, Partner 1 and Partner 2b will read, and Partner 2a will monitor. On the fourth day, Partner 1 and Partner 2a will read again, and Partner 2b will monitor. **Note:** If there are fluency triads in a classroom, the teacher would need to implement partner fluency **four times a week** so that each member of the triad would have an opportunity to read the *Practice Passage* three times during the week.

Q4. **What happens if a student's skills are so far below that of the rest of the class that he/she cannot be matched with a partner?**

ANSWER: In that case, the "outlying" student could be paired with a student tutor, a classroom volunteer, or a paraprofessional. Another possibility would be to audiotape the reading material and have the student work independently listening to the tape rather than reading to a partner.

Q5. **Should a student who reads fewer than 40 cwpm still engage in reading *Practice Passages*?**

ANSWER: Students who read fewer than 40 cwpm most likely need to increase their sight-word vocabulary. These students could benefit from fluency practice at the single-word level with *Automatic Word Lists* (see *Fluency Building Sheets*). The goal would be for the student to eventually read 60 cwpm of high-frequency words.

It is important to have students reading *Practice Passages* for fluency building as soon as possible to encourage skill generalization. It is possible that some students might need to practice both types of fluency—single-word and *Practice Passage*—on an alternating basis.

Q6. **What if neither partner knows some of the words in their *Practice Passage*?**

ANSWER: On Mondays, all student partnerships are given new *Practice Passages* to work with during the week. Before students begin fluency practice, they preview the entire passage for accuracy and underline unknown words. The teacher should monitor carefully, supplying any unknown words to either partner. It is important to make certain that students are accurate *before* they begin fluency building practice. **Note:** A properly placed student is 91%–96% accurate at his/her instructional reading level. If the accuracy rate is below that range, the student needs to be reassigned a *Practice Passage* at a lower readability level.

Q7. **How often should the teacher review partnership folders?**

ANSWER: At least once a month. Keep in mind, though, that during the daily six-minute fluency practice, the teacher should be walking around the room and monitoring students very closely. Daily monitoring is essential because it enables the teacher to have a good idea of how each partnership is functioning and progressing.

Q8. **How does the teacher know when to move a partnership up to the next readability level?**

ANSWER: Generally speaking, students will work at the same readability level for at least six weeks. However, some students will need to remain on the same level much longer. When a teacher notices that partners are reaching the upper range of fluency at their level, it is time to conference with the partners and discuss moving up to the next level.

Remember that students must practice fluency building on material they are reading 91%–96% accurately. On the other hand, they need to progress to the next level as soon as they are ready in order to accelerate their reading gains.

Q9. **How often should partnerships be changed?**

ANSWER: We recommend that students be assessed for fluency three times during a school year. Based on that fluency data, partnerships are then reassigned. During the intervals, some partnerships may remain the same while others may need to be changed. As a general rule, change partnerships if:

- Partners are progressing at very uneven rates.
- Partners are not cooperating with each other, even after teacher intervention and conferencing.

Q10. **Should students practice fluency at their *independent* or *instructional* level?**

ANSWER: As with many situations in education, the answer depends on the circumstances. Generally speaking, younger students and those reading close to grade level can easily practice fluency building at their independent reading level.

However, for older students and those reading significantly below grade level, time is of the essence! These students need to close the reading gap as quickly as possible. Therefore, it may be more appropriate for them to practice fluency building at their instructional reading level.

Keep in mind that students need to practice fluency with material they can read with a high degree of accuracy. Accuracy should *always* be stressed before fluency; therefore, it is imperative that teachers make certain that all fluency partners are accurate in reading their respective *Practice Passages* before they begin fluency practice. This is accomplished during an accuracy check on the first day of fluency practice with a new *Practice Passage*.

Fluency Assessment Report

STUDENT NAME: _____   GRADE: _____

TEACHER: _____   DATE: _____

EXPECTED CWPM FOR THIS GRADE LEVEL: _____

Dear Parent,

    Fluency training is an important part of our language arts program. We assess students _____ times a year and report the scores as correct words per minute (cwpm). Reading smoothly, efficiently, and accurately is a focus of our reading program. We practice our reading fluency skills in many ways. By the time students reach the fourth grade, they should be able to read at least 100 words per minute orally and their reading rates should increase every year. You can use this figure as a yardstick to measure your child's oral reading fluency rate.

Date	1 Timing Correct Words per Minute	Date	2 Timing Correct Words per Minute	Gain in Correct Words per Minute	Date	3 Timing Correct Words per Minute	Gain in Correct Words per Minute	Percent of Improvement During the Entire Year

Initial Assessment Record

TEACHER: _____

CLASS: _____ DATE: _____

STUDENT NAME	ASSESSMENT 1—ORAL READING RATE (CWPM)	ASSESSMENT 2—INSTRUCTIONAL READING LEVEL

Rank students according to oral reading rate and then instructional reading level.

Fluency Record

NAME: _____ CLASS: _____

PASSAGE NUMBER: _____

PARTNER: _____ DATE: _____

PASSAGE #	DATE	CWPM	DATE	CWPM	DATE	CWPM	DATE	CWPM	DATE	CWPM

CWPM = correct words per minute

Fluency Graph 1

NAME: _____ CLASS: _____

PARTNER: _____ DATE: _____

Correct Words Per Minute															
200															
195															
190															
185															
180															
175															
170															
165															
160															
155															
150															
145															
140															
135															
130															
125															
120															
115															
110															
105															
100															
95															
90															
85															
80															
75															
70															
65															
60															
55															
50															
45															
40															
35															
30															
25															
20															
15															
10															
5															
DATE															
PASSAGE NUMBER															

The Six-Minute Solution: A Reading Fluency Program (Intermediate Level)

Fluency Graph 2

NAME: _____   CLASS: _____

PARTNER: _____   DATE: _____

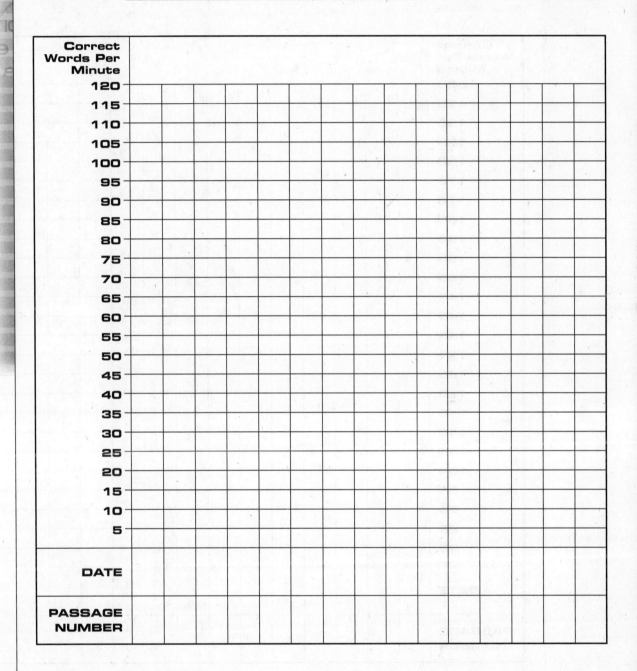

Correct Words Per Minute

120
115
110
105
100
95
90
85
80
75
70
65
60
55
50
45
40
35
30
25
20
15
10
5

DATE

PASSAGE NUMBER

Fluency Graph 3

NAME: _____ CLASS: _____

PARTNER: _____ DATE: _____

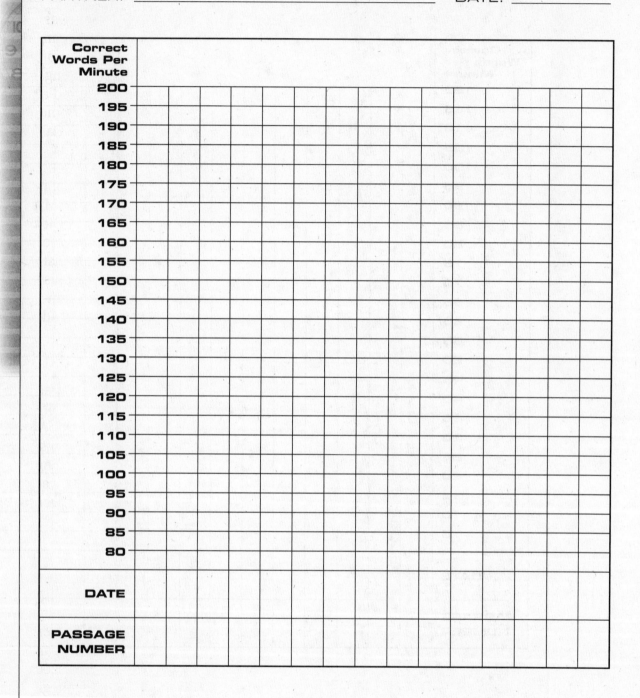

Correct Words Per Minute															
200															
195															
190															
185															
180															
175															
170															
165															
160															
155															
150															
145															
140															
135															
130															
125															
120															
115															
110															
105															
100															
95															
90															
85															
80															
DATE															
PASSAGE NUMBER															

Three *Six-Minute Solution* Field Tests

Field Test I

A description of the *Six-Minute Solution* intervention program was published as "Working with Words: A Summer Reading Intervention Program" (Adams, Brown, and Van Zant, 2000) and as "Summer Reading Intervention Program Prepares Fifth Grade Students for Middle School Reading Challenges" (Adams, Brown, and Van Zant, 1999). *Six-Minute Solution* is also featured as part of "Teaching Reading in Every Classroom," an online staff development program, at the San Diego County Office of Education, San Diego, California.

Location

In the summer of 1999, the authors developed a summer reading intervention program for at-risk middle school readers at Meadowbrook Middle School (in Poway, California, a town 20 miles north of downtown San Diego). The *Six-Minute Solution* model was a critical component. Meadowbrook, built in 1964, is the oldest middle school in the Poway Unified School District. The 1,515 students represent a rich diversity of cultural, ethnic, linguistic, and religious backgrounds. Thirty-one percent of the students are non-Anglo, the largest ethnic group being Filipino. Of the 1,515 students, 108 students speak a language other than English in their homes.

Participants

Fifty-two students (who were reading at least two years below grade level) were selected to attend this 24-day summer school intervention program. Additionally, 30 of the 52 intervention program participants (58 percent) had previously been identified as eligible for special education services or English Language Learner (ELL) support. Students were in this reading class two hours a day, Monday through Friday. The teacher-student ratio was 1 to 26 for each class. Students were divided into two homogeneous classes based on instructional levels.

Procedure

Using the assessment procedures described in this book, students were assigned fluency partners. These student partners practiced fluency daily—either with *Automatic Word Lists* or with *Practice Passages* at their instructional reading levels. Students also were taught a multisyllabic word decoding strategy using the *REWARDS: Reading Excellence, Word Attack, and Rate Development Strategies* program (Archer, Gleason, and Vachon; 2000). Students received direct instruction in reading comprehension strategies and in paragraph writing. Additionally, students participated in "novel partnerships" in which they read trade books to each other in five-minute segments and practiced oral comprehension strategies.

Reading gains recorded by the summer school intervention students were outstanding in many cases. Pre-assessment fluency scores on a sixth-grade passage ranged from a low of 40 correct words per minute (cwpm) to a high of 136 cwpm. Post-assessment rates ranged from a low of 61 cwpm to a high of 195 cwpm. The average reading fluency gain was 36 percent.

Comprehension gains were also considerable. Pre-assessment reading comprehension scores ranged from a Lexile level of 260 (first grade) to a high of 905 (fifth grade). Post-assessment scores ranged from a low of 395 (second grade) to a high of 1,050 (sixth grade). One class gained an average of 166 Lexile points (a gain equivalent to between one and two grade years). The second class gained an average of 133 Lexile points (a one-half to one-year grade equivalent). As measured by pre- and post-Lexile readability scales, the overall growth in reading comprehension was 26 percent.

Note: A **Lexile** is a measure of the reading difficulty of a text. It is a number on a scale representing the semantic difficulty and the syntactic complexity of the text. The Lexile scale ranges from 0 to 2,000 and can be correlated to a text's readability. Instead of assigning a readability level to a text such as "4.2" or "6.7," signifying a grade level, the Lexile assigns a number such as 853. This Lexile means that the text is on a fifth-to-sixth-grade reading level. When an assessment reports a score as a Lexile, the Lexile reading score can then be matched to a list of titles that fall within the Lexile reading range. The Lexile Framework Web Site, www.lexile.com, offers a wealth of information about this reading tool.

Field Test II

Location

In the 2000–2001 school year, teachers from Dana Middle School in the San Diego Unified School District, San Diego, California, were trained in the *Six-Minute Solution* fluency-partner model as part of their participation in the "Teaching Reading in Every Classroom" online staff development program. Dana Middle School has 864 fifth- and sixth-graders. Fifty percent of the student body is Caucasian. Twenty-nine percent are Hispanic, and 9 percent are African-American. A Title I school, Dana Middle School is one in which 48 percent of students qualify for the free and reduced lunch program. Dana Middle School identified its lowest performing readers by examining their Scholastic Achievement Test (Harcourt, 2001) and Stanford Diagnostic Reading Test (Bjorn and Gardner, 2001) scores from the 1999–2000 school year.

Participants and Procedure

Of the 864 students who attend Dana Middle School, 120 were placed into six groups of 20 students each. They formed six sections of an elective class called Dana Readers' Club (DRC). These students received one additional hour of reading support, four days a week. Students were paired with partners and practiced reading both instructionally appropriate passages and sight words using the *Six-Minute Solution* model. Students received additional instruction in reading multisyllabic words and specific skill instruction in the form of mini-lessons and guided practice.

Data was collected on 92 students. Students in quartile one made an average of 1.52 years growth during the span of one school year. Students in the other groups did not make as impressive growth, but 91 of the 92 students (99 percent) demonstrated measurable growth in oral-reading fluency, with 61 of the 92 students (66 percent) evidencing a 25 percent or better increase in their oral reading rate. Moreover, 42 of the 92 students' (46 percent) post-reading-fluency scores placed them within the average oral-reading-fluency

range for sixth-grade students. The teachers who participated in this project became convinced of the power of repeated readings, timed sight words, and word study. Anecdotal reports by teachers and students
suggest that students spent more time actively reading, showed more pleasure in reading, and were more likely to perceive themselves as readers.

Field Test III

Location

In the 2001–2002 school year, the *Six-Minute Solution* was implemented in two upper-grade classrooms at Los Penasquitos Elementary School over a three-month period. Los Penasquitos Elementary School is in the Poway Unified School District in California. At Los Penasquitos, there are 635 students, representing 21 languages, in grades kindergarten through five. Los Penasquitos is a Title I school, with 41 percent of students qualifying for the free and reduced lunch program.

Participants and Procedure

The *Six-Minute Solution* was implemented in two classrooms: a heterogeneous fourth-grade classroom of 31 students and a combined fourth–fifth grade class in the Los Penasquitos Academy. In the fourth-grade classroom, the smallest gain was 18 percent and the largest gain was 91 percent. The average gain in oral reading fluency for the class was 38 percent. Twenty-six of the 31 students (84 percent) increased their oral reading rates by more than 25 percent. In the fourth–fifth grade Academy class, students attend school 48 percent more hours than do students in traditional classes (1,600 hours vs. 1,080 hours). Both a longer school day and a longer school year give Academy students the extended time necessary to acquire the knowledge, skills, and character traits that are essential for success in rigorous high school programs, and for admission to competitive universities. In the fourth–fifth grade Academy classroom, 24 of the 25 students (95 percent) demonstrated a significant gain in oral reading fluency as measured by a comparison of pre- and post-cwpm scores on grade-level passages.

Summary Paragraph Frame 1

This passage was about _____

_____.

First, I learned _____

_____.

Next, I learned _____

_____.

Finally, I learned _____

_____.

Summary Paragraph Frame 2

After you read the *Practice Passage* with your teacher, write a paragraph about the passage. First name the who or what in a topic sentence. Then add three important facts relating to the topic sentence to complete the paragraph.

Example:

_____ is/was _____. One

important fact is _____. Another important

fact is _____. A final important fact is

_____.

What Is Reading Fluency?

The ability to read text:

- ■ Accurately

- ■ Quickly

- ■ With expression

Why Is Reading Fluency Important?

It is directly related to:

- Reading comprehension
- Independent reading
- Work completion

Bibliography

Adams, G., Brown, S., & Van Zant, S. (1999). Summer reading intervention program prepares fifth grade students for middle school reading challenges. *Educational Research Service Successful School Practices*, *22*(1), 6–8. Arlington, VA: Educational Research Service.

Adams, G., Brown, S., & Van Zant, S. (2000). Working with words: A summer reading intervention program. *Principal*, *80*(1), 59–60. Alexandria, VA: National Association of Elementary School Principals (NAESP).

Allington, R.L. (1977). If they don't read much, how are they ever gonna get good? *Journal of Reading*, *21*, 57–61.

Allington, R.L. (1983). Fluency: The neglected reading goal in reading instruction. *The Reading Teacher*, *36*, 556–561.

Archer, A.L., & Gleason, M.M. (2002). *Skills for school success series*. North Billerica, MA: Curriculum Associates, Inc.

Archer, A.L., Gleason, M.M., & Vachon, V.L. (2000). *REWARDS: Reading excellence, word attack, and rate development strategies*. Longmont, CO: Sopris West Educational Services.

Carnine, D., Silbert, J., & Kame'enui, E.J. (1997). *Direct instruction reading* (3rd ed.). Upper Saddle River, NJ: Prentice-Hall.

Carpenter, P.A., & Just, M.A. (1983). What your eyes do while your mind is reading. In K. Rayner (Ed.), *Eye movements in reading: Perceptual and language processes* (pp. 275–307). New York: Academic Press.

Carroll, J., Davies, P., & Richman, B. (1971). *The American heritage word frequency book*. Boston: Houghton Mifflin, American Heritage Publishing.

Consortium on Reading Excellence (CORE). (1999). *Assessing reading: Multiple measures*. Novato, CA: Arena Press.

Cunningham, A.E., & Stanovich, K.E. (1998). What reading does for the mind. *American Educator*, *22*(1–2), 8–15.

Cunningham, P. (2000). *Phonics they use*. Longman, NY: Addison Wesley.

Dowhower, S.L. (1987). Effects of repeated reading on second-grade transitional readers' fluency and comprehension. *Reading Research Quarterly*, *22*, 389–406.

Dowhower, S.L. (1994). Repeated reading revisited: Research into practice. *Reading and Writing Quarterly*, *10*, 343–358.

Farstrup, A.E., & Samuels, S.J. (Eds.). (2002). *What research has to say about reading instruction* (3rd ed.). Newark, DE: International Reading Association.

Foorman, B.R., & Mehta, P. (2002, November). *Definitions of fluency: Conceptual and methodological challenges*. PowerPoint® presentation at A Focus on Fluency forum, San Francisco, CA.

Fuchs, L.S., Fuchs, D., Kazlan, S., & Allen, S. (1999). Effects of peer-assisted learning strategies in reading with and without training in elaborated help giving. *Elementary School Journal*, *99*(3), 201–220.

Good, R.H., & Kaminski, R.A. (2003). *DIBELS: Dynamic indicators of basic early literacy skills*. Longmont, CO: Sopris West Educational Services.

Greenwood, C.R., Delquadri, J.C., & Hall, R.V. (1989). Longitudinal effects of classwide peer tutoring. *Journal of Educational Psychology*, *81*, 371–383.

Harcourt, Inc. (2001). Stanford achievement test series (9th ed.) (SAT-9). San Antonio, TX: Author.

Hasbrouck, J.E., & Tindal, G.A. (2005). *Oral reading fluency: 90 years of measurement* (Tech. Rep. No. 33, Behavioral Research and Teaching [BRT]). Eugene: University of Oregon, College of Education. Retrieved January 24, 2006, from http://www.readnaturally.com/pdf/oralreadingfluency.pdf

Hasbrouck, J.E., & Tindal, G.A. (in press). Oral reading fluency norms: A valuable assessment tool for reading teachers. *The Reading Teacher*.

Hudson, R.F., Lane, H.B., & Pullen, P.C. (2005). Reading fluency assessment and instruction: What, why, and how? *The Reading Teacher*, *58*(8), 702–714.

Johns, J.L., & Lenski, S.D. (2001). *Improving reading: A handbook of strategies* (2nd ed., p. 164). Dubuque, IA: Kendall/Hunt Publishing Co.

Karlsen, B., & Gardner, E.F. (1995). *Stanford diagnostic reading test* (4th ed.). San Antonio, TX: Harcourt, Inc.

LaBerge, D., & Samuels, S.J. (1974). Toward a theory of automatic information processing in reading. *Cognitive Psychology*, *6*, 293–323.

La Pray, M., & Ramon, R. (1969). The graded word list: Quick gauge of reading ability. *Journal of Reading*, *12*(4), 305–307.

Levy, B.A. (2001). Moving the bottom: Improving reading fluency. In M. Wolf (Ed.), *Dyslexia, fluency, and the brain* (pp. 357–379). Timonium, MD: York Press.

Levy, B.A., Nicholls, A., & Kroshen, D. (1993). Repeated readings: Process benefits for good and poor readers. *Journal of Experimental Child Psychology*, *56*, 303–327.

MacGinitie, W., MacGinitie, R., Maria, K., & Dreyer, L. (2003). *Gates-MacGinitie reading tests*. Itasca, IL: Riverside Publishing.

Mercer, C.D., Campbell, K.U., Miller, M.D., Mercer, K.D., & Lane, H.B. (2001). Effects of a reading fluency intervention for middle schoolers with specific learning disabilities. *Learning Disabilities Research and Practice*, *15*, 179–189.

Meyer, M.S., & Felton, R.H. (1999). Repeated reading to enhanced fluency: Old approaches and new directions. *Annals of Dyslexia*, *49*, 263–306.

Moats, L.C. (2001, March). When older kids can't read. *Educational Leadership Report*.

National Institute of Child Health and Human Development (NICHD). (2000). Report of the National Reading Panel: *Teaching children to read: An evidence based assessment of the scientific research literature on reading and its implications for reading instruction. Chapter 3: Fluency* (NIH Publication No. 00-4754). Washington, DC: U.S. Government Printing Office.

Pinnell, G.S., Piluski, J.J., Wixson, K.K., Campbell, J.R., Gough, P.B., & Beatty, A.S. (1995). *Listening to children read aloud: Data from NAEP's integrated reading performance record (IRPR) at grade 4* (Report No. 23–FR–04). Washington, DC: U.S. Department of Education, National Center for Education Statistics, Office of Educational Research and Improvement.

Rosenshine, B., & Meister, C. (1994). Reciprocal teaching: A review of research. *Review of Educational Research, 64*, 479–530.

Samuels, S.J. (1979). The method of repeated readings. *The Reading Teacher, 32*, 403–408.

Scholastic, Inc. (2003). *Scholastic reading inventory (SRI)*. New York: Author.

Shapiro, E.S. (1996). *Academic skills problems: Direct assessment and intervention* (2nd ed.). New York: Guilford Press.

Stanovich, K.E. (1986). Matthew effects in reading: Some consequences of individual differences in the acquisition of literacy. *Reading Research Quarterly, 21*, 360–407.

Stanovich, K.E. (1990). Concepts in developmental theories of reading skill: Cognitive resources, automaticity, and modularity. *Developmental Review, 10*, 72–100.

Stevens, R.J., Madden, N.A., Slavin, R.E., & Famish, A.M. (1987). Cooperative integrated reading and composition: Two field experiments. *Reading Research Quarterly, 22*, 433–454.

Stieglitz, E. (2002). *Stieglitz informal reading inventory: Assessing reading behaviors from emergent to advanced levels*. Boston: Allyn & Bacon.

Topping, K. (1987). Paired reading: A powerful techniques for parent use. *The Reading Teacher, 40*, 608–614.

Torgesen, J.K., Rashotte, C.A., & Alexander, A. (2001). Principles of fluency instruction in reading: Relationships with established empirical outcomes. In M. Wolf (Ed.), *Dyslexia, fluency, and the brain* (pp. 333–355). Timonium, MD: York Press.

Wolf, M. (2001). *Dyslexia, fluency, and the brain*. Timonium, MD: York Press.

Woodcock, R.W. (2000). *Woodcock reading mastery test*. Circle Pines, MN: American Guidance Service.